Sicilian
SEAFOOD
COOKING

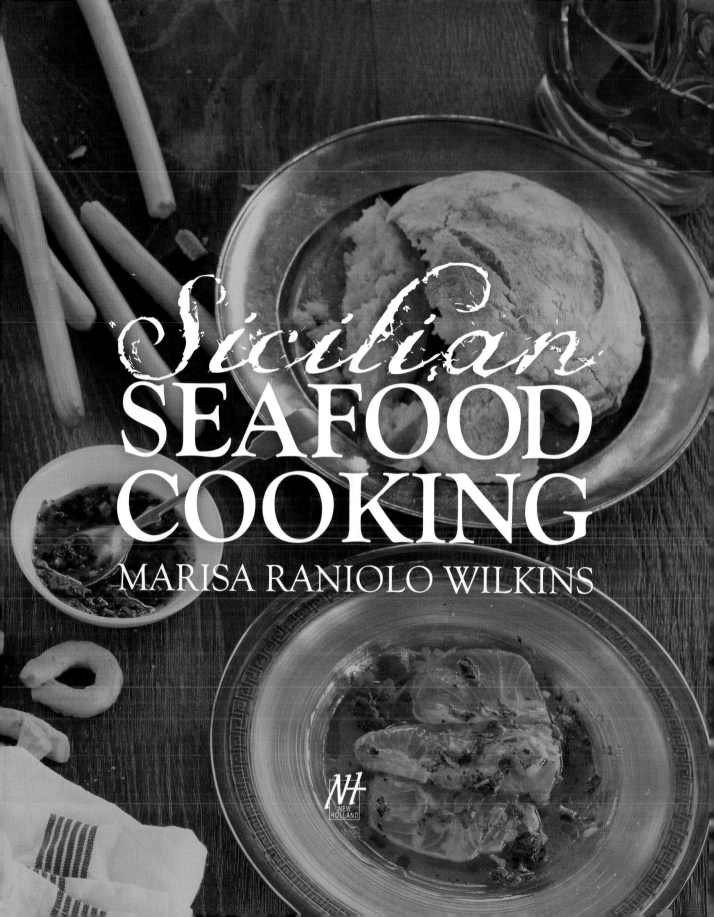

Sicilian
SEAFOOD
COOKING

MARISA RANIOLO WILKINS

NH
NEW
HOLLAND

*For my father who has always loved Sicily
and never stopped being Sicilian*

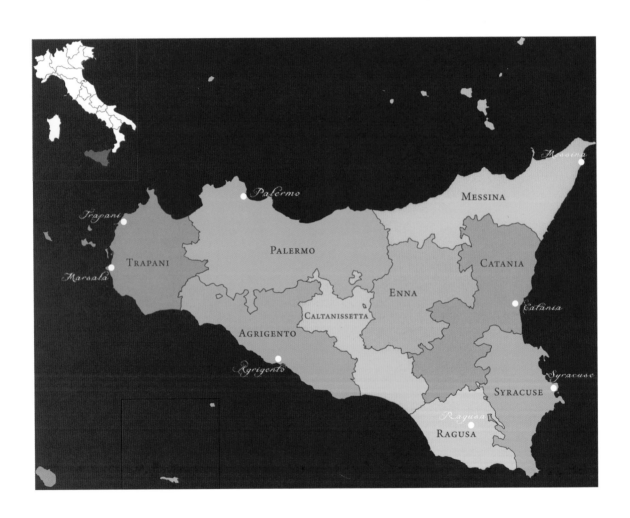

Contents

The Sicilian language 6

A Leone in the kitchen 7

CHAPTER 1
Ieri, oggi e domani – Yesterday, today and tomorrow 8

CHAPTER 2
Comu primu – As first course 32

CHAPTER 3
Comu sacunnu – As second course 120

CHAPTER 4
Come fare una bella figura – How to make a good impression 252

CHAPTER 5
Festa – Feast 274

CHAPTER 6
'U cuntuonnu – Vegetable dishes 292

CHAPTER 7
Una caponata per ogni stagione – A caponata for every season 356

The menu 380

Index 380

Acknowledgements 384

The Sicilian language

Sicilians still think of Sicily first, and Italy second.

Whether Sicilian is a language or a dialect is probably more a matter of politics or patriotism than of linguistics. The answer is much less certain because of the lack of written records. But there is more support for Sicilian being a language than an extreme Meridional dialect. (A southern Italian person is referred to as a Meridionale, the northerner is a Settentrionale).

Just like the food of Sicily, the Sicilian language is a blend of the linguistic and cultural influences from the different people who occupied the island. The Sicilian language, like every other aspect of Sicilian culture, is unique and the language is a blend of the Latin of the Romans and innumerable expressions and inflections derived from Greek, Arabic, Catalan, French and Spanish, as well as words from the ancient Siculi (ancient Sicilian tribe that occupied the eastern part of Sicily).

There are at least ten regional dialects spoken in Sicily: three in the west, three in the centre and four in the east.

Italian is the official language in all of Italy and as a traveller in Sicily you will almost certainly be spoken to in Italian and everything you read will be written in Italian. But Sicilians frequently speak their own language among themselves. You may hear Siciliano spoken between fellow Sicilians, just as you will hear the Napoletano dialect around Naples, Veneto spoken around Venice or any of the other numerous dialects spoken in the different regions of Italy.

C'è acchi cosa di cchiù beddu p'un populu d' 'a lingua di so' 'ntinati!
(Sicilian saying)
What could be more beautiful for the populace than the language of their forefathers!

I palori nimici fannu ridiri, chiddi di l'amici fanni chianciri. (Sicilian proverb)
Le parole dei nemici fanno ridere, quelle d'amici fanno piangere.
(Italian)
The words of enemies make you laugh, but those of friends can make you cry.

A Leone in the kitchen

Ogni cani è liuni a la sò casa.
(Sicilian proverb)
*Ogni cane nella sua casa si sente
un leone.* (Italian)
*Every dog feels like a lion in his
own house.*

Every cook and professional chef has a way of doing things.

It is said that you don't leave your life behind, you take it with you. With regard to cooking and eating I have maintained my lifelong interest in using and eating fresh (newly picked or harvested or caught) produce. Fresh, seasonal produce is more likely to equate to optimum flavour, nutrition and enjoyment.

My mother's surname is Leone. Often daughters acquire some of their knowledge and skills in the kitchen from watching their mothers and, like the Sicilian proverb, I am a *leone* (a lion) in control of my kitchen.

Ieri, oggi e domani

Yesterday, today and tomorrow

La storia

The story

STOP FOR A MOMENT AND REFLECT ON THE NAME 'MEDITERRANEAN': IT IS THE SEA IN THE MIDDLE OF THE EARTH. THEN PICTURE THE TRIANGULAR-SHAPED ISLAND IN THE CENTRE OF THAT SEA: SICILY. IS IT ANY WONDER THAT SICILY, THIS ISLAND IN THE CENTRE OF THE SEA IN THE MIDDLE OF THE EARTH, SHOULD BE THE MEETING PLACE OF SO MANY CULTURES OVER SO MANY CENTURIES?

Sicily has been endowed with the geography, climate and terrain that made it the grain-store of the Greek and Roman empires. In the long centuries when the lights of learning sputtered out in northern Europe, Sicily was a beacon of knowledge and tolerance, where Jews, Christians and Mohammedans lived in harmony. The food of Sicily reflects this overlay of cultures and the profusion of ingredients that have flourished in its dark, volcanic soils. It is the food that Sicilians cook and eat that perpetuates the dynasties and empires, that incorporates the religious rituals and the articles of faith.

In ancient times the island's greatest attraction was its strategic location – an easy sail from the imperial centres of three great continents (Europe, Asia and Africa), making it an essential port of call on one of the world's most important trade routes. The first inhabitants of the island in Neolithic times were the Sicani, who may have come from North Africa, and settled in the west. The Siculi, who occupied the eastern part of Sicily, are thought to have Indo-European origins. Archaeologically, there is no substantial difference between Sicani and Siculi but the Sicanians are considered to be indigenous to Sicily because theirs is the earliest society that can be identified.

When you eat something you eat
culture.
Regina Schrambling (food
writer)

Murriali, città senza cunfortu,
o chiovi o mina ventu o sona a
mortu. (Sicilian saying)
Monreale, a city without comfort,
either it rains, or the wind blows,
or bells toll for the dead.

Throughout its history, Sicily has been coveted, occupied and invaded by many civilisations – the Phoenicians and the Greeks were among the earliest settlers. Then came the Romans and Carthaginians followed by the Byzantines and Saracens. Next were the Normans, French and Spaniards and, for short periods, Germans, Austrians and Piedmontese.

The diversity and richness of Sicilian cultures, the layering and blending of influences, make the food of Sicily different from that of all other Italian regions. The colonists from each culture brought new ingredients and cooking methods that were adapted and incorporated, creating an increasingly eclectic and unique cuisine.

Sicily is a relatively small island, but each part has its own cultural history and, not surprisingly, its own culinary traditions. The food of Palermo (northwest coast) is very different from that of Syracuse (southeast coast) or Trapani (west coast). It is fascinating to identify some of the cultural factors that may have influenced the localised cuisine on these coastlines.

Seasonal fishing, often accompanied by elaborate rituals and traditions, was well established in ancient times – long before it became the most important industry of the medieval Mediterranean. Plentiful and free, fish was the most available food for Sicilians living on the coast. Christianity provided another boost to the fishing industry. The Catholic Church banned eating meat on days of fasting and abstinence, which amounted to almost a third of the year, so fish was always in demand, whether it was freshly caught or salted.

The past affects the present and the future. The Church has relaxed its laws and Sicilians are more prosperous than they were, but they continue to eat loads of fish prepared in interesting ways. Food culture is the consequence of local conditions and resources. Recipes are influenced by the species of fish, and seasonal and culinary variations that reflect changes in time and place. But from this profoundly divided island, with distinct regional variations, there is a united, shared ethic of eating fresh local and seasonal food.

Fishing has always been vital to the Sicilian economy and Sicilian vessels make up nearly a quarter of the Italy's total fishing fleet. Sicily also has significant processing and distribution industries: fresh, salted, dried and canned fish – especially canned tuna – forms one of the largest export industries in Europe.

A rapidly growing aquaculture industry is also developing in the provinces of Syracuse, Agrigento and Trapani and others are underway on the islands of Filicudi (Messina) and Favignana (Trapani).

In the waters around Sicily, as in the other oceans of the world, the number of species of economic value has reduced considerably. But even though the size of the catch has decreased significantly, Sicilian fishing boats catch about 25 per cent more marketable product annually than the Italian national average. This is because the currents circulating around Sicily mix deeper waters with surface layers, assuring favourable feeding conditions for fish larvae.

SICILY, PIECE BY PIECE

The northwest coast

The northwest coast of the island, centred around Palermo, is thought to be strongly influenced by the Saracens. They occupied Siqilliah (the Arabic name for the island) in the 9th, 10th and 11th centuries. The Saracens introduced sophisticated methods of irrigation and excelled at fishing, salting and preserving fish. They bought new culinary traditions and bold flavours which strongly influenced the cuisine of Sicily. Some claim that the Saracens also introduced produce such as rice, sugar cane, raisins, oranges and lemons, as well as spices like cloves, cinnamon and saffron. This helps explain the distinctive *agro dolce* (sweet and sour) flavours in Sicilian cuisine and the use of spices, dried grapes and nuts. However, there are conflicting views. Some argue that the cultivation of oranges and lemons did not begin until the Spanish occupation and that the wide range of spices was an essential ingredient in the cuisine of the Roman Empire.

Palermo has always been an important fishing town and many fish recipes originate from there. Palermo was called Ziz by the Catherginians, Balem by the Arabs and Panarmus ('spacious harbour') by the Romans. Sicilians refer to Palermo as *la più nobile* (the most noble), *la più superba* (the proudest), of Sicilian cities. It was the seat of government for various ancient wealthy courts – the Saracen, Norman, French and Spanish.

The cuisine of Palermo is living archaeology: as the wealthy urban elites traded with the world and with other important Sicilian cities, they swapped recipes. Each royal court, aristocracy and mercantile class developed and added to the already varied existing culinary traditions. The peasant class, of

SOME PALMERMO SPECIALTIES

Cauliflower fritters (*Brocculi a pastetta*)

Pumpkin with vinegar, mint, sugar and cinnamon (*Ficato ri setti cannola*)

Eggplant caponata

Pasta with sardines, from Palermo, with fennel, pine nuts and currants (*Pasta chi sardi*)

Soused fish with vinegar, garlic and mint (*Agghiata*) *or* sauce of onions sugar and vinegar (*Cippudata*)

Sardines a beccafico(*Sardi a beccaficu*)

Salmoriglio dressing (*Salamurrigghiu*)

Grilled tuna with oregano (*Tonnu rigatanu*) with Sicilian green sauce (*Sarsa virdi siciliana*)

Baked baccalà

Fried sardines (*Fritto misto di pesce*)

Eggplant or zucchini parmigiana (*Mulinciani a la parmiciana* or *Cucuzzeddi a la parmiciana*)

Baked stuffed tomatoes (*Pumarori chini*)

course, had to make do with what they could get. Fresh 'poor' ingredients go a long way in *cucina povera* (the art of transforming meagre, frugal ingredients into satisfying and even sumptuous dishes).

Most of the food culture of Sicily – and Italy – developed in cities, not in the countryside. The ingredients in the rural areas were fresh, but limited. The largest markets with the greatest range of produce were in the cities. This is where culinary ideas were swapped and blended and recipes were recorded, and where the kitchens of the well-to-do competed to cook new recipes.

Monks and nuns were also responsible for developing and recording some fine Sicilian recipes. Mediaeval monasteries and convents often had large, well-staffed kitchens and many of the monks and nuns came from rich families and were used to lavish feasting. They frequently held large banquets, and tried to outdo their neighbours with the magnificence of their feasts. Perhaps boredom was also a factor; many sweet delicacies, especially those made with marzipan, were developed in convents. In *I Viceré* (*The Viceroys*), Federico De Roberto describes the monks of that period as 'living the life of Michelasso; eating, drinking and going out'. This is where the Italian proverb about the life of the rich and idle – *Fare l'arte di Michelasso: Mangiare, bere e andare a spasso* – comes from.

The Normans first settled in Sicily towards the end of the 11th century. They were mainly meat eaters and made few culinary additions of their own. They embraced some of the Saracen culture they supplanted – Arab chefs prepared Arabic food alongside their Norman counterparts in the royal kitchens, but some of the sophisticated agriculture the Muslims had introduced went into decline. The Normans brought dried cod with them from Scandinavia and it is still very much a part of Sicilian cuisine, popular for its flavour and long-lasting qualities.

The next major influences come from France and Spain. These new elites brought butter and pastry and the dishes of the poor were refined with expensive ingredients. With the French came onions instead of garlic, butter roux, slow braises, stuffed meats, the use of sauces and the *monzù* (a corruption of the word 'monsieur'; they were master chefs and a status symbol in 18th-century Sicily and Naples).

The Spanish introduced chocolate, peppers, potatoes, zucchini, other squashes and tomatoes from the new world. Many of the tomato-based sauces probably have Spanish origins. The Spanish aristocracy established *cucina baronale* with lavish foods and complex flavours.

Lettu di Duminicani, tavulu di Cappuccini, lussu di Biniottini.
(Sicilian proverb)
The Domenicans for a bed [their beds were reputed to be soft] the Capuchins for food and the Benedictines for luxury.

La terra dici: Dùnami ca ti dugnu. (Sicilian proverb)
The earth says: Give to me and I'll give to you.

Some Trapani Specialties

Fish Couscous (Cuscusu)
Tuna balls in salsa (Purpetti di tunnu ca` sarsa)
Raw marinated tuna (Tonno cunzato)
Tuna poached in oil and vinegar (Tunnu sutt' ogghiu vugghiutu cu acitu)
Caponata con bottarga
Pesto made with tomatoes, basil, pine nuts or almonds (Ammogghia e mataroccu)
Pasta with a tuna stew (Pasta cu tunnu no sucu)
Pasta with raw tomatoes and fried fish (Pasta co pumaroru cruru e pisci friuti)
Pasta with bottarga (Pasta ca buttarga)
Tuna ragout with cinnamon (Tunnu a' raù ca canneddà)
Stuffed calamari with fresh cheese, almonds and nutmeg in marsala (Calamaricchi chini cà marsala e mennuli)
Boiled tuna as the Capo Rias ate it (Tunnu vugghiutu d'u capu rais)
Small braciole stuffed with herbs (Braciulittini)
Sardines a beccafico (Sardi a beccaficu – Sarde a beccafico)

Three important cities round the coast from Palermo – Trapani, Marsala and Mazara del Vallo – each have well-established fishing industries and have been strongly influenced by the Tunisians and other North African cultures. Many recipes, especially for tuna, come from this part of Sicily.

Trapani, which has the most important harbour on the west coast, is a cosmopolitan centre. Having been ruled by Carthaginians, Romans, Saracens and Normans, Trapani also had an extensive commercial trade, especially with Tunisians and other African cultures.

The traditional and popular Sicilian fish dish of couscous evolved in Trapani. This North African dish was originally made with meat but the Trapanesi adapted it into a seafood dish. Because fresh fish was only available near the sea, the people living inland needed preserved products for days of Lenten and religious fasting. Salted fish became an important commodity and processing industries to preserve and salt anchovies, sardines and tuna began in Trapani, and continue today.

In the early 1800s, wealthy English merchant families named Ingham, Whitaker, and Woodhouse lived in Trapani and the surrounding ports and contributed to the prosperity of the region.

John Woodhouse recognised that marsala (named for the town where it is made) shared similarities with madeira and port. Woodhouse bargained on marsala being able to successfully compete with the popular Spanish fortified wines; he shipped some casks of marsala to England and the trade soon became an important component of the local economy. In fact the name 'marsala' comes from 'Mars-al-Allah', meaning 'harbour of God' and was given to the town by the Saracen rulers in the 9th century.

Mazara del Vallo, a seaport in the province of Trapani, was another safe haven for boats with a history reaching back thousands of years. In ancient times Mazara was a port for the Phoenicians, a military position during Roman times and a staging post for the Saracen conquest of the rest of the island. Later Mazara attracted trade from Pisa, Barcelona and Majorca. Today it is the most important fishing port in Italy. The history of fishing here began on the banks of the local river, the Mazaro, which is navigable for long tracts and had plentiful fish stocks.

Just west of Sicily, between Trapani and Marsala among the Egadi Islands, is the island of Favignana where migrating bluefin tuna were harvested throughout the centuries. Favignana is famous for the *mattanza*, an annual fishing ritual where the tuna are trapped in a maze of nets.

The *mattanza* is Saracen in origin. The word comes from an old Spanish word *matar* (to kill), which in turn comes from the Latin verb *mactare* (to slaughter). The leader of the Favignana tuna fishermen is known as the *rais* (from the Arab word meaning commander or head) and he directs and coordinates the team of *tonnarotti* (tuna fishermen). Two long barrier nets, measuring several kilometres, are laid into the migratory path of the tuna, which have come to the Mediterranean to spawn, channelling them into the mouth of the trap that leads to *la camera della morte*. When the *rais* considers this 'death chamber' to be full, he calls for *la mattanza* (the slaughter) to begin. The fishermen, chanting traditional songs, surround the chamber with their boats, pull up the net and gaff the tuna.

The fishermen follow the seasons and respect the tuna's breeding patterns and life cycle; they hoist into their boats only the mature tuna and leave the younger ones till they are ready for the next harvest. Bluefin tuna are no longer plentiful globally, but the *mattanza* still takes place, albeit on a much reduced scale, more as tourist spectacle than a fishing frenzy.

The east coast

The eastern side of Sicily with its coastal cities of Messina, Catania and Syracuse was historically part of the Greek Empire centred on Athens. Four of the greatest minds of the ancient world lived in Syracuse: Archimedes, the mathematician and physicist; Plato, the philosopher; and the playwrights Aeschylus and Pindar. Less well known were Miteco, who wrote about gastronomy, and Epicharmus, the writer of comedies. Empedocles, the philosopher, lived in Agrigento and Archestrato, another gastronomist, in Gela.

The cuisine of the eastern side of Sicily is a world away from the west coast. The Greeks developed sophisticated agricultural systems but preferred simple produce from the land and sea. Their cooking techniques were straightforward and aspired to preserve the flavour and texture of fresh produce. In their writings on gastronomy, Archestrato and Miteco cautioned against making sauces too rich. Rather than masking the food's natural flavours, they recommended reducing cooking juices and simply enhancing the food with chopped fresh herbs, good olive oil and salt. Grilled food, simply dressed with *salmoriglio* (salt, oregano, olive oil and lemon juice) is still very common in Sicily.

A focaccia-style pie (*'Mpanata*)
Rich fish soup from Syracuse cooked in the oven (*Zuppa di pisci a sirausana 'o fornu*)
Fish soup with a soffritto of garlic and parsley (*Zuppa di pisci*)
Spaghetti with sea urchins (*Spaghetti chi ricci*)
Vermicelli as cooked in Syracuse with anchovies and peppers (*Virmicieddi a la sirausana*)
Tuna *alla stemperata* with onions, vinegar, capers, green olives and mint (*Tunnu 'a stimpirata*)
Tuna *alla ghiotta* with peppers and eggplants (*Agghiotta di tunnu cu pipi e mulinciani*)
Fish, poached in broth with capers (*Pisci chi chiappareddi*)
Trout with olives and wild fennel (*Trota in padella con olive e finocchio selvatico*)
Trout from the Manghisi River with garlic, tomatoes, myrtle and croutons (*Trotta d' u manghisi*)

When the Aragonese (Spanish) made Messina the seat of government in the 14th century, they introduced sauces, elaborate pastry and a wealth of braised fish dishes. Messina today is an important commercial port. One of its signature dishes is *stoccafisso* (air-dried cod). This air-dried technique contrasts with other parts of Sicily which use *baccalà* (salt-processed, dried cod). Both *stoccafisso* and *baccalà* are still very popular in Sicily (as in Spain and Portugal) and were originally traded for salt by the Danish and Norwegian sailors. The old Catholic rule of eating only fish on Friday made the salt cod trade very profitable. Perhaps not coincidentally, *stoccafisso* is also a culinary specialty in other large commercial ports in Italy – Genova, Livorno, Taranto and Venezia.

Midway down the eastern coast is Catania. The second most important city in Sicily, it was founded by Greeks who named it Katane.

Catania is where my mother's family, the Leones, come from. Her family – mother, father and four brothers (Alfio, Orazio, Stefano and Pippo) and one sister (Graziella) – moved to Trieste in the north of Italy in 1932 when my mother Elena was five years old. The whole family lived in Trieste until my grandfather died. Then my grandmother, aunt and two uncles returned to Sicily. My mother as a teenager chose to remain in Trieste with her older brother, my uncle Alfio, and his wife Renata (from Rovigo near Trieste). My mother's youngest brother Pippo also stayed in Trieste and married a Triestina.

During World War II, the whole Leone family once again lived in Trieste for most of 1943 and 1944. By this time Stefano and Orazio had married and they brought their Sicilian brides with them. They remained in Trieste until Sicily was considered safe. Then Orazio moved back to Catania and my grandmother, Nonna Maria, and my mother's sister, Graziella, went with Stefano and his wife Assunta to Augusta, on the east coast halfway between Catania and Syracuse.

My father met my mother when he was very young and stationed in Trieste as a policeman during the war. His family lived in Ragusa, in southeast Sicily. When they married, he and my mother stayed in Trieste until we came to Australia.

As a child in Trieste, I was always being told by all my mother's Leone relatives that although Palermo was the historic capital of Sicily, Catania is the cultural capital and, most importantly, the culinary capital of Sicily. If only Catania had a port! The Leone family have always lived by the sea. They are great lovers of fish and much of what I know about cooking fish I have learned from these relatives.

SOME MESSINA SPECIALTIES

Impanata
Stuffed mussels with
besciamelle (Cozzuli chini)
Spaghettini with mussels
(Spaghettini e cozzuli)
Pasta or rice with black ink
sauce *(Pasta cu niuru di sicci)*
Pasta with swordfish and mint
(Pasta con spada e menta)
Fish *alla ghiotta* from Messina
with tomatoes, green olives,
capers, pine nuts and currants
(Agghiotta di pisci a missinisa)
Small braciole, stuffed with
herbs *(Braciulittini)* braised in
tomato or baked
Grilled fish *(Pisci 'nta braci)*
Stockfish *alla ghiotta* with green
olives, capers and potatoes
(Agghiotta di piscistoccu)

*Si Catania avissi u portu,
Palermu saria mortu.* (Sicilian
proverb)
*Se Catania avesse un porto,
Palermo sarebbe morta.* (Italian)
*If Catania had a port, Palermo
would be dead.*

Potato croquettes *(Cuzzili)*
Eggplant croquettes *(Purpetti ri
mulinciani)*
Cauliflower fritters *(Brocculi a
pastetta)* or made with zucchini
flowers
Raw marinated fish *(Crudo e
cunzato)*, especially sardines
(Anciovi cunzati)
Roasted or grilled peppers *(Pipi
arrustuti)*
Roasted or grilled artichokes
(Cacocciuli arrustuti)
Grilled eggplants, zucchini
and mushrooms *(Mulinciani,
cucuzzeddi e funci 'nta braci)*
Caponata from Catania
(Caponata catanese)
Pasta with tomatoes, eggplants
and bottarga *(Pasta a la norma
ca bottarga)*
Bad weather pasta with
anchovies and zucchini *(Pasta
ro' malutempu)*
Soused fish with vinegar, garlic
and mint *(Agghiata)*
Cauliflower braised in red wine,
cheese, olives and anchovies
(Vrucculi affucati)

Catania has a huge fishing industry and equally large market to sell the catch of the day. But Catania is not just another Sicilian coastal city. It is spread out on the flanks of Mount Etna, one of the most active volcanoes of the Mediterranean, along with Stromboli and Vesuvius. Etna's slopes sometimes tremble, threatening to erupt, and are seared by rivers of lava. The molten rock is the source of the Catania's fertile and bountiful soil, which in tune with the climate produces vegetables, nuts, fruit and herbs.

As with other Sicilian towns, Catania has its own ways of cooking fish – the regional specialty is *alla brace* (grilled over hot coals), and I hope this is not because Catania's patron saint, Sant' Agata, was martyred by having her breasts cut off and then being rolled on hot coals.

Siracusa (Syracuse) is south of Catania. When the southern part of Sicily was colonised by Greeks, it became known as Magna Graecia (Greater Greece) and by the 5th century BCE, Syracuse was at the centre of the Mediterranean trade routes, the richest and most powerful of all Greek cities. The strong tradition of eating seafood in Syracuse began then and continues today – fish is prepared in various ways, from simple grills to the lavish *zuppa siragusana* (fish soup) made from a variety of fish.

Travelling west from Syracuse and towards the most southern end of the island, you come to Ragusa: this is the capital of the province called by the same name. Ragusa began as a Siculi settlement, but was soon hellenised by Syracuse and it was an important trade centre between the coastal towns and the rural centre. It was conquered by the Romans (around 258 BCE), who united the whole of Sicily as a Roman province.

Other main towns in the Ragusa region are Modica, Scicli and Noto and each of these southeastern baroque towns are not too far from the coast (about 20 minutes by car).

Ragusa is where my father's family, the Raniolo, come from. When I taste the cooking of my father's relatives, I notice sharp, piquant or sweet flavours when you least expect them. For example, they add vinegar to produce strong, sharp flavours or use chilli instead of pepper. They add sugar to pastry for savoury dishes and in delicate *ricotta ravioli* served with a strong *ragù* or with a sauce of squid and black ink (see fish cooked *alla stemperata*, page 136, and ricotta ravioli with black ink sauce, page 80).

The Ragusani use fewer and simpler ingredients in their cooking, mainly local produce, which is rich in meat (especially pork), vegetables and fruit. I particularly enjoy their bitter greens and wild vegetables and, like the

Ragusani, I could not do without fresh cheeses – ricotta, *formaggio fresco* and *caciocavallo ragusano*.

I have spent far more time, both in my childhood and as an adult, with the Raniolos than with my mother's Leone family and, although they may not be as widely represented in the fish recipes, they have contributed significantly to my passion about and overall knowledge of Sicilian cuisine and culture. Zia Niluzza is my father's only surviving sister and throughout the years has been a great source of information.

The south coast

SPECIALTIES OF AGRIGENTO, SCIACCA AND ENNA

A focaccia-style pie (*'Mpanata*)
A sauté of spring vegetables (*Frittedda*)
Raw marinated fish (*Crudo e cunzato*)
Baked fish with meat broth (*Pisci o'furnu co bruoru ri carni*)
Fish in a bag (*Pesce al cartoccio*)
Fish with broad beans (*Pisci che favi*)
Sautéed mushrooms (*Funci trifulati*)

Following the southern coast and heading northwest again brings you to Gela, Licata, Agrigento and Selinunte, all centres founded by the Greeks, as is evident by the impressive ancient ruins in these areas.

Sciacca is a small town between Agrigento and Selinunte. Originally a Sicani settlement, it was later colonised by the Romans, who enjoyed bathing in its spring waters. After the destruction of Selinunte by the Carthagians in 409 BCE, the town became a leading agricultural and commercial centre and the principal Sicilian port for the export of grain to North Africa. The town's fishing industry thrived and it has remained a busy fishing port, exporting fish to other parts of Sicily, Italy and other countries.

Many believe that Homer's lines in Book 7 of the *Odyssey* may be a description of Sicily.

Here luxuriant trees are always in their prime,
pomegranates, and pears, and apples glowing red,
succulent figs and olives swelling sleek and dark.
And the yield of all these trees will never flag or die
neither in winter nor in summer, a harvest all year round.

And here is a teeming vineyard planted for the kings,
beyond it an open level bank where the vintage grapes
lie baking to raisins in the sun while pickers gather others:
some they trample down in vats, and here in the front rows
bunches of unripe grapes have hardly shed their blooms
while others under the sunlight slowly darkened purple.

And there by the last rows are beds of greens,
bordered and plotted, greens of every kind,
glistening fresh, year in, year out.

Homer referred to Sicily as Thrinakie, which means triangular-shaped isle (which changed to Trinakria), a reference to the three promontories on the island: Capo Peloro (Messina) in the northeast, Capo Boéo or Lilibéo (Marsala) and Capo Passero, the southeastern extreme of Sicily. The name later became Trinacria, which the poet Dante Alighieri used to refer to Sicily in the *Divine Comedy*. It is also the name of the three-legged figure, the symbol of Sicily.

Plenty has made me poor.
– Ovid

Per domani: Festa o fame

For tomorrow: feast or famine

Sicilians have always indulged in eating fish, and as long as there are fish to catch, they will continue to enjoy it. Sicily is the only Italian region that is surrounded by three seas – the Ionian, Tyrrhenian and Mediterranean.

For centuries, the seas around Sicily teemed with all manner of fish and the bounty of the Mediterranean seemed inexhaustible. Inevitably, fishing was industrialised: large motorised fleets joined the countless small fishing boats. The rapid development of hi-tech fishing brought higher yields but it also resulted in unsustainable fishing methods and put the marine ecosystem in danger.

It wasn't long ago that fish were only eaten close to where they were caught. Today every ocean is accessible to trawler fleets which can ship their catch all over the world, creating the impression that fish are plentiful.

Sicily, like many other fishing cultures, has exploited its marine resources with little thought of the consequences. Many species are in danger of being lost forever.

In the 1980s concern about the reduced numbers of marketable fish led Sicily to pass a law prohibiting fishing in particular areas during specified periods to allow stocks to recover. Financial compensation was also offered to Sicilian fishermen who could no longer continue fishing and quotas for specific fish species and open and closed seasons were established.

Festo die si quid prodegeris,
profesto egere liceat nisi
peperceris. (Latin)
Feast today makes fast tomorrow.
– Platus, *Aulularia*

Menu for the ancients and wise

The ancients would have eaten simply cooked fish, pulses, olives, figs, cheese, radishes, honey, grapes, garlic, onions, olive oil, wheat and wine. Guests are: Empedocles (c. 490–430 BCE), a scientist and philosopher who lived in Agrigento and is best known for his theory that all matter is composed of four elements; Archimedes of Syracuse (c. 287–212 BCE), whi is said to have run naked through the streets of Syracuse, shouting 'Eureka!' after discovering the principle of hydraulics while taking a bath; and Aeschylus (c. 524/525–455/456 BCE), one of the greatest Greek playwrights and a regular guest of Hieron of Syracuse.

❧

Sweet and sour onions
(*Cipudduzzi all'auruduci*)
Olives dressed with oil and
fennel seeds
Grilled tuna with oregano
(*Tonnu rigatanu*) or eel if you
can get it
Wild greens (*Erbe spontanie*),
boiled and dressed with olive
oil, a little lemon juice and
garlic

Over time, these regulations have become more stringent, but they do not appear to be sufficient. There is evidence to suggest that wide-scale illegal catching and selling of protected or endangered fish is still happening. Some Sicilians believe that the penalties for ignoring closed fishing areas, exceeding quotas and catching undersized fish are not consistently enforced, and that there are many unreported, unlicensed fishers selling directly to the public.

As in other parts of the world, some Sicilian fishermen are significantly understating their catch – they do not keep records and sell without documentation. Another concern is that some vessels are operating outside their own country's fishing limits and are venturing illegally into Sicily's territorial waters (a problem that is prevalent worldwide). This illegal activity affects the ways fish stocks are assessed and how species are managed. For example, the endangered bluefin tuna has been over-fished for many years, especially in the eastern Atlantic and Mediterranean. The European Commission put measures in place to limit bluefin tuna fishing in September 2007, but so far they have not been effective. Other governing bodies and conservation groups are attempting to control its exploitation. The International Commission for the Conservation of Atlantic Tuna (ICCAT), an inter-governmental fishing organisation responsible for the conservation of tuna and tuna-like species in the Atlantic Ocean and its adjacent seas, has imposed strict measures to reduce the catch, although some conservation groups are urging a ban on the international trade in bluefin tuna.

A century ago in Sicily, it was easy to catch thousands of tuna during the season, each weighing as much as 300 kilograms (660 lb). Because of their size they were referred to as *maiali del mare* ('pigs from the sea'). Today their numbers have fallen drastically and the maximum weight for a wild caught tuna may now be about 100 kilograms – and these are rare.

Swordfish (*pesce spada*) has been part of the Sicilian diet for centuries. As its name implies, this is characterised by an upper jaw that extends to form a flat, sharp-edged sword shape. Italians call swordfish *il pesce cavalliere* (the cavalier fish) partly because of the courage the fish displays as it fights to protect itself and its fellow species with its sharp, luminous sword. It is an impressive jumper and a powerful fighter and is considered exciting to catch. The swordfish is also admired for its faithfulness to its lifelong companion.

Unfortunately, the situation with swordfish is much the same as that of bluefin tuna. In the past it would not have been unusual for fishers to haul swordfish measuring more than 5 metres (16½ feet) long into their boats. Now, especially in the Mediterranean, stocks have rapidly reduced. Swordfish fisheries in the southwestern Indian Ocean are still moderate compared with the Atlantic and the Mediterranean Sea, mostly because of the lack of modern vessels and infrastructure, but it may not be long before *il pesce cavalliere* is extinct.

Sicilians love fingerlings (*neonata*, 'just born') of fish and molluscs. These miniscule young fish are often transparent and gelatinous. Most are less than 4 centimetres (1½ in) long and are eaten whole and uncleaned. During the long, open fishing season *neonata* are widely available and are considered a delicacy and a staple. Despite the ethical and sustainable problems of harvesting juvenile fish, and legal restrictions, there seem to be so many *neonata* available – it is hard to believe the quotas are being followed. When I visit Sicily I am amazed to see so much juvenile fish on sale in the markets and on restaurant menus.

Of the many restaurateurs I have spoken to in Sicily, only one family business, a small trattoria in Sciacca, refused to include juvenile fish on the menu. They explained that the issue with *neonata* could be related to the fact that vendors and restaurateurs deal directly with the fishers so there is little observance and enforcement of fishing regulations.

Although I have never ordered *neonata* in a restaurant in Sicily, I have often been presented with a complimentary platter of tiny fish – sometimes of a single species, at other times a mixture (the minute fish are known by different names, which vary from region to region and often within the same provinces).

I have also spoken to many vendors in the fish markets in Sicily. Some were also the fishers. Although they all acknowledged that the supply of fish in Sicilian waters has diminished, none appeared willing to accept any responsibility. Fishers, vendors and restaurateurs all claimed that their livelihoods were at stake: customers expect to buy juveniles and, if they do not provide them, other suppliers would.

Many Sicilian fishers and vendors justify selling juvenile fish on the grounds that they are 'bycatch' (taken while fishing for other species). They argue that the fish are already dead or injured, so there is no point in throwing them back. It seems that for Sicilians, 'sustainability' means that all fish are fair game as long as they can catch their quota. However, it is important to acknowledge that the traditional fishing for juveniles is an important activity for small-scale fishers. It only takes place for

Amara a cu nun avi travagghiu.
(Sicilian proverb)
Is a succinct way of saying
in Sicilian: *Life is tough (and desperate) if you don't have a job.*

Il portafolio vacante, levati davanti. (Italian proverb)
If your purse is empty, go away.

60 consecutive days during the winter and therefore has a high socio-economic impact at local level.

ABOUT THE COLLECTION OF RECIPES

Whether it is a blessing or a curse, Sicily has a rich and varied history, which is reflected in the island's cuisine. It is that variety and that tradition I most value and enjoy. In present-day Sicily, many local communities are recording authentic recipes before they are lost, and more restaurants are presenting localised traditional food, which supports growers in the region and builds relationships within the community.

Because Sicily is an island, the focus of the recipes in this book is on fish *in primi* (first course) and *secondi* (second or main course), with accompanying sauces and vegetables (*contorni*).

Not every meal has to feature the most popular or fashionable fish on the market nor do I associate cost with taste, but I am prepared to pay more for premium, sustainable seafood when I can get it. I buy a variety of sustainable fish and use a cooking method that best complements the taste and texture of the fish I buy.

Not just in Sicily, but also in many other parts of the world, the Slow Food Movement has been influential in linking ethics, ecology and pleasure. In 2005 the Slow Fish Fair, the first gastronomic convention entirely dedicated to fish, was held in Genoa in northern Italy. The Slow Fish Fair is now a biennial event to promote the lesser known varieties of fish as alternatives to those that have been endangered by unsustainable and irresponsible fishing – usually fish with high market value, which is partly due to scarcity and partly due to fashion. Slow Fish also raises awareness of the need to protect small fishing communities that still respect marine ecosystems. This is similar to the eco-label certification awarded to some fisheries around the world by the Marine Stewardship Council (MSC). These are fisheries that catch sustainable seafood, are well managed, do not overfish and work to minimise damage to the marine ecosystem. Some seafood companies supply fish that are certified with the eco-label and this means that each member of the supply chain can be traced.

Readily accessible guides to sustainable seafood are available from leading organisations and scientific institutes in most parts of the world. The MSC is the principal non-government body. Check the websites of your national marine conservation organisations too, as well as the government departments responsible for regulating fishing catches. Some of the information can quickly become outdated as fish stocks and new fisheries are assessed. Keep in mind that stocks of a species might be healthy in one part of the world and seriously depleted in another.

How fish is caught is crucial to ecological sustainability and these sustainability guides review the major fishing methods and their impact on the marine environment. The species of fish are usually grouped into categories. with a traffic-light colour grading system to guide consumers' choices: green to indicate a good sustainable choice; orange to show there may be some concern, and red for the least sustainable – say no, do not buy these fish.

It may come as a surprise that aquaculture industries are not regarded as sustainable. In light of all the well-documented problems associated with fish farms, only non-polluting, on-land aquaculture facilities that do not release pollutants into the sea or rivers should be considered sustainable.

Many Sicilian fish recipes, as you might expect, are for the aristocrats of Sicilian fish – the bluefin tuna and swordfish – but they can be easily replaced by sustainable alternatives cooked in the exactly the same way.

Although I have used the original names for the recipes – for example, pasta with swordfish – I have suggested sustainable alternatives. None of the species are from the endangered list and my personal choice is to use 'green-light' fish only. For example, I have included many recipes that suggest albacore tuna – this tuna is sustainable and can be used for all tuna recipes and for those intended for swordfish or marlin.

However, I have included some fish from the orange category to take account of seasonal and regional variations that may occur.

Sardines (also known as pilchards) are still very plentiful in the seas around Sicily, especially in the summer months, and feature prominently in Sicilian cuisine. Sardines are commonly called *pesce azzuro* (blue fish). This is not a scientific definition of the species but refers to the colour of the ventral and lateral scales – dark blue (often there is also green). This category also includes mackerel, garfish and bonito. They are also called 'blue' because they are part of the seasonal, migratory fish species, which visit the *acque azzurre* – the term used for Sicilian coastal blue waters. These fish are generally cheap

GOOD, CLEAN AND FAIR FISH

The Slow Food philosophy is based on everyday gastronomic pleasure for everyone. To emboy this philosophy, Slow Food has developed a concept of food quality divided into three fundamental and interdependent principles:
Good: fresh, delicious and seasonal, satisfying the senses and connected to our culture and local identity.
Clean: produced using methods that respect the environment and human health.
Fair: accessible prices for consumers, but also fair earnings that can guarantee decent working and living conditions for small-scale producers and workers.

These principles correspond to a global vision of food production, taking into consideration the environment's ability to renew itself and the need for people to live together in harmony, and are as applicable to fish as any other food.
– Slow Fish in Action,
The Slow Food Presidia

because they are plentiful. Bluefin tuna and swordfish were originally included in this category, but they are no longer plentiful or cheap.

It may seem a little tricky to match sustainable fish from other countries with those caught in Sicilian waters, but I have tried to fit certain characteristics, for example the texture, level of oiliness and the range of flavours (from mild to strong) of the fish used in Sicilian recipes and the sustainable fish found in other waters. Refer to specific websites to find out what species of fish represent a better seafood choice in your country and substitute accordingly.

For me, it is vitally important to have a good fishmonger, just as it is to have a good butcher; I know I can request different cuts or ask to vary the size of the portions without feeling embarrassed. I have always established and maintained a good relationship with all the businesses from whom I buy my produce and have been well rewarded – I get very good service and the freshest produce. My fishmonger is a great example. The seafood is always fresh. The small business is family run, and the sellers show respect for the product. I always know what I am buying because the names of the fish are clearly displayed. Sometimes there is information about where it has been caught and even how it was caught, but I know I can ask questions about the fish I buy and always get straight, courteous answers.

Il portafolio vacante, levati davanti (if your purse is empty, go away), a fish vendor in the Catania fish market said to me when I was taking photographs of his fish. I laughed because his statement was unexpected, succinct and it rhymed. So he realised I could speak Italian. We then had a long and amicable conversation.

The oceans are the planet's last great wilderness, man's only remaining frontier on Earth, and perhaps his last chance to prove himself a rational species.
– John L Cully, *The Forests of the Sea; Life and Death on the Continental Shelf*

U pesci feti ra testa. (Sicilian proverb)
Il pesce puzza dalla testa. (Italian)
Fish start smelling from the head (i.e., corruption starts at the top).

Tomu primu

Its first course

MOST SICILIANS CANNOT CONTEMPLATE A MAIN MEAL THAT DOES NOT BEGIN WITH *UN PRIMO*, A FIRST COURSE. AND, WHETHER EATING AT HOME OR IN A RESTAURANT, THEY USUALLY START WITH SOME FORM OF PASTA, WHICH IS OFTEN THE HIGHLIGHT OF THE MEAL. SOMETIMES A SOUP (*MINESTRA* OR *BRODO*) OR RISOTTO IS SERVED AS AN ALTERNATIVE, BUT GENERALLY SOUP IS MORE COMMON IN THE EVENINGS – AND EVEN THIS IS LIKELY TO CONTAIN PASTA. MY RELATIVES SAY THAT IN SICILY EVEN DOGS EAT PASTA EVERY DAY. AND THEY DO.

In the north of Italy, the first course is just as important, but the *primi* will include more soups, risotti, gnocchi (not only those made with potato) and polenta. Sicilians love to eat fish, especially when they eat out. In the numerous fish restaurants in Sicily, the *primi* are likely to be pasta or rice with seafood. Sicilians often precede the pasta with a small antipasto but Italians (and that includes Sicilians) would never order pasta or risotto or a soup as a main course.

PASTA

Good-tasting pasta is made with hard durum wheat. flour. Outside Italy, pasta may come in many shapes and sizes but it means only one thing: something that is made out of wheat and is boiled and eaten dressed with a sauce. But in Italy pasta is the word for dough, pastry or paste – for example, *pasta di mandorla* (almond paste), *pasta di pane* (bread dough) and *pasta frolla* (short pastry).

Dry pasta is just called pasta. Fresh pasta is *pasta fresca*, which you make or buy and cook fresh. Sicilians typically eat commercially made dry pasta, unless they have a *nonna* (grandmother) to make *pasta fresca* for them. *Pastasciutta* means 'dry' (*asciutta*) pasta, but the term is used for any kind of pasta dressed with a sauce and eaten with a fork, rather than in a wet dish such as a soup.

Each time I stay with my relatives in Ragusa, I am reminded just how easy pasta is to make. Nothing gives my elderly aunt, Zia Niluzza, more pleasure than to cook and feed people, and for my benefit, she makes fresh pasta every day in a variety of shapes and sizes. She keeps her wooden board, sawn-off broomstick (which she uses as a rolling pin) and her sack of durum wheat flour within easy reach in her kitchen.

Shapes of pasta

Commercially made pasta comes in many shapes and sizes. Because pasta sauces made with fish are light, long thread-like pasta of varying thicknesses are preferred. The general rule is the lighter the sauce the thinner the pasta.

The most common pasta for fish sauces are spaghetti to spaghettini (from *spago*, Italian for string) to vermicelli (from *vermi*, meaning worms) and the thread-like pasta shapes with holes through their entire length – bucati to bucatini (from *buco*, hole).

Un giorno senza pasta è un giorno sprecato. (Italian proverb) *A day without pasta is a day wasted.*

The long wide (tagliatelle to linguine) or wide pasta (lasagne to pappardelle) may have straight or curled edges and are usually eaten with sauces made with meat. The short tubular (penne, rigatoni) or the twisted or spiral (fusilli) shapes, rings (anelli), shells (chiocciole or conchigle) or butterflies (farfalle) are shaped to retain and trap the ingredients in the sauce and therefore are used for thicker sauces.

There is no classification system to determine the sizes or common names for the endless pasta types. Identical shapes can have different names according to regional preferences or those of particular manufacturers. The best policy is to go for shape and size (such as short and tubular).

The essential ingredients are flour made out of hard wheat (*semola di grano duro*) and good-quality water – the best water is said to come from Naples and this is why Italians believe the best pasta and the best coffee are Neapolitan. Dough strength and high-protein content are the qualities of pasta made with 100 per cent durum wheat.

According to Giuseppe Coria, a respected Sicilian food authority, there are three rules to follow for a good plate of pasta. It must be *olurusu* (perfumed), *sapuritu* (have excellent flavour) and *insucatu* (well dressed). For Italians, a sauce is a *condimento* and it never overpowers the main ingredient, which is the pasta. Which is why in Italy a little sauce goes a long way. This means that the quality of the pasta is paramount and everything depends on how it is cooked and drained.

Amounts

In Italy 100g (3½oz) of dry pasta and 125g (4oz) of fresh pasta per person is the general rule. Taking into account small and large eaters, I find that 500g (17½oz) of dry pasta is sufficient for *primo* portions for six people or 600g (1lb 5oz) of fresh pasta. If I am serving the pasta dish as a main course (do not tell any Italian that you do this), I increase the amounts accordingly (750g/1lb 12½oz if they are big eaters).

To cook pasta

Add the pasta to plenty of boiling salted water. Stir the pasta gently to separate the pieces and keep them from sticking to the bottom of the pot.

The pasta needs to be drained when it is *al dente* – which literally means 'to the tooth' and refers to the pasta's consistency when it comes in contact with the teeth. I have also heard the term *pasta in piedi* ('pasta standing up'). When bitten, there should be some resistance from the dough in the centre – the whitish area, about the size of a pinprick, that is partially cooked – called the *anima*, or soul of the pasta. On my last visit to Sicily I was reminded just how firm *al dente* is compared with what is eaten, even in reputable Italian restaurants, outside Italy. When pasta is overcooked, all the wheat turns to sugar and loses that nutty wheat flavour.

Manufacturers usually give a cooking time, but test the pasta a couple of minutes before it is supposed to be ready and bite into it – it continues to cook with the residual heat. Fresh pasta cooks in a fraction of the time of dried pasta: it is ready when it rises to the surface. Because the pasta is fresh, there will not be the *anima* in the centre. The pasta needs to be smooth and silky. In either case, keep checking. How things change over time! In Maestro Martino's 15th-century manuscript, *Libro de arte coquinaria*, there are recipes for sun-dried pastas that could be stored for up to three years and needed to be cooked for one to two hours.

Pasta must be drained well (in a colander) and is always mixed with sauce before being brought to the table. It is best to return the drained pasta to the saucepan it was cooked in and then add the sauce, or add the pasta to the pan with the sauce – both methods help retain the heat.

A contrary view

It is difficult to believe that any Italian could hate pasta, but one person did, and he tried to persuade others to change their habits.

Dissi lu Zu'Nicola: si nun vugghi la pignata, nun si cala. (Sicilian proverb)
Disse lo zio Nicola: se la pentola non bolle, non si cala. (Italian)
Uncle Nicola said: Don't lower the basket until the water is boiling.

As first course

Filippo Tommaso Marinetti hated pasta. He was a poet and one of the founders of Futurism, an artistic and literary movement that began in Italy and spread to other countries in the first decade of the 20th century. Enthused by modernity (the world should be new, shiny, steely and speedy), Futurists repudiated the past, especially political and artistic traditions. Their manifesto *Le Futurisme* was published in Paris in 1909. In 1930 the Italian Futurists launched their *Manifesto of Futurist Cooking* in Milan and in 1932 Marinetti published *Cucina Futurista* (*The Futurist Cookbook*).

Marinetti argued that Italians should replace pasta with rice because pasta was making his compatriots passive and lethargic. He wrote:

We call for the abolition of pastasciutta, an absurd Italian gastronomic religion. It may be that a diet of cod, roast beef and steamed pudding is beneficial to the English, cold cuts and cheese to the Dutch and sauerkraut, smoked pork and sausage to the Germans, but pasta is not beneficial to the Italians. For example, it is completely hostile to the vivacious spirit and passionate, generous, intuitive soul of the Neapolitans. If these people have been heroic fighters, inspired artists, awe-inspiring orators, shrewd lawyers, tenacious farmers it was in spite of their voluminous daily plate of pasta. When they eat it they develop the typical ironic and sentimental scepticism which can often cut short their enthusiasm.

– F T. Marinetti, T*he Futurist Cookbook* (translated by Suzanne Brill)

RISU – RISO (RICE)

Rice was introduced to mainland Italy via Arab-occupied Spain and Sicily. Rice was grown in Sicily before 1000 BCE. The Arabs used irrigation to grow rice and it was cultivated around the area south of Catania until the early 18th century. But in the rest of Sicily rice growing dwindled after the Normans established their 'kingdom in the sun' in the 11th century. Interest in eating rice was only revived by the Aragonese 450 or so years later and was then carried on by the Spanish during their rule of Sicily.

Risotto is a northern Italian dish. If you see it on Sicilian menus it will be a modern recipe or an adaptation of a traditional recipe.

Traditional Sicilian rice dishes consist of boiled rice dressed with a sauce. The *risu* (Sicilian for rice) is cooked and treated like pasta – cooked in boiling salted water, drained and dressed with the sauce. The other, less common method is to add the rice to the ingredients being cooked (usually a braise with sufficient liquid), cover, and leave it to cook.

Modern recipes are more like risotto and suggest using stock instead of water. Butter is another modern addition. My relatives very rarely, if ever, purchase butter and never margarine.

In Sicily the standard rice is *originorio*, which is short and round with a pearly appearance. Unavoidably, rice traditionally used for risotto has also found its way into Sicilian homes, and *arborio*, *vialone nano* and *carnaroli* are now preferred in Sicily.

Amounts

As a general guideline I use half a cup of rice per person. Again I increase or decrease the amounts accordingly, depending on whether it is to be served as a *primo* or a main course and particular appetites.

To cook rice

Cook rice like pasta until *al dente* so that the grains remain separate instead of clumping. Drain and dress like pasta.

Taste is like an umbilical cord. We all return to our grandmothers, no matter how many detours we take along the way.
– Carlo Petrini, the founder of the Slow Food movement

ABOUT THE RECIPES IN *COMU PRIMU*

Recipes are never finished, they change all the time. To put them in writing would be to standarise them, kill them.
– Fulvio Pierangelini, fabled Italian chef referred to as 'the great singer of Italian cuisine'

On a recent trip to Sicily, I went looking for some of the dishes of my childhood and found them in the homes of my friends and relatives, as well as in small homely restaurants and *trattorie*, which offer a simple cuisine and use local produce. Some of them are not just presenting old favourites, but are proudly rediscovering many original recipes and linking up tradition and innovation.

It is very difficult not to eat Sicilian food in Sicily. Even the more modern, stylish and expensive restaurants with professionally trained chefs use and promote the best local produce and combine their international knowledge to create new approaches to traditional recipes. As a cook, I am innovative too and I have included these as variations with the recipes.

COMMON INGREDIENTS IN SAUCES

There is an obvious affinity of tastes and flavours in Sicilian recipes, bound to the region, the resources and the local traditions – some common flavours combine well with fish, and some should never be mixed.

Extra virgin olive oil is the cooking medium and is also added for taste, as are herbs and the stronger flavours of garlic, chilli, capers, olives, anchovies and sometimes lemon zest. But generally the list is limited to a few ingredients – to enhance the taste of the pasta (and the fish), not to overpower it.

I always use fresh herbs (mainly parsley, fennel, mint, basil and bay leaves) except for oregano, which becomes more pungent when dried.

Although most recipes say to chop herbs, they should be finely cut. The chopping action bruises the leaves and alters the taste.

I have refrained from calling salt 'sea salt' because even common iodised salt is technically sea salt, as it is derived from seawater, refined and processed with the addition of iodine. For general cooking I use what is called sea salt, which is harvested naturally by channelling seawater into shallow ponds and allowing the sun and wind to evaporate the water. This unrefined salt has no additives and still contains traces of other minerals to varying degrees, including iron, magnesium, calcium, potassium, manganese, zinc and iodine. It can be ground finely or used in coarser small grains.

I generally add rock salt to boiling water when I cook pasta. It is just a habit, a family tradition.

For the table and salads, I generally use crystal salt flakes. These are derived from the brine seabeds or riverbeds or, in some cases, from underground. The way the crystals form and their shape, as well as the other chemicals that are present, affect the taste of the salt and the dish they are dressing.

I've noticed that Sicilian restaurants nowadays seem very fond of cherry tomatoes (*ciliegine*, from *ciliegia*, the local word for cherry, but sometimes *pizzitelli* or 'little'). They look more stylish than cooked tomatoes and provide an explosion of flavour in the mouth.

Probably the most unusual additions to *primi* made with fish are the final sprinklings of grated cheese (pecorino, *caciocavallo* or salted ricotta), a taste shunned by the rest of Italy who never eat cheese with fish.

A very Sicilian thing to do is to sprinkle breadcrumbs toasted in olive oil on top of pasta. These add crunch, texture and taste.

Come diavolo e l'aqua santa.
(Italian proverb)
Like the devil and holy water.

&

Come pane duro e coltello che non taglia. (Italian proverb)
Like hard bread and a knife that does not cut.

– Favourite sayings of my Zia Niluzza

FISH USED IN PASTA AND SOME RICE *PRIMI*

Italians use a variety of terms to describe various fish – for example *pesce azzurro* (blue fish), *pesce povero* (poor or common fish) and *pesce sostenibile* (sustainable fish).

Sardines, anchovies, bonito and mackerel are included in the category known as *pesce azzurro*. But these fish are also known as *pesce povero* (literally 'poor fish' – inexpensive because they are common). Swordfish and tuna are also members of this group, but they cannot be classed as inexpensive or prolific. Interestingly, inexpensive fish are often used in Sicilian restaurants. There are numerous pasta dishes made with *pesce povero*, especially sardines in various stages of maturity.

Unfortunately Sicilians are very fond of all types of *neonata*, or 'new born' (see pages 26) – *nunnata* and *muccu* are two of the many local names for the minute fish.

In these recipes for *primi* I have used simple categories: those related to size, *pesci piccoli* (small fish) and *pesci piu grandi* (bigger fish); shellfish, which include the crustaceans group and the molluscs group, and *pesce salato* (salted fish).

Crustaceans and molluscs are often grouped on restaurant menus as *frutti di mare*. *Crostacei* (crustaceans) include various familiar animals, such as crabs, lobsters, crayfish, prawns and shrimps. *Molluschi* (molluscs) are invertebrates – without backbones – including oysters, mussels, squids and octopuses. Sea urchins are also prized as a condiment for pasta.

Pesce salato (salted fish), especially anchovies, are commonly used to flavour sauces and give the characteristic Sicilian flavour to dishes. Other popular salted fish found in restaurants are *bottarga* and *tonno salato* (see pages 102–19).

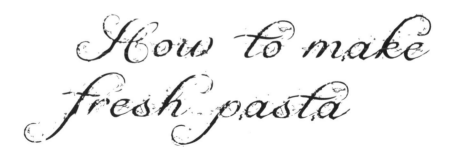

How to make fresh pasta

Avere le mani in pasta. (Italian proverb)
To have one's hands in the dough (the literal translation): to have one's finger in the pie.

LIFE STILL SEEMS TO BE THE SAME IN SICILY WHEN IT COMES TO DOING THINGS WITH THE FAMILY. SUNDAY IS USUALLY FAMILY DAY – THE DAY OF REST WHEN THE FAMILY GETS TOGETHER FOR A LONG LUNCH. IF THERE IS A DAY TO MAKE FRESH PASTA, SUNDAY IS IT, AND OFTEN, THE OLDER WOMEN IN THE FAMILY – THE GRANDMOTHERS (*LE NONNE*) AND THE AUNTS (*LE ZIE*) WILL MAKE IT – IT IS LIKE SECOND NATURE, SO EASY. IT IS THE REST OF THE MEAL THAT WILL TAKE TIME.

I have never seen anyone in Sicily make pasta with a food processor or electric mixer; even in restaurants people make it by hand. They may mix the dough and set it to rest before they go to Mass and afterwards roll out the dough and cut it into shape. Some may even have time for a short *passegiata* and a chat with friends or to buy cakes from the *pasticceria*. The men, the daughters and daughters-in-law may get to go to the bar for a coffee and an extended chat before helping the elderly women. In Sicily on a Sunday, the streets will look pretty much deserted by lunchtime. On occasion the extended family will go to a restaurant; often it will be out of their town. There they are likely to order a *primo* of *pasta fresca* because restaurateurs also follow the tradition.

Pasta may be made without eggs, but generally eggs are used for taste, colour and to bind the flour (most commercial pastas do not contain eggs). Pasta with a high proportion of eggs is more common in northern Italy.

Measurements are not the Sicilian way – it's the look, feel and smell of something that guide the cook. It's difficult to give the exact quantities of flour and eggs, as it depends on how large the egg is and how much the flour will absorb, but the standard proportions for making egg pasta are 1 large egg and 1 eggshell full of water for every 100g (3½oz) of flour. Pasta with a high proportion of eggs may not require any water. Zia Niluzza generally uses more eggs if she is making tagliatelle or lasagne and less when she is making the shorter Sicilian shapes.

Flour made from hard durum wheat (strong protein flour) is sold under different names. 'Hard' is high in gluten and is best for pasta and bread. 'Soft' is good for cakes, pastry and biscuits. In Italy flour is milled and classified as *farina* 1 or 0, or 00. This is the degree of the grind – 00 is the most highly refined but is not necessarily the highest in protein, so it is best to ask when you purchase it.

The following is the method Sicilians prefer for making pasta.

METHOD

FORM THE PASTA

On a flat surface

Shape the flour and salt into a mound, make a well in the centre and crack the eggs in one at a time. Add about 1 cup of water and, using a fork, whisk the eggs until combined (Zia Niluzza cannot resist adding about a tablespoon of extra virgin olive oil at this stage). Start drawing in some of the flour with your fingertips – begin at the inner rim of the well, and gradually mix the liquid into the flour as you continue to add very little amounts of water

Keep a little flour to the side so you can add it to the dough if it feels a little sticky. Keep incorporating flour and liquid until the dough is no longer wet and feels stiff.

Knead the dough for 10–15 minutes, using your palm and pushing the dough away from you, then folding it back onto itself until it feels elastic (press the dough with your finger – it will spring back). It will eventually form into a ball. If your hands begin to stick when you're kneading, dip them in a little flour.

Coat the dough with oil and wrap it in plastic film. Leave it to rest in a cool place for at least 40 minutes before shaping.

INGREDIENTS

For 6–8 people

700g (1lb 9oz) plain flour (made from hard durum wheat)

2–5 eggs (I use organic, free range)

1 tablespoon extra virgin olive oil

½ teaspoon salt

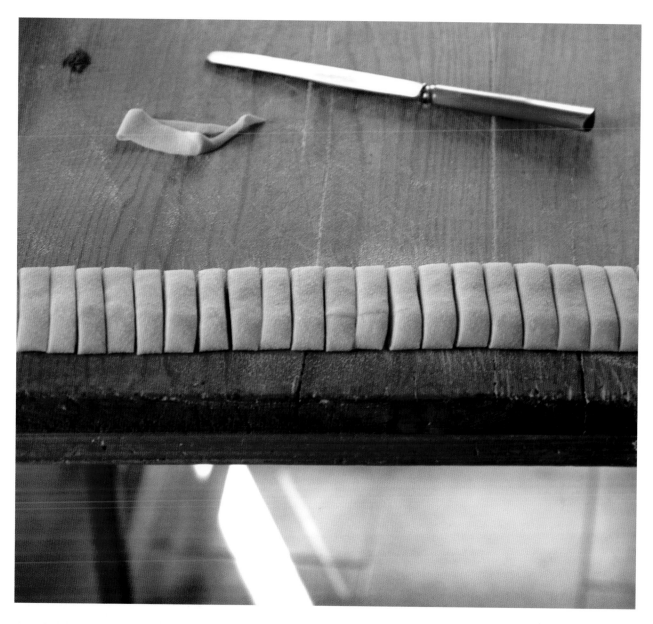

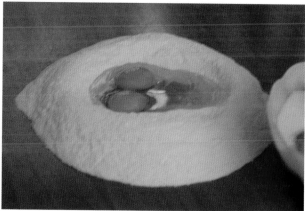

With a food processor or electric mixer with a paddle attachment
Process flour and salt for a few seconds. Add eggs and oil and as much water as it takes for the mixture to resemble fine breadcrumbs and the dough to start coming together. A food processor with a bread hook will do the kneading.

THE PASTA IS NOW READY TO BE ROLLED

With a rolling pin
Divide the dough into eight pieces. Work one piece at a time (keep the others covered with plastic wrap as you work). Dust the work surface and dough with a little flour. Flatten the dough with the palm of the hand and then, using a rolling pin, roll it forwards then backwards to even it out. If it begins to stick, dust the rolling pin with flour. Turn the dough regularly to keep its circular shape and roll it to about 2mm (⅛in) thick (depending on how thick you want it: sheets of lasagne are usually slightly thicker than ribbon pasta such as papardelle).

With a pasta rolling machine (a small one with a handle)
Prepare the pasta as above. Lightly flour and feed separate pieces of dough through the rollers of the pasta machine on the widest setting, folding the sheet once or twice and feeding through the rollers again until the sheet is smooth. Reduce the setting notch by notch, feeding the sheet through until you reach one of the last notches and it is about 2mm (⅛in) thick.

LONG PASTA SHAPES

If using a pasta machine, its cutters will determine the width of the strips.

There are various methods for cutting long ribbon pasta by hand. Roll up each sheet of pasta and with a knife and cut the rolls into required widths. Zia Niluzza rolls the dough around a thin rolling stick, then pulls out the stick and has a roll of pasta ready to be sliced and unfurl into strips.

Cut the pasta with a sharp knife or pastry wheel. Rest for at least 10 minutes before cooking. The width of ribbon pasta varies. These are rough estimates:

lasagne: 12 x 17cm (5 x 7in) squares
ravioli: 8cm (3½in) discs or squares
pappardelle: 2cm (¾in) strips
fettuccine and *tagliatelle* (generally interchangeable): 1cm (½in) strips
taglierini: 2–3mm (about ⅛in) strips

As first course

maltagliati ('badly cut') or *stracci* ('rags'): 2–3cm (¾–1¼in) strips, unfurled and randomly sliced diagonally; or tear into 10–12cm (4–5in) pieces.

SICILIAN SHORT PASTA SHAPES (MACCARRUNA)

Maccarruna (*maccheroni* in Italian) is sometimes used as the generic word for pasta and is still common, especially in Naples and Sicily. It is also the term used in ancient recipe books. Most pasta, of whatever sort, was labelled *maccheroni* until about 1870, after which local folk names were widely adopted by producers and consumers.

Some researchers believe *maccarruna* comes from *maccare*, to squash. Others think it comes from *maccu*, a thick Sicilian soup of pulses and pasta. There are also Greek words: *macron* meaning long; *makaria*, a dough of barley and broth, and *makar*, very happy – presumably the state *maccarruna* eaters experience. Whatever its origins, Sicilians consume large quantities of *maccarruna*.

There are many small shapes of fresh pasta made in Sicilian homes. Some of the favourites are the gnocchi or *gnocchetti* (smaller gnocchi) shapes.

Gnocchi (dumplings) in mainland central and northern Italy are made of potatoes, pumpkin or ricotta (often with spinach). There are also bread gnocchi and ones made of fine cornmeal or semolina. Sicilians prefer *gnocculi* or *gnucchiteddi* (a smaller one) made with pasta dough – these have different names in different regions in Sicily. In Ragusa, they are called *causanedda*. The most common local names are *gnocculi*, *gnucchiteddi*, *cavati* and *caviateddi*. All have an indentation in the centre to ensure even cooking. Some are *rigati* (have ridges) and some are *lisci* (smooth). Also popular in Ragusa and Modica are *lolli* – these are 6–7cm (2½–3in) long and are often included in soups made with dried legumes.

MAKING GNUCCHITEDDI (OR CAUSANEDDA)

For *gnucchiteddi* (or *causanedda*), my Ragusa relatives use 1–2 eggs for 800g–1kg (29–36oz) of durum wheat flour and as much water as the dough absorbs, but the standard practice in other parts of Sicily is to use no eggs.

Mix the flour, water, salt and oil according to instructions on page 46. Shape and knead the dough until it feels hard and compact. Because there are fewer eggs (or no eggs) in the mixture, the dough will benefit from extra kneading (15–20 minutes). Rest the dough for at least 30 minutes.

Divide dough into several pieces. Use your hands to roll out long cords (1–2cm/½–¾in in diameter). My relatives like the smaller ones in thick

soups and the larger (2cm) ones for pasta eaten with a fork (*pastasciutta*). Cut thinner cords into 2cm pieces, the others into 4cm (1½in) pieces.

Shape each piece of dough individually. For *causanedda,* shape on a flat board with the index and middle fingers. For *gnocculi* and *gnucchiteddi* use the inner side of a cheese grater (or a finely ridged wooden block, such as a butter pat): start by holding the piece of dough at the top of the grater and with the index and middle fingers of one hand lightly press and draw the piece of dough in a curved, concave shape so it has a hollow in the centre. Some shape the *gnocculi* with a fork. Usually all the women and children contribute to the shaping. My relatives make these shapes very quickly and I am always embarrassed because even the youngest shape them faster than I can. It is just practice.

Zia Niluzza sometimes uses her grandmother's special device (it looks like a narrow loom) for making *gnucchiteddi*. Small, fine strips of pasta (4cm) are rolled on a long, thin reed. By rolling the reed on the loom, she makes grooves on each piece of dough.

Busiate are popular in the area around Trapani and are made by wrapping flat pieces of dough (usually 4.5–9cm/2–4in) around a double-pointed knitting needle and curling the dough into shape. The needle is then removed rapidly so the pasta maintains its form.

In Naples, these shaped pasta are sometimes called *fusilli*, which is also the common name of commercial pasta of this shape. Other commercial types of pasta (that look homemade) are *fusilli busiate* or *maccheroncelli*. *Casarecci* or *pasta casareccia* (from *casa*, 'home') comes from the Puglia region in southeast Italy and, like the Sicilian pasta, is shaped by being rolled around a wooden dowel. Also originating from Puglia are *orecchiette*; when homemade, they are shaped with one finger. The shape resembles a small ear (*orecchio* means ear). Once I watched women in the town of Bari sitting in the lane outside their homes making *orecchiette* for one of the local restaurants.

STORING FRESH PASTA

If you have any dough left over, cut it into strips (1–2cm/½–¾in wide) and freeze it well wrapped in plastic between layers of greaseproof paper, or dry before you store. I use a broomstick suspended between two chairs to dry long pasta. It should be brittle when completely dry. To cook frozen pasta, simply add to boiling water.

Pesce piccolo
Small fish

EXCEPT THE LARGE FISH SUCH AS TUNA AND SWORDFISH, THIS GROUP ENCOMPASSES ALL THE OTHER FISH OF VARIOUS SHAPES AND SIZES. THERE ARE THE ROUND SHAPED ONES (BREAMS AND JOHN DORY) AND THE LONG FISH (RED MULLETS AND SNAPPER) AND THE OILY FISH (HERRINGS AND SARDINES). THESE FISH CAN BE FIRM OR FLAKY. THE OILY FISH HAVE A LOT OF FLAVOUR THAT CAN TASTE UNPLEASANT IF THEY ARE NOT ABSOLUTELY FRESH.

As first course

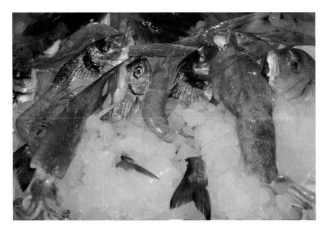

Pasta chi sardi

Pasta con le sarde

PASTA WITH SARDINES FROM PALERMO, MADE WITH FENNEL, PINE NUTS AND CURRANTS

MENU FOR LEONARDO SCIASCIA

In his intricately plotted novels, Sciascia (1921–89) scrutinised the Mafia's evil influence on his island's culture. A member of the communist party, he was elected to the Italian Parliament and then the European Parliament. I ate in a trattoria in Porta Carini, one of the ancient sections of Palermo, where Sciasia and Andrea Camilleri used to meet and have heated discussions over lunch.

&

Rolled eggplants with stuffing
(*Mulinciani ammugghiati*)
Pasta with sardines from
Palermo (*Pasta chi sardi*), baked
version
Fish in a bag (*Pesce al cartoccio*)
with *salmoriglio* dressing
Zucchini sautéed with tomatoes
(*Cucuzzedda cu pumaroru*)

You cannot go to Sicily and not eat *pasta con le sarde*, the national dish of Sicily (the others would have to be caponata, cassata and cannoli). There are many regional variations of pasta sauces made with sardines, all called by the same name, but the most famous is an ancient dish from Palermo.

I like how Sicilians often skip between the sweet and savoury tastes – the sour and/or salty is often combined with the sweet. What makes this dish unusual is the combination of textures and strong fragrant tastes: the strong oily sardines, the cleansing flavour of the fennel, the sweetness of the raisins (or currants) and the delicate aromatic pine nuts.

Pasta con le sarde is served with toasted breadcrumbs, in the same way that grated cheese is used (the breadcrumbs may have been a substitute for cheese for the poor). In some versions the cooked ingredients are arranged in layers in a baking dish, topped with breadcrumbs and baked .

Unfortunately, it may be difficult to buy bunches of wild fennel (*finucchiu sarvaggiu*) outside Italy, but wild fennel does grow in neglected areas such as on the side of the road, vacant land and along banks of waterways. It has a strong aniseed smell and taste, strong green colour and fine fern-like fronds. I collect the soft young shoots of this plant, recognised by their lighter colour. Unlike Florentine fennel, wild fennel has no bulb. Always make sure that the plant looks healthy before you collect it – it is a weed and may have been sprayed. Florentine fennel can be used but the taste will not be as strong – try to buy bulbs with some of the green fronds attached and you enhance the taste by using fennel seeds as well.

The addition of almonds is a local variation – it brings another layer of taste and texture to the dish. Alternatively, you could double the quantity of pine nuts.

The origins of *pasta chi sardi* are said to be Arabic. In one story, an Arab cook was instructed to prepare food for the Arab troops when they first landed in Sicily. The cook panicked when confronted by such a large number of people, so the troops were instructed to forage for ingredients. He made do with what they found – wild herbs (fennel) and fish (freshly caught and plentiful sardines) to which he added Arabic flavourings (the saffron, dried fruit and the nuts).

The first time I ate *pasta con le sarde* was at the famous La 'Ngrasciata (meaning dirty/the dirty one) in Palermo, an incredible restaurant not only because of what they served but because of the characters patronising it, at the tables and standing in the car park. There was no menu, just a waiter who rattled off what he suggested we eat (in Sicilian because he was speaking to locals). Amazing food.

The pasta can be eaten hot or at room temperature – Italians believe that piping hot food prevents the tastebuds from functioning effectively and mutes the individual flavours. I particularly like to serve it at a cool temperature in summer. Take it out of the fridge a couple of hours before serving.

Pasta con le sarde is fairly substantial. In Sicily it is a first course, in other parts of the world where it is not a mortal sin to eat pasta as a *secondo* you could increase the quantities of fish and follow it with a green salad as a separate course (I never serve pasta and salad together). In Italy a salad is a *contorno* (a side dish) and accompanies a main course. Pasta, risotto and soup (all *primi*) cannot be served with a side dish.

Traditionally the sauce is made with sliced fillets of sardines. Sardines are not difficult to clean, but buying fillets save time. Leave about a third of the fillets whole, to decorate the pasta. If using whole sardines for decoration, Sicilians butterfly them.

You could substitute other oily fish such as small mullet. In the hinterland, before transportation, salted sardines were used – an authentic variation.

METHOD

Place the wild fennel in cold, salted water and boil for 10–15 minutes. Remove the fennel and reserve the green-tinged, fennel-flavoured water. If using fennel bulb, boil the quartered bulb with the fennel seeds until tender. Drain the fennel in a colander, then gently squeeze out the water. Strain the cooking liquid, discarding the seeds and reserve.

INGREDIENTS

about 300g (10½oz) wild fennel (stalks and foliage); or 1 large bulb cut into quarters, the green fronds, and 1 teaspoon fennel seeds
700g (1lb 9oz) sardines
about 1 cup extra virgin olive oil
2 onions, finely sliced
4 anchovies, finely chopped
1 cup pine nuts
1 cup almonds, toasted and chopped (optional)
¾ cup currants, or seedless raisins or sultanas
½–1 small teaspoon saffron
500g (17½oz) bucatini
4–5 tablespoons coarse breadcrumbs
salt and freshly ground pepper to taste

Chop the fennel roughly.

Cut about two-thirds of the sardine fillets into thick pieces, reserving whole fillets or butterflied fish.

Heat oil in a wide shallow pan large enough to fit all the ingredients including the pasta. Sauté the onions over medium heat until golden. Add pine nuts, raisins and almonds (if using). Toss gently. Add the sliced sardines, salt and pepper and the remaining raw fennel. Cook on gentle heat for about 5–10 minutes, stirring gently. Add the anchovies and, as they cook, crush them with the back of a spoon to dissolve into a paste. Add the cooked chopped fennel and the saffron dissolved in a little warm water. Continue to stir and cook gently.

Boil bucatini in the fennel water until *al dente*. Drain.

Fry the whole fillets of sardines or butterflied sardines in a separate frying pan, keeping them intact. Remove from the pan and put aside.

In a separate pan, toast the breadcrumbs in a little olive oil over medium heat, watching them carefully so they don't burn.

To assemble, place the pasta in the saucepan with the fish and fennel sauce. Stir gently off the heat. Add the pasta and leave for 5–10 minutes to incorporate the flavours and to preserve some warmth. Gently fold in the whole fillets.

When ready to serve, tip the pasta and fish mixture into a serving bowl, arranging the whole fillets or butterflied sardines on top. Sprinkle the dish with the toasted breadcrumbs.

IF YOU ARE BAKING THE PASTA

Oil a baking tray or ovenproof dish (traditionally a round one) and sprinkle with breadcrumbs (that have been dry-toasted in the oven) to prevent sticking. Place a layer of the dressed pasta on top, add more breadcrumbs and another layer of pasta; finish with breadcrumbs.

Cover with some fresh breadcrumbs, sprinkle with extra virgin olive oil and bake in preheated 200°C (400°F) oven for about 12–15 minutes. A teaspoon of sugar can be sprinkled on top of the breadcrumbs – this, with the oil, will help the bread form a crust, adding yet another contrasting taste and a different texture. Five minutes before the dish is cooked, place the whole or butterflied fillets on the top to warm through.

VARIATION

PASTA WITH SARDINES FROM SYRACUSE

There are many regional examples of *pasta con le sarde*. In a trattoria in Sciacca (on the southwest coast), I ate a version made with wild fennel, fennel seeds and a little *strattu* or *estratto di pomodoro*, a wonderfully thick and rich strong-tasting tomato paste (see opposite). This version is also popular in and around Catania and the sauce is made very quickly – the pasta can be cooked at the same time as you are making the sauce.

Soften the onion in ½ cup of olive oil, then add the sardine fillets and seal. Add the raw fennel fronds (Sicilians cook these first in boiling water, but I do not think this is necessary), tomato paste, fennel seeds, salt and pepper. Add a splash of water (or white wine) and cook for 5–10 minutes.

Heat the remaining olive oil in another pan, add the anchovies and stir vigorously to dissolve. Add the breadcrumbs and stir until golden.

Cook pasta. Combine the pasta, the sauce and the breadcrumbs and serve hot.

In some parts of Sicily, the pasta is served with grated pecorino cheese rather than the breadcrumbs and anchovy mixture. Or substitute fresh parsley for the fennel greens and seeds, and use 2–3 cloves of chopped garlic instead of the onion.

INGREDIENTS

1 onion, finely sliced
1 cup extra virgin olive oil
500g (17½oz) sardine fillets
1 cup fennel fronds, finely sliced and closely packed
2 tablespoons tomato paste
1 tablespoon fennel seeds
3–4 anchovies
1 cup breadcrumbs
500g (17½oz) bucatini
salt and freshly ground pepper to taste

Estratto di pomodoro

TOMATO PASTE

In summer, thick tomato pulp is spread out on shallow trays or boards to dry in the fierce Sicilian sun. My great-grandmother and my grandmother in Ragusa used to dry the pulp in large platters – the type with ancient patterns and designs now reproduced by the Sicilian ceramicist company called Alessi from Caltagirone. These beautiful platters are still used by my cousins in Ragusa.

The tomato pulp is stirred regularly so that it dries evenly. When it achieves a deep red, almost black, colour and a very thick texture – so thick that when it is spooned onto a surface it will hold its shape – it is packed into preserving jars by the spoonful and covered with extra virgin olive oil. If the paste is to be stored for longer, the contents are covered with a heavy sprinkling of coarse salt and some muslin.

Strattu is available commercially in specialised places in Sicily and some is still made at home; I bought some at the Syracuse Market. But obviously, if you can't be in Syracuse a good quality tomato paste will just have to suffice.

Pasta chi trighi o'rau

Pasta e trigle al ragu

PASTA WITH BRAISED RED MULLET

Sicilians love *trigle* (red mullet, called *rougets barbets* in France) and so do I. The skin of red mullet remains red even after it is cooked – I try to keep the fish pieces whole and use some of the fish on top of the pasta as decoration.

This pasta dish is particularly flavourful. The sauce is a braise made with red mullet, tomatoes, garlic, parsley, fronds of wild fennel (when in season) and perhaps a few fennel seeds.

When I last travelled to Sicily, I visited as many restaurants listed in one of the Slow Food publications as possible. I ate this dish in a seafront restaurant in San Leone near Agrigento. It was in autumn, so the purée of fresh broad beans they add in springtime was missing. I feel sure that the purée is a chef's innovation and not a traditional thing, but it sounded appealing.

If I am fortunate enough to find young broad beans, I leave them whole and I am not inclined to double-peel them (removing the outer skin), even though the peeled beans are sweeter, smoother and have a beautiful colour. If the beans are blanched, the degree of difficulty and the tedium scale lessens considerably, but this is not enough to convince me.

In this recipe there are four different cooking processes: the making of the tomato sauce, the sealing of the fish before it is added to the salsa, the cooking of the broad beans (and puréeing if you wish to do this) and the cooking of the pasta.

INGREDIENTS

¾ cup extra virgin olive oil

800g (1lb 13oz) red tomatoes, peeled and chopped

3 cloves garlic, chopped

1 cup wild fennel or fronds from bulb fennel, finely chopped

½ teaspoon fennel seeds (or more if fresh fennel is not available)

500g (17½oz) red mullet, whole or fillets, cut into 8–10cm (3½–4in) pieces

1 onion, chopped

500g (17½oz) shelled broad beans (optional)

1 cup finely cut parsley

500g (17½oz) tagliatelle or bavette

salt and freshly ground pepper to taste

METHOD

Make a sauce using some of the oil, the tomatoes, garlic, fresh fennel and fennel seeds. Reduce, uncovered, over medium heat until thick.

Heat some of the olive oil in a frying pan, seal the fish on both sides and

season. Braise on gentle heat until the fish is cooked (it will only take a few minutes). Carefully add the fish to the pan containing the sauce.

Soften the onion in some more olive oil. Add the broad beans and parsley, and braise slowly, covered, for about 10 minutes. Add salt and pepper and a little liquid so that the beans do not stick. Purée the beans (optional).

Cook the pasta.

To serve, place the broad beans or the broad bean purée on the bottom of each plate and top it with the dressed pasta. Place a fillet of fish on top.

VARIATION

Replace the purée of broad beans with one made of fresh peas.

Pasta co pumaroru cruru e pisci friuti

Pasta col pomodoro e pesce fritti

PASTA WITH RAW TOMATOES AND FRIED FISH

Around Trapani, on the northwest coast, it is quite common to serve hot pasta with an uncooked sauce of ripe tomatoes. When the pasta is dressed the fragrant smells of summer are released. This is topped with small fried fish (hot or warm). Use short shaped fresh pasta or what is called *pasta casareccia* (commercially produced dry pasta, but shapes look homemade) or spaghetti or bucatini. Once the pasta is cooked and dressed, it is topped with small fish, first dipped in flour then fried (see page 55).

To dress the pasta

Use either Sicilian pesto (*pesto trapanese*) made with tomatoes, olive oil, garlic, almonds and basil (see page 271); or *sarsa a friddu* (*friddu* means 'cold' in Sicilian) in which the raw ingredients – tomatoes, olive oil, garlic, parsley and/or basil – are chopped very finely and mixed (see page 258).

Suitable fish

Use 600g (1lb 5oz) of small whole fish or 500g (17½oz) of fish fillets – sardines or sprats. Use small fish such as mullet, red mullet, sand whiting and leatherjackets.

Pesce più grande
Larger fish

THESE ARE THE LARGE MEATY, FIRM FISH SUCH AS SWORDFISH AND TUNA THAT HAVE QUALITIES SIMILAR TO MEAT. KINGFISH AND MACKEREL ALSO BELONG TO THE TUNA FAMILY.

As first course

Maccarruna che cacocciuli

Maccheroni coi carciofi

PASTA WITH ARTICHOKES AND TUNA

MENU FOR LUIGI PIRANDELLO

Born in the village of Caos, a poor suburb of Girgenti, Agrigento, Pirandello (1867–1936) settled in Rome and won the Nobel Prize for Literature in 1934. When I think of him I think of the almond festival in the Valley of the Temples in Agrigento.

Raw marinated sardines
(*Anciovi cunzati*)
Pasta with artichokes and tuna
(*Maccarruna che caccocciuli i*)
Swordfish with citrus and almonds (*Pesce spada con agrumi e pistacchi*), almonds instead of pistachios
Stuffed calamari with cheese, almonds and nutmeg braised in marsala (*Calamaricchi chini cà marsala e mennuli*)
Salad of cauliflower

What I particularly like about this dish is that the taste of the artichokes remains distinctive – the only ingredients are artichokes, a little parsley, garlic and tuna with a small amount of wine and cheese. The wine sharpens the taste, the sweetness of the *formaggio fresco* is a contrast to the slightly bitter flavours of the artichokes and the pecorino gives it bite.

Formaggio fresco is a fresh, unripened cheese. It has different names depending on its regional origins, and is sometimes called *pecorino fresco* even if it is made with cow's milk – pecorino is the generic name for cheese made with ewe's milk and is mostly associated with southern Italy – the farther south you go, the more *piccante* (sharper) the cheese. The dry variety can be a table cheese and is used for grating. Sicilian pecorino is often flavoured with peppercorns and is sometimes called *pepato*. *Pecorino stagionato* is the matured version.

This dish is assembled and baked for a short time, mainly to enhance the flavours and to fully melt the *formaggio fresco,* but baking is optional.

The artichokes are cut into thin slices so they almost dissolve into the sauce. It is always better to use fresh young artichokes. If I have to use a mature artichoke I use the tender hearts, the meatier *fondi* (bases) and the stalks (their fibrous covering stripped, see page 68). The stalks will produce a more flavourful and thicker sauce. The number of artichokes needed will depend on their size and degree of tenderness.

Suitable fish
This recipe requires a white mild-tasting fish that will not compete with the taste of artichokes. I use albacore tuna, King George whiting, whiting

or leatherjackets. Blue-eye travella, red emperor, pink ling and kingfish are also suitable. Shellfish add sweetness to the dish. I use crab meat or yabbies (freshwater crayfish).

METHOD

To prepare the artichokes, remove the tough outer leaves, then cut into quarters, and each quarter into thin slices. If using mature artichokes, remove the tough leaves and choke. Strip the stems of their fibrous outer layer and slice. Place the artichokes in acidulated water until ready to use.

Heat ½ cup of the oil in a saucepan and when the oil is warm, add the garlic and sauté for a couple of minutes. Drain the artichokes, add them to the pan and sauté for about 5 minutes. Add a splash of wine and allow to reduce. Season, add the parsley and about ½ cup water. Cover the pan and cook slowly till the artichokes are tender (up to 20–30 minutes, depending on how tender they are); if necessary, add more water.

Heat about 2 tablespoons of oil in another frying pan, seal the fish, add the bay leaves, seasoning and a splash of white wine (or water) and reduce until it has evaporated. It is a small amount of fish, so will cook quickly. If it needs more cooking, add a splash of water, cover and cook for longer. Add the fish to the artichokes.

Preheat the oven to 190°C (375°F). Generously coat a baking dish with oil.

Cook the pasta and drain about 5 minutes before it is *al dente* (it will have about 10 minutes more cooking in the oven.) Dress the spaghetti with the artichoke and fish sauce. Add the fresh cheese and about half the grated cheese. Mix gently but thoroughly.

Assemble the pasta in a baking dish. Sprinkle the rest of the grated cheese on the pasta. Bake for about 10–15 minutes and serve.

INGREDIENTS

3–6 artichokes, depending on
    size and maturity
1 lemon for acidulated water
¾–1 cup extra virgin olive oil
3 cloves garlic, chopped
500g (17½oz) bucatini,
    spaghetti or spaghettini
2 splashes of white wine
¾ cup parsley, cut
250g (9oz) fish, cut into
    mouth-sized pieces
1–2 fresh bay leaves
200g (7oz) formaggio fresco
    or bocconcini or fresh
    mozzarella, cut into cubes
grated pecorino or pepato to
    taste
salt and freshly ground
    pepper or chilli flakes to
    taste

Spaghetti e tunnu chi linticchi

Spaghetti e tonno con le lenticchie

SPAGHETTI WITH TUNA AND LENTILS

Pulses (*legumi*) feature in many wet pasta recipes (or thick soups) especially in the south and inland in places like Agrigento, Ragusa, Modica and Syracuse. This recipe can be made with lentils (*lenticchie*) or beans (*fagioli*). If I use beans, for taste and colour, I prefer borlotti beans. In season I always use fresh borlotti – 2 kilograms (4lb 6oz) will give you a sufficient quantity of shelled beans. Fresh borlotti beans do not need to be soaked, but lose their colour when cooked.

The brown lentil is widely used in Sicily – southern Italy used to be one of the most important lentil producers in the Mediterranean basin. Italy's smallest lentils are grown on the southern Sicilian island of Ustica and cultivated almost entirely by hand. The production is supported by the Presidia of Slow Food, which is concerned with sustaining crops at risk of extinction, protecting unique regions and ecosystems, recovering traditional processing methods and safeguarding local plant varieties. Ustica lentils are included in the compendium of *The Ark of Taste* launched in 1977 to catalogue thousands of edible species and traditional products in danger of extinction.

Although lentils do not need soaking, I like to soak them for about an hour before cooking. Do not add salt to the water when cooking pulses – it makes them tough. Wet pasta dishes with pulses are commonly cooked plain and presented with a drizzle of oil. In Ragusa it is common to use strips of pork skin. This version made with fish is from Trapani.

Suitable fish
Sicilians would not buy the finest cuts of tuna for this recipe; one of the inferior parts of the fish is suitable for this dish (such as the tail, which is less

The Egyptians, whose ideas were sometimes most eccentric, imagined it was sufficient to feed children with lentils to enlighten their minds, open their hearts, and render them cheerful.
– Alexis Soyer, *The Pantropheon, or, History of Food and its Preparation*, 1853

bloody). At fish markets, the whole carcass of tuna is displayed in different cuts, or the fish is kept whole and the vendor cuts the appropriate piece of tuna for particular methods of cooking. You could substitute any mild-tasting white fish. I use albacore tuna, flathead or snapper.

INGREDIENTS

450g (16oz) lentils or
  borlotti beans
1 carrot, finely sliced
1 celery stalk, in bite-sized
  slices
2 fresh bay leaves
500g (17½oz) short pasta
  (600g/1lb 5oz if using
  fresh pasta)
1 onion, finely chopped
½ cup extra virgin olive oil
300–500g (10½–17½oz)
  tuna
1 large tomato, peeled and
  diced
1 cup white wine
1 cup finely cut parsley
salt and freshly ground
  pepper or chilli flakes

METHOD

Soak beans in cold water overnight – they will swell so it is important to put them in plenty of water. If using lentils, soak for an hour (optional). Drain. Place sufficient water to cover the pulses and add the carrot, celery and bay leaves (this will be the broth).

Bring the pulses to the boil. Cook the pulses until soft but preferably still whole. The lentils will cook quickly but the beans will take 20–40 minutes, depending on how fresh they are.

Cook the pasta.

Soften the onion in the oil in a different saucepan. Add the fish and sauté until it begins to colour. Add the tomato, wine and salt. When the wine has evaporated, add the pulses and vegetables and as much broth as you need (1–2 ladlefuls). Heat through.

Combine the pasta and sauce. Add the parsley. Drizzle with extra virgin olive oil and freshly ground pepper or chilli flakes and serve.

VARIATIONS

꙾ Wild fennel (or the green fronds from cultivated fennel) and/or fresh basil leaves may be added to the traditional wet pasta dish from Ustica. Instead of tossing the pasta with oil and parsley, garnish with a *soffritto*: heat about ½ cup of olive oil in a wide pan, add a clove of finely chopped garlic and the parsley. Fry on high heat – it should sizzle and the parsley turn bright green – then pour over dressed pasta. Enjoy the aroma.

꙾ This dish can also be eaten as a very thick soup. In many parts of Sicily, it is customary to add broken spaghetti to the boiling broth and pulses. The fish is cooked and added to the soup. Drizzle with extra virgin olive oil. Serve the dish with some grated pecorino cheese.

Pasta con spada e menta

PASTA WITH SWORDFISH AND MINT

Ci erano tempi ch' i pisci
mirievano ri vicchiai.(Sicilian
proverb)
C'erano tempi che i pesci
morivano di vecchiaia. (Italian)
There was a time when fish
died of old age.

Mint is not a common herb in the rest of Italy and generally most unexpected in a pasta dish anywhere but Sicily.

When I first ate a version of this in Sicily in the 1980s, it was made with *pesce spada* (swordfish). Since then I have cooked it many times using sustainable fish (*pesce sostenibile*). I replicated it from memory, but later found a similar recipe which included fresh cubed cheese. I use *formaggio fresco* or fresh pecorino, failing this, fresh mozzarella or bocconcini.

Suitable fish
This recipe is particularly good with dense-textured fish. I use albacore tuna, mackerel, rockling or flathead. Shellfish also enhances the sweetness.

INGREDIENTS

¾ cup extra virgin olive oil
400g (14oz) fish, in 4cm (1½in) pieces
500g (17½oz) rigatoni or other short ribbed, tubular pasta
3 cloves garlic, chopped
½ cup white wine
10–15 mint leaves
300g (10½oz) formaggio fresco, diced
salt and freshly ground pepper to taste

METHOD

Heat the olive oil, add the fish and lightly seal it.
   Cook the pasta.
   Add the garlic, wine, 4–5 mint leaves and seasoning to the fish. Cover and cook gently until the fish is ready. Combine the pasta, fish, cheese and mint leaves (large leaves cut into smaller pieces) and serve.

VARIATION
- Add a few slices of zucchini lightly fried in extra virgin olive oil (cooked separately and added at the end). Add any juices from the zucchini.
- Add pistachio nuts to complement the sweet taste and the green of the mint and zucchini.

Pasta cu tunnu 'nno sucu

Pasta col tonno nel sugo

PASTA WITH A TUNA STEW

A *stufato* is a slowly cooked stew, similar to a *ragù*. Often in Sicilian cooking, fish is treated like meat and braised. Most of the time tomato is included as an ingredient, or tomato paste is used for a stronger taste.

For a braise, Sicilians would use the cheaper cuts of tuna, but in other places you may be restricted to thick fish steaks. Buy the largest pieces of fish you can find so they won't fall apart. Sicilians cook this for a long time – the texture will be flaky, like canned tuna. In other countries and in modern recipes we may prefer it less cooked.

Boiled rice could replace the pasta in this dish.

Suitable fish
I use solid, meaty fish like albacore tuna, bonito, flathead and mackerel.

METHOD

Sauté the onions in the oil, add the tuna and when the ingredients begin to brown add the wine, mint and bay leaves. Toss it around in the pan on high heat for a few minutes. Reduce the heat and allow the wine to evaporate.

Cook the pasta.

Add the tomatoes or paste to the fish and season. Cook uncovered on slow heat until the liquid reduces. Combine the drained pasta with the sauce. Top with the breadcrumbs and fresh mint leaves.

INGREDIENTS

2 onions, finely chopped
1 cup extra virgin olive oil
500g (17½oz) short, tubular, ridged pasta
500g (17½oz) tuna, cut into large pieces
1 cup red wine
1 cup finely chopped mint
2 bay leaves
400g (14oz) red tomatoes, peeled and chopped, or 2 tablespoons tomato paste
1 cup toasted breadcrumbs (see page 57)
mint leaves for garnish
salt and chilli flakes to taste

As first course

Spaghetti al cartoccio

SPAGHETTI IN A BAG

This is a show-off dish that restaurants love to serve. But more than that, it is a way of using up left-over fish stews. Use the previous recipe (Pasta with a tuna stew) or any of the wet cooked recipes in the *secondo* chapter. Individual packages are easier to handle, but if cooking for two people, make one large package. The ingredients must be hot when they are packed in the bag. You could fold the package in the shape of a fish.

I ate this pasta in Caltagerone, a town which specialises in ceramics and is well inland. The maître d' assured me the fish had been caught that same morning. What about the distance from the sea? I said. He looked up to the ceiling, shrugged his shoulders, arms out, palms turned up. Enough said. So I did what the locals were doing and I was not disappointed.

INGREDIENTS

100g (3½oz) spaghetti per person
3–4 tablespoons ragù per person
1 tablespoon extra virgin olive oil per serve
extras: basil leaves, cut parsley or herb used in the sauce, halved cherry tomatoes, stoned olives, capers, fennel seeds, anchovies, small cubes of pecorino fresco, ricotta salata or bocconcini

METHOD

To prepare the packages, use two layers of baking paper or aluminium foil, leaving extra for folding; if using foil, lay a sheet of baking paper on top. Coat the paper with olive oil.

Cook the pasta for three-quarters of the normal time, then mix with the *ragù*. Place an individual portion in the centre of each prepared package, scatter any extra ingredients (if using) through the mixture and seal well.

Place on a tray and cook in 210°C (410°F) oven for 15–20 minutes.

Place packages on individual plates and bring to the table. Make a hole in the centre of the foil, then peel it back. Make air vents in the baking paper to release the steam before the package is opened – take care because the steam will be hot.

Calamari e seppie

Squid and cuttlefish

CALAMARI, CUTTLEFISH AND SQUID ARE CEPHALOPODS, A MOLLUSC GROUP OF THE SHELLFISH FAMILY. THEY ARE GENERALLY FAST GROWING AND FOR THIS REASON ARE CONSIDERED SUSTAINABLE. CALAMARI AND CUTTLEFISH ARE VERY POPULAR WITH SICILIANS. CALAMARI REFERS TO THOSE SPECIES OF SQUID WITH LONG SIDE FINS; THOSE WITH SHORTER SIDE FINS ARE SEPPIE (CUTTLEFISH). THE TWO SPECIES MAY BE SOLD INTERCHANGEABLY. CUTTLEFISH IS FAVOURED FOR BLACK INK SAUCES.

Purpi (*polpi* in Italian, octopus) and *moscardini* (baby octopus, 2–3 cm/ ¾–1¼in long and considered a delicacy) do not seem common in pasta sauces on their own, but are often part of the mixture in a *marinara*.

Cooking squid can be tricky. There is a fine line between tender and rubbery. It can be cooked on high heat for a short time (1kg /2lb 4oz squid in no more than 5–8 minutes) or a long time on slow heat (for at least 30–40 minutes). When you cook squid for a short time, it may still look a little shiny, but the residual heat completes the job and the flesh will turn opaque. If you cook the squid for longer, the juices will have more taste. For Sicilians, cooking calamari is not tricky – they just cook it for a long time.

THE INK OF SQUID AND CUTTLEFISH

Cuttlefish (*seppie*) seems to contain more ink and is preferred to squid for black ink sauce in Italy. Both squid and cuttlefish have the potential to contain ink sacs in their bodies. When you clean squid you will find

Take the squid, open it, and take out the ink, and keep it: then take the squid cut in slices and fry it in oil with spices. And when it is fried, put in a bit of water, and boil it: then colour this with the reserved ink, which is called squid salt, with good wine, and put it in a broth with savoury herbs and spices, and serve it.
Note that squid ink should be tied off at the head, so that it does not leak; and smoke it, so that when you want to make dressing, sauce, broth or other food black, you come back to this.
– Anonimo Toscano, Libro della Cocina (Cookery book), late 14th or early 15th century (translated by Vittoria Aureli)

a pea-like swelling filled with black ink in some of the cavities, although sometimes the ink bladder is empty. When you fish for squid, the moment you try to lift them out of the water, most will squirt a cloud of dark brown ink in their attempt to get away, and so it is hardly surprising the ink supply is limited. Because the ink is very thick and concentrated you only need 1–3 ink sacs. The ink is not harmful to eat – it has been used in cooking throughout the centuries and is composed mostly of melanin. (It was once used as the artist's pigment sepia.)

I always buy the blackest looking squid or cuttlefish, hoping that the squid will have sacs intact. I freeze any sacs I don't use. You can purchase sachets or jars of squid ink from specialist food stores, fishmongers and fish markets.

Pasta o risu cu niuru di sicci

Pasta o riso al nero di seppie

PASTA OR RICE WITH BLACK INK SAUCE

Pasta with black ink sauce is eaten all over Sicily and with very little variation in the recipes. The ingredients are *seppie* (cuttlefish), tomatoes and garlic or onion. Some include bay leaves, white wine and red chili flakes. The variations are mostly in the type of pasta – most prefer spaghetti but linguine or bucatini are also common. Plain boiled rice is also dressed with black ink sauce.

Risotto or spaghetti with black ink sauce and *seppie* braised with black ink and served with polenta are also specialties of Venice and the Veneto region. The northern Italian version does not usually contain tomatoes. This is not surprising – tomatoes are grown mostly in the sunny south of Italy.

Fans of the television series *Montalbano* (a big hit in Italy) are likely to be enchanted with the beauty of the Sicilian landscape and the array of specialty Sicilian food featured in the series. Commissario Salvo Montalbano lives in the southeast of Sicily, near Marina di Ragusa where my relatives have their holiday houses. The series is adapted from the books by Andrea Camilleri which are full of delicious Sicilian food references.

Montalbano loves to eat. He savours his food, relishing every dish, readily accepts dinner invitations and has his favourite *trattorie*. He uses food to cheer himself up, plan his next moves and weigh up the evidence. In the evenings he anticipates what Adelina, his housekeeper, has left for him to eat. He hates to be interrupted over his dinner, although the phone often rings. He always seems to be thinking about what he will eat next or what he has just eaten and often forms opinions about people based on the food they eat. Camilleri describes almost every dish Montalbano eats. And every dish is traditionally Sicilian.

'By the way Inspector,' Beatrice said with a smile, 'I have a confession to make. When I am eating, I'm unable to speak. So you should interrogate me now, before the risotto comes, or in between courses.'
Jesus! So it was true: the meeting of one's twin did sometimes happen. Too bad that, at a glance, she looked to be twenty-five or so years younger than him.
– Andrea Camillerie, An Excursion to Tindari

As first course

One of Camilleri's favourite dishes must be pasta or rice with black ink sauce – there are references to these dishes in a number of his books. The *trattorie* and restaurants in southeastern Sicily where the series was shot have capitalised on Montalbano: you can always find pasta or rice with black ink sauce (*cu niuru di sicci*) on the menus.

Boiled rice and *ravioli di ricotta* are dressed with the same sauce.

Ingredients

500g (17½oz) spaghetti,
    linguine or bucatini
600g (1lb 5oz) squid or
    cuttlefish, plus 2–3 ink sacs
1 medium onion and/or
    2 cloves garlic
½ cup olive oil
100g (3½oz) ripe tomatoes,
    peeled and chopped
1 large tablespoon tomato
    paste
1 cup finely cut parsley
1 cup white wine
grated pecorino or ricotta to
    serve (optional)
a little salt
chilli flakes or freshly ground
    pepper to taste

Method

Clean the squid or cuttlefish carefully and extract the ink sac (see page 76). Cut it into 1cm (½in) rings and set aside. The tentacles can be used also.

For the sauce, sauté the onion and garlic in the olive oil. Add the tomatoes and tomato paste, parsley, white wine and salt. Bring to a boil and reduce until the salsa is thick.

Cook the pasta.

Add the ink and chilli flakes to the sauce and mix well. Add the squid rings and cook over a medium-high heat until the squid is cooked to your liking (for me squid only takes a few minutes, cuttlefish a little longer). If you prefer to cook it further (as the Italians do), add a little water or white wine, cover the pan and braise for longer.

Serve the pasta with grated pecorino.

Variations

- Keep the squid white: sauté it in a little oil for a few minutes, then add 1 chopped clove of garlic and 1–2 tablespoons of finely cut parsley. Fold through the dressed pasta gently and reserve some for on top.
- Add 1 cup of shelled peas at the same time as the tomatoes.
- Add bay leaves at the same time as the squid or cuttlefish.
- The most delectable variation is to add fresh ricotta to the finished dish. Reserve some of the sauce and serve the black pasta with a spoon of sauce and one of ricotta on top. Call it Etna!

Ravioli di ricotta cu niuru di sicci

Ravioli di ricotta col nero di seppie

RICOTTA RAVIOLI WITH BLACK INK SAUCE

Once in Syracuse I dined in a relatively new restaurant and ate large ravioli stuffed with ricotta and covered with black ink sauce. It was wonderful. The restaurant owner told me that the recipe was her version of her father's favourite dish, pasta with black ink sauce, which he always topped with fresh ricotta. Indeed pasta with black ink sauce and ricotta is common in various locations in Sicily, especially in the south.

Ricotta is generally made with cows' milk in the southeastern part of Sicily. The ricotta made from sheep's milk is sweeter and more delicate and is used in the most famous Sicilian desserts: cannoli and cassata.

The word *ri-cotta* means 're-cooked'. After the curd has been removed to make the cheese, the leftover whey is recooked to make the ricotta. Interestingly, in Italy ricotta is not considered a cheese because the curd has been removed to make the cheese.

Ricotta salata (which has been salted, drained and dried) is used as a grating cheese in the same way as a mature pecorino. These two local cheeses are preferred to parmesan.

Ricotta is frequently baked (*ricotta frisca 'nfurnata – ricotta fresca infornata*). I make the authentic baked ricotta – unadulterated, white and fresh tasting with a beautiful golden crust. Baked ricotta is made with the solid shaped ricotta, usually sold by the weight and cut into slices. I leave it on some paper or cloth overnight in the fridge if I think it needs draining.

Ravioli di ricotta are a specialty of Ragusa and environs, so I can understand why I found them in nearby Syracuse as well. Sicilians are very competitive and each locality strives to 'own' a particular speciality. My relatives in Ragusa like to tell the legend of the miracle performed in ancient times when the

A worthy cook will be learned in all matters, in harmony with the diversity of animal and vegetable kingdoms and will be able to vary and flavour foods, as he deems proper.
– 14th century culinary text, author and title unknown

ANDREA CAMILLERI

Camilleri (born 1925) is best known for his series of books about Inspector Montalbano, who is based in a fictitious Sicilian town of Vigata. Montalbano is passionate about food, so Camilleri deserves at least two menus. These are based on some of the foods in the novels. Montalbano often dissolves bicarbonate of soda in water and he drinks this to help his digestion

❦

MENU 1
Caponata recipe from the
Leone family
Spaghetti with sea urchins
(*Spaghetti chi ricci*)
Octopus braised with tomatoes
(*Purpi' no sucu*)
Potato croquettes (*Cuzzili*)

❦

MENU 2
Whitebait fritters (*Crispeddi di nunnata*)
Pasta with black ink sauce
(*Pasta cu niuru di sicci*)
Grilled fish (*Pisci 'nta braci*)
a mixed platter, with *Sarsa di chiappareddi*)
Salad of boiled green beans
(*Fasulinu vugghiutui*)

hermit Brother Guglielmo in Scicli (near Ragusa) was invited by a rich man to eat *maccheroni* that were filled and coated with mud, and he miraculously turned the mud into ricotta. In another version of the same event the pasta presented to Brother Giglielmo are lasagne and he turned these *lasagne cacate* (shat-upon lasagne) into pasta with a thick *sugo* and ricotta.

The ravioli served at the restaurant were an impressive *primo* and the progressive courses were just as memorable. I particularly liked the large leaves of prickly pear used as platters, breadbaskets, fruit bowls and plates for peeled prickly pears or biscuits. The staff said they had been using the same leaves since the restaurant first opened, about seven months before. Some of the leaves had started sprouting new shoots – with no water. Another miracle!

Fresh lasagne sheets can be used to make ravioli. I dare not tell my Sicilian relatives I have a friend who uses another cheat method – wonton wrappers. Although made without eggs, each square can be stuffed with ricotta filling, sealed with another wrapper, and presto, *un grande raviolo*.

TO MAKE RAVIOLI DI RICOTTA

The *ravioli di ricotta* are traditionally presented with a strong *sugo* (meat and tomato-based sauce, which here is made with pork and pork sausages). Local variations include a little orange peel or finely cut marjoram to the ricotta stuffing. In Ragusa they add a little sugar (1 teaspoon per cup of ricotta). It is interesting to hear locals arguing over these variations. I remember praising my aunt's ravioli in a shop in Ragusa and discussing the pros and cons of adding sugar or marjoram with the owner. Soon all the customers joined in. Discussions about food are always passionate in Sicily but the sweet-or-savoury debate would have been meaningless in mediaeval times when sugar was an expensive imported luxury and was added to almost every dish in a rich household. Sugar, or marjoram or peel may not be as common with ravioli dressed with black ink sauce, but adding them enhances the ricotta stuffing.

METHOD

Drain the ricotta
Place it in a colander lined with cheesecloth and refrigerate for at least 2 hours or overnight.

Mix the ricotta with a little salt and any of the extra flavourings.

Ingredients

2½ cups ricotta
salt to taste
extras: sugar, citrus peel
*   or finely cut marjoram*
*   (optional)*
1 quantity pasta (see recipe,
*   page 45)*
black ink sauce, (see recipe,
*   page 78)*

Make the ravioli

The most authentic and quickest way to cut the ravioli is by hand. There is no prescribed size – they can be either round or square (about 7cm/3in across) or half-moon shaped (a 9cm/4in circle folded over).

To make individual ravioli, cut pasta into circles or squares. Place heaped teaspoons of stuffing in the centre of each, continuing until all the stuffing is used. For half-moon shapes fold the pasta over the filling. For others, lay another circle or square on top, then moisten the edges with a little water and press together carefully to seal properly (press hard on the edges and spread the pasta to a single thickness, so they cook evenly).

Set the finished ravioli on a lightly floured cloth. They can rest in a cool place for up two hours.

To make more than one raviolo at a time

Cut the pasta into long rectangular strips about 9cm wide. Place heaped teaspoons of stuffing about 5 cm apart (beginning about 2cm/¾in from the margin of the sheet). Cover with another strip of pasta of the same size.

Cut each raviolo free with a knife or serrated pasta wheel. Repeat the process, until all the pasta and the stuffing is used up.

Cooking

Cook ravioli as you would any pasta. Lower them into the water a few at a time and scoop each out when it floats to the surface.

Dress them carefully with the black ink sauce so as not to break them. Serve as is or with a scoop of ricotta or some grated pecorino (they use *caciocavallo* or *ricotta salata* in Ragusa, see pages 80 and 96).

Frutti di mare

Fruits of the sea

YOU CAN FIND MANY DIFFERENT TYPES OF SHELLFISH IN THE FISH MARKETS AND RESTAURANTS OF SICILY. AND *FRUTTI DI MARE* (FRUITS OF THE SEA) – A MIXED PLATTER OF SHELLFISH, BOTH *MOLLUSCHI* (MOLLUSCS) AND *CROSTACEI* (CRUSTACEANS) – IS A FEATURE OF MANY RESTAURANT MENUS.

Any double-hinged shells are molluscs (sometimes referred to as clams), as are *ricci di mare* (sea urchins), which have a prickly exterior and are usually eaten raw like oysters. Squid, octopus and cuttlefish are cefalopods, a subgroup of molluscs. Crustaceans – lobsters, scampi, crabs, prawns and marrons and freshwater crayfish – have a hard outer shell, which is discarded as the animal grows. Molluscs are found all around the Sicilian coast and are gathered mostly by mechanical harvesting (includes by suction). This inevitably disturbs the sea floor and affects the habitat of other species. Sicilians are now aware of the consequences and fishers are required to rotate sites, create fallow areas, and follow seasonal harvesting. The most common clams are oysters, scallops, cockles and mussels. Abalone is also a clam, and if farmed is sustainable. There are many varieties of soft-shelled or hard-shelled clams harvested in sustainable ways or grown on certified sustainable farms in other parts of the world.

Do not worry if some clams are open when you buy them. They may not be dead but will be very unhappy at being out of the water. Ask whether they are being sold clean of sand. If they need to be purged, place in cool water and sea salt (30g/2oz salt to each 4 cups of water) for several hours, or overnight, at room temperature – if they are refrigerated they'll close up and won't expel the sand. Rinse in two or three changes of water. If they are particularly gritty, repeat the process and soak for 5–10 minutes in-between rinses.

As first course

Scallops are called *cappe sante* in Italian. They are not common in the fish markets and restaurants of Sicily.

Clean mussels by rubbing them against each other in cold water (or use a plastic scourer). Pull the beards sharply towards the pointy end of the shell. When cooking mussels, give them sufficient time to open – closed ones are not necessarily dead. They just need more time.

Prawns (or shrimp) of all sizes are known in Sicily as a scampi. Lobsters are not as common: the terms lobster and crayfish are used interchangeably in some places, but the marine species are lobsters and the freshwater species are crayfish. The true scampi is also called Norwegian lobster, Dublin Bay prawn or langoustine. They are abundant and very popular in Sicily. Not many nations farm scampi; fishing for the species using pots or creels rather than trawling increases sustainability, although this method of harvesting is not common.

We once ploughed our way through numerous dishes of a set menu in a fish restaurant in Mazara del Vallo on the west coast of Sicily. One of the dishes was large prawns and scampi, still in their shells. What we found disturbing was that most of these creatures still had eggs attached under their tails. In many countries catching or selling females in this condition is prohibited. We discussed this with the owner of the restaurant, and once again listened to the same old story we had heard in numerous restaurants and fish markets when asking about *neonata*. His words: 'If you have caught a female in this condition, you keep it. There is no point throwing it back because the creature has probably already been damaged. And, besides, have you tried sucking the eggs before you peel the prawns or scampi? They are so sweet!'

COMMON TERMS FOR PASTA *CON FRUTTI DI MARE*

A spaghetti or risotto *alla marinara* generally will include fish as well as shellfish, squid or cuttlefish and sometimes octopus. Spaghetti or risotto *allo scoglio* is common in Italian menus (*scoglio* means rock, those found by the seaside where shellfish hide). It contains a selection of molluscs – all sorts of clams with maybe a few crustaceans (such as unpeeled prawns). In the past the organisms and sea mosses attached to the rocks were also added and this is where the name originated. In Trapani sailors cooked a wet pasta dish *con piccole pietre* (with small stones). These were used like soup bones and removed when serving. I have seen mosses for sale in Sicilian fish markets.

Complimenti alla cuoca [feminine] or *al cuoco* [masculine]. *Compliments to the cook.*

Risu cull'anciuli

Riso con gli angeli

RICE WITH ANGELS

There are many versions of rice with seafood, all with a variety of sea-inspired names. Many are modern recipes cooked like a risotto with butter and wine. In *risu cull'anciuli* (rice with angels) the angels are mussels, fanned to look like angel's wings, but the name is more likely to refer to the fresh, light taste and texture of the dish .

My grandmother used to tell us about cooking a seafood rice dish in Catania. Her husband, my nonno (he died before I was born) would go off to the boats very early every Sunday morning to buy seafood for the *primo* for lunch. He would bring back a range of molluscs – cockles, mussels and often razor fish, cigar-shaped clams and any other clams he could find. He also used to bring home a little container of seawater, which was added to the dish. Apparently seawater is still used in some recipes. The ingredients listed are a rough guide to quantities and variety.

METHOD

Clean the cockles and mussels (see pages 84 and 87). Steam in a covered frying pan coated with a little oil. Once opened, shell them, but reserve some mussels in their shells. Cut up the flesh and save the juice.

While you are preparing the seafood, cook the rice (add the rice to plenty of rapidly boiling, salted water). Drain and place in serving bowl.

In a wide pan, sauté the garlic and parsley in extra virgin olive oil. Add prawns, squid (and any other seafood) and season. Stir for a few minutes, then add the clam juice. Toss for a few minutes without reducing the liquid. Add mussels and cockles (shelled and unshelled) and heat through.

Mix the seafood with the rice. Arrange some mussels in their shells on top to look like angels with open wings. Serve with grated cheese.

INGREDIENTS

400g (14oz) cockles
400g (14oz) mussels
3 cups arborio, carnaroli or vialone rice
3 cloves garlic, chopped
½ cup finely cut parsley
¾–1 cup extra virgin olive oil
200g (7oz) prawns (shrimp), shelled and de-veined, cut into pieces; some left whole
200g (7oz) squid (small with tentacles), cut into slices
100g (3½oz) of one or a mixture of: crabs, lobster, Moreton bay bugs, scallops (optional)
grated pecorino
salt and red chilli flakes to taste

Spaghettini e cozzuli

Spaghettini e cozze

SPAGHETTINI WITH MUSSELS

I love mussels. In aquaculture farms, mussels are grown on ropes in clean, flowing ocean currents suspended metres above the seabed – they are clean from sand and grit and need very little preparation. Farmed mussels seem to be readily available. They grow wild in dense clumps and are fairly prolific – the shells can be seen attached to exposed reefs, rocks and jetty pylons. All the flesh inside the shell is edible; females tend to be more orange in colour.

Mussels were not for sale when we first came to Australia. But word spread among the Italian community in South Australia that mussels could be found in Wallaroo, a small country town in the Yorke Peninsula, so we drove out and collected them from the pier. Mussels in Italy are also eaten like oysters, *all'ostrica*, opened live and dressed with a squeeze of lemon juice. Naturally, the fresher the better – so we opened them as soon as we pulled them off the pier. We had our knives and our lemon juice ready.

This is not a complicated dish. It is simply made with mussels and a few fresh tomatoes, but not so much that they mask the taste of the other ingredients. Spaghetti and mussels are cooked all over Sicily, but the best I have eaten were in Taormina, which is reputedly the most beautiful town in Sicily, with mesmerising views of hills and sea and an incredible heritage.

Spaghettini are used for this – the thin strands result in a greater surface area and allow greater absorption of the sauce. Like many of the sauces for pasta, it is prepared quickly while the spaghettini are cooking.

METHOD

Clean the mussels as described on page 87. Heat 2 tablespoons of olive oil in a deep frying pan and add the mussels. Cover and cook over a brisk flame, shaking the pan every now and then until the mussels have opened.

Turn off the heat and let them cool slightly, then remove and discard the shells

INGREDIENTS

2 kg (4lb 6oz) fresh live
  mussels
½–¾ cup extra virgin olive
  oil
3 cloves garlic, finely chopped
1 cup finely cut parsley
2–3 anchovies, finely
  chopped
15–20 black olives, whole
  and pitted
500g (17½oz) red
  tomatoes, peeled and
  chopped
basil, stalks and leaves
500g (17½oz) spaghettini
grated pecorino to taste
  (optional)
salt and freshly ground
  pepper to taste

of about three-quarters of them. Reserve the whole mussels for decoration.

Place the mussel meat with the garlic, parsley and seasoning in a bowl and set aside (save the juice from the mussels in a separate bowl).

Add the rest of the oil and the anchovies to the frying pan. Reduce to a paste by pressing them with the back of the spoon.

Add the olives and the chopped tomatoes and some basil stalks with leaves attached (reserve some leaves for garnish). Simmer the sauce for about 8 minutes to blend the flavours and to reduce the liquid.

Cook the spaghettini. Drain and return to the saucepan.

To the pasta, add the mussels, parsley and garlic and the sauce and as much mussel juice as you need for lubrication. Gently mix in the mussels in their shells and warm through.

Remove the cooked basil (it has done its job). Toss through some fresh basil leaves. Serve with pecorino (if wanted).

Shellfish are the prime cause of the decline of morals and the adaptation of an extravagant lifestyle. Indeed of the whole realm of Nature the sea is in many ways the most harmful to the stomach, with its great variety of dishes and tasty fish.
– Pliny the Elder (23–79 CE)

Spaghetti a vonguli

Spaghetti alle vongole

SPAGHETTI WITH COCKLES

My fondest memories of collecting cockles are from beaches in Goolwa, Middleton and the Coorong in South Australia – large succulent cockles that we ate raw like oysters, prized open on the beach and eaten with a squeeze of lemon. Aboriginal Australians loved cockles – their discarded empty shells form the middens found in the sandhills of the Coorong.

I cook them in a large frying pan or a wok to ensure even cooking.

METHOD

Rinse the cockles, rubbing to remove sand, and discard any open ones that don't close after being gently squeezed or tapped.

Heat the olive oil in a frying pan and fry the garlic and chilli lightly. Add the cockles and parsley and shake the pot for 1–2 minutes. Add wine, cover and gently cook for a few minutes until the cockles are open. Remove some cockle meat from the shells for ease of eating (I do not always do this).

Cook the pasta, then drain and combine with the cockles. Gently mix the spaghetti through the sauce.

VARIATION

* When frying the garlic and chilli, add either 3 anchovies, finely chopped, or 2 peeled and chopped tomatoes (or both).

INGREDIENTS

2kg (4lb 6oz) cockles
  (vongole)
½ cup extra virgin olive oil
3–4 cloves garlic, crushed
1 red chilli, deseeded and
  finely chopped, or chilli
  flakes
1 cup finely cut parsley
¼ cup dry white wine
500g (17½oz) spaghetti
grated pecorino to taste
  (optional)

Spaghetti chi ricci

Spaghetti con le uova di ricci di mare

SPAGHETTI WITH SEA URCHINS

Sea urchins are members of the phylum Echinodermata, which includes starfish and sea cucumbers. They are considered a delicacy by Italians, who call them *ricci* (the word means 'curly', after the curly ends of the sea urchin spines). The gonads of both sexes of sea urchins are referred to as roe (which sounds nicer than testes and ovaries).

When I was a child visiting Sicily, we used to find sea urchins under rocks on the beach – we would wrap our hands in newspaper and go looking for them at low tide. It was easy to find four to six each. We'd eat them raw with a squeeze of lemon juice, cutting them in half and revealing the yellow-orange roe that is easily removed with a teaspoon.

Our next favourite method of eating them was as a dressing for pasta.

Now fishing for sea urchins is regulated by season and harvesting can only be done when the roe is of a marketable quality. Restrictions in particular areas and defined quotas are also in place.

Because sea urchins are expensive, some recipes also include anchovies. So as not to make a *brutta figura* (a bad impression), estimate at least three roes per person (six or eight are preferable) and a little crustacean oil added to the sauce enhances the taste.

Spaghetti are traditionally used for this recipe, but I also like *ricci* with fresh narrow ribbon-shaped pasta made with eggs – a delicate taste which complements the sweet, fresh taste of the roe. The ingredients are simple – oil, garlic, chili and parsley.

When cleaning the sea urchins, hold the prickly shell with a towel or gloves to protect your hands from the spines.

And one last thing – the sea urchins are not cooked, but are mixed with the hot pasta at the time of serving. The aroma is indescribable.

The object of desire is no longer the food available in abundance but the one that is rare; not the food that fills you and alleviates hunger but the one that whets the appetite, inviting you to eat more.

– Massimo Montanari, *Food is Culture, Taste is a Product of Society*

INGREDIENTS

*3–8 sea urchins per person
  (see note, page 93)*
*500g (17½oz) spaghetti
  (600g/1lb 5oz) if using
  fresh pasta)*
*4–5 cloves garlic, finely
  chopped*
¾ cup extra virgin olive oil
*3 anchovies, finely chopped
  (optional) salt*
*¾ cup finely cut parsley
  freshly ground pepper or
  chilli flakes*

METHOD

Cut into the shell using a short, very sharp knife or use scissors and enter it via the mouth (you will see the opening). Work your way around the shell in a circle until half of the shell can be removed. Split in half and, very carefully using a spoon and avoiding the dark matter, remove the soft yellow flesh. Place the roes in a bowl and discard all the rest.

Cook the pasta.

Heat olive oil, add the garlic and cook over slow heat until it becomes translucent. Add anchovies if using; dissolve in the hot oil. Add pepper. Place the pan back over high heat. Add pasta and toss to coat.

When about to serve, add the drained pasta to the pan, then the parsley, the sea urchins and the pepper. Toss well to combine. Serve immediately.

VARIATIONS

- I ate my best-ever pasta with sea urchins in a restaurant in Mondello. It included lemon: add finely grated zest or juice of 1 lemon; or ½ cup of best extra virgin olive oil to the roes before adding them to the pasta.
- *Bottarga* is sometimes grated on top of the pasta.
- Add a little crustacean oil to the sauce to enhance the taste

CRUSTACEAN OIL (TO ENHANCE PARTICULAR DISHES)

When I remove the flesh from crustaceans shells, I save any juices that escape. Nothing need be wasted. The yellow-brown cream 'mustard' (tomally) inside lobsters, crays and crabs, is very flavoursome and should be added to sauces. The shells make excellent stock. This recipe is not necessarily Sicilian, but is very useful. The oil will keep for at least three weeks in the fridge. Add it to any of dishes made with shellfish. The quantities are sufficient for the shell(s) of 1 large lobster or 1kg (2lb 4oz) of prawns (shrimp). Crush the shell(s) into manageable pieces with 1 tablespoon of sea salt and 3 cloves of garlic.

Cut into small dice 100g (3½oz) each of carrots and onions and 30g (1oz) celery; sauté in 2 tablespoons olive oil. Add 2 bay leaves, a teaspoon of fennel seeds, a little salt, the crushed shells and 2 cups of white wine. Cook on medium heat until most of the wine has reduced. Add a500ml (16fl oz) of extra virgin olive oil and cook on a slow simmer for about 45 minutes. Leave overnight in a cool spot. Pour off the oil, strain through muslin, bottle and keep in the fridge.

Pasta e gammareddu ca ricotta

Pasta e gamberi colla ricotta di capra

PASTA AND PRAWNS (SHRIMP) WITH GOATS' MILK RICOTTA

Ragusani will add ricotta to just about anything. This recipe is from Vittoria in Ragusa province. Goat's milk ricotta tastes completely different to ricotta made with cows' milk or sheep's milk. I have also used fresh goat's cheese curd and goat's milk feta for a stronger taste. *Lolli* is the name of a pasta shaped by rolling it around a knitting needle. It is popular in Modica and in the Ragusa province. In other parts of Italy it is more commonly called *busiate*.

METHOD

Cook the pasta.

Heat the olive oil in a frying pan and then fry the garlic lightly. Add the prawns and toss around in the hot oil before adding the parsley. Stir over high heat until the prawns begin to change to red, 3–5 minutes. Add the wine and reduce.

Drain the pasta, reserving about ½ cup of the cooking water to mix with some of the ricotta – this warms the ricotta and prevents it from solidifying with direct heat. If you are using feta, cube it before adding it to the pasta and stir. It will melt very successfully.

Mix the pasta and prawns together. Gently blend in the ricotta and place a little on top. Serve immediately.

INGREDIENTS

500g (17½oz) busiate,
  linguine or spaghetti
½ cup extra virgin olive oil
3–4 cloves garlic, crushed
500g (17½oz) green prawn
  meat
1 cup finely cut parsley
¼ cup white wine
200g (7oz) goat's milk
  ricotta, cheese curd or feta
  (see above)
salt and freshly ground
  pepper

Spaghetti c'arausta

Spaghetti con l'aragosta

SPAGHETTI WITH CRAYFISH

The terms lobster and crayfish are often used interchangeably, but the marine species are lobsters and the freshwater species are crayfish. There are many types of lobsters known by a variety of local names.

Lobsters (*aragoste*) are popular around Trapani, although they are expensive. When making pasta with *aragosta*, I often buy spiders (the legs) – they can be quite meaty and very suitable for a pasta dish that requires cooked lobster. When buying lobster, select a heavy specimen with a good strong shell. They molt several times in their life cycle and, if they are pale with a thin shell, they are not likely to have much flesh. As for size, anything less than 1.5 kg (3lb 5oz) is not worth buying – a lobster under that size doesn't have enough meat, especially from the spiders.

There is no comparison between the taste of a freshly cooked lobster and one purchased already cooked.

This dish requires cooked lobster and it is added last. The other ingredients are raw and pounded in a mortar and pestle (or pulsed in a food processor). The raw ingredients can also be finely chopped and mixed together. Use fresh ripe tomatoes.

Although this recipe is especially suited for lobsters, other crustaceans can be used.

This pasta dish is fantastic for the hot weather and it could be part of a celebratory lunch (such as Christmas in the Southern Hemisphere).

Mancia di sanu e vivi di malatu.
(Sicilian proverb)
Eat with gusto but drink in moderation.

METHOD

If you would like to cook your own, see opposite.

Remove the flesh from the lobster, tear or cut into small portions and place it in a bowl with the juice of 1 lemon and some of the oil.

INGREDIENTS

lobster, no less than 50g
(1¾oz) of meat per person
juice of 3 lemons, plus grated
zest of 1 lemon
about ½ cup extra virgin
olive oil
2 cloves garlic
600g (1lb 5oz) ripe
tomatoes, peeled, seeded
and drained, chopped
1 small bunch of basil
½ cup finely cut parsley
½ cup capers; if salted
soaked and thoroughly
rinsed
500g (17½oz) spaghetti or
spaghettini
salt and freshly ground
pepper to taste

Use a mortar and pestle to combine the rest of the ingredients. Begin with the garlic, then add the tomatoes, seasoning, and some more oil. Then stir in the basil, parsley capers and, lastly, the zest of 1 lemon – stir these into the pesto. Add some of the lemon juice, taste the pesto and add more if necessary (you may not need all of the lemon juice).

Cook and drain the spaghetti. Arrange in a serving bowl, add the pesto and lobster and mix it gently. I like to add more grated lemon zest on top.

TO COOK LIVE CRUSTACEANS

There are humane ways to dispatch a live lobster. Place in the freezer for about 40 minutes until it shows no signs of life – this renders it unconscious and ready to be killed with a knife or in the pot. The Royal Society for the Prevention of Cruelty to Animals in Australia recommends that crustaceans be spiked after being stunned in the ice before cooking.

Use a large pot full of boiling salted water; use seawater or 80g (2½ oz) of salt per litre (4 cups) of water. Some Sicilians add white wine and bay leaves to the poaching liquid of salted water. Make sure the lobster is well covered so it is killed quickly. Plunge it into the pot and keep the water boiling on very high heat – it takes about 10 minutes per 1kg (2lb 4oz) to cook. Switch off the heat and leave in the water for an extra 5 minutes. Remove from the water and leave to cool. The meat will keep on cooking and will set.

To remove the flesh from the tail I prefer to hold the body (with a tea towel) and cut the body and tail lengthways with a large, heavy, sharp knife. Keep a bowl underneath it while doing this to catch the tasty juices and then remove any coral and mustard and set that aside to add to the sauce. One friend prefers to flatten the tail and then twist it off from the body using her thumb to push out the meat.

Spaghetti cu granciu fritta

Spaghetti col granco fritto

SPAGHETTI WITH FRIED CRAB

The Sicilian coast is quite rocky in places and crabs can be found easily on some beaches. Crabs of various sizes are easily available for sale. The small ones with soft shells cook quickly and are eaten whole.

There was a time in Sicily when you could find very large crabs, the size of mud crabs or the Italian *granseola*. Unfortunately the large crabs are no longer seen. The medium-sized crabs are known by a variety of local names – *aranciu pilusu* (hairy orange), *migrociu* or *granciufudduni*. They are popular cooked whole, either grilled on coals or fried in hot oil. They are also popular in pasta sauces, as in this recipe.

In most fish restaurants in Sicily it is customary to display fish and for the customer to select the ones they would like to be cooked. I ate *pasta con granchi* in a restaurant on the waterfront overlooking the fishing boats in Mondello close to Palermo and I can only assume that the fresh sweet taste was mostly due to the very fresh ingredients. It was cooked very simply with a little tomato sauce and a generous amount of crabmeat.

Wild crabs are caught in traps and pots and some are caught commercially by trawling and by-catch. They have a high reproduction rate and therefore are sustainable.

As well as spaghetti, I have eaten this dish made with fresh pasta – *tagghiarini* (*taglierini* or *tagliolini* in Italian, pasta cut into 2–3mm/⅛in strips wide). In Trapani I ate a version of this made with *spaghettoni* – thick spaghetti – fun to eat! Save some of the legs to decorate the pasta.

INGREDIENTS

¾ cup extra virgin olive oil

500g (17½oz) red tomatoes,
  peeled and chopped

5 cloves garlic, finely chopped

500g (17½oz) spaghettoni
  to spaghettini

600–800g (21–29oz) crab
  meat

1 cup finely cut parsley

7–10 basil leaves (I like to
  use several small sprigs
  with the leaves attached)

salt and freshly ground
  pepper or chilli flakes to
  taste

METHOD

In a saucepan, place ¼ cup olive oil, tomatoes, 2 cloves of garlic and a little salt and pepper and cook, uncovered, until it has reduced to a cream-like consistency. Remove from the heat.

Cook the pasta.

In a frying pan, heat the remaining olive oil, add the crab meat and the rest of the garlic and sauté for a few minutes.

Add the crab mixture to the hot sauce (you may need to reheat it) and toss it through. Add the parsley to the hot drained pasta and mix well.

Combine the pasta and the sauce, add basil and serve.

VARIATION

- Use any or several varieties of crustaceans. I like to add uncooked prawn meat and freshwater crayfish (yabbies).
- One whole crab could be used for decoration.

Pesce Salato

Salted Fish

SALTED FISH HAS BEEN GREATLY VALUED AND AN IMPORTANT INDUSTRY IN SICILY. DURING MEDIEVAL TIMES THE STANDARD LENTEN DIET WAS BASED ON PULSES AND DRIED SALTED FISH. STILL POPULAR IN SICILY, SALTED FISH WERE POPULAR WITH THE ANCIENT ROMANS. ANCHOVIES, WHICH STILL FLAVOUR MANY DISHES, PROBABLY REPLACED THE GURUM USED WIDELY BY ANCIENT ROMANS.

Gurum was made by crushing and fermenting fish innards. It was very popular during Roman times, an import from the Greeks. It was a seasoning preferred to salt and added to other ingredients like vinegar, wine, oil and pepper to make a condiment used for meat, fish and vegetables – much like the fish sauce used in some Asian cuisines.

Two early cookery books, *The Art of Cooking: The First Modern Cookery Book* by Martino of Como and *On Right Pleasure and Good Health* by Platina, praise the taste and quality of salted tuna (particularly the middle section of tuna called *tarantellum* or *terantello*). Salted tuna (sometimes called *mosciame* in Sicily) was introduced by the Arabs (who called it *muscamma*) in about the 10th century. It has firm, deep red-brown flesh that needs only paper-thin slicing and is mainly eaten softened in oil with a sprinkling of lemon juice. Salted tuna is also produced in southern Spain; they refer to it as air-dried tuna or sun-dried tuna and Mojama tuna). *Bottarga* (called *buttarica* or *buttarga* in Sicilian) are the eggs in the ovary sacs of female tuna. These are pressed into a solid mass, salted and processed. The name *bottarga* is thought to have evolved from the Arabic *buarikh* – raw fish eggs, once made made by dipping the sac

AUTUMN MENU

&

Bad weather pasta from
Palermo *(Pasta ro' malutempu)*
Fish in a bag *(Pesce al cartoccio)*
Green leaf salad *('Nzalata virdi)*
with fennel and orange

in beeswax and leaving it to dry. Making *bottarga* is a much more complicated process now and is only produced in Favignana. It is grated to flavour dishes, mostly pasta, or sliced finely and eaten as an antipasto. *Bottarga* can also be made with mullet. The Sardinians also produce *bottarga*.

Italian and Spanish salted tuna and *bottarga* are available from specialist food stores. It is expensive, but if you are using it for a pasta dish you will not need very much – the flavour is very concentrated. Other parts of the tuna are also salted (see page 114), and I have used them like *bottarga*.

SALTED ANCHOVIES

These small, aromatic preserved fish appear in numerous Sicilian pasta sauces. Anchovies are smaller than sardines and are lighter tasting; they are found in Sicily around April to September. In Italian they are known as *alici* or *acciughe* , although they are generally called *masculini*, and are eaten raw and marinaded or cooked. Preserved anchovies are usually sold in large vats, packed in salt or in oil or in smaller quantities in a tin or jar.

Preserving anchovies in salt uses an ancient technique: top-quality fish are cleaned and washed in salt brine, then dried. They are then packed in large round tins in sea salt and left to cure over a specified time; the tins are then sealed. Salted anchovies only need to be soaked in cold water for about 15 minutes. The backbone and tail is easily removed.

Anchovies packed in olive oil are cured by a similar process, but once cured the fish are rinsed in salt water to remove scales and skin. They are filleted before they are packed in oil. Most Sicilians still prefer the anchovies packed in salt because, once soaked, they are less salty than most of the oil-packed anchovies.

It is worth shopping around for *filetti di alici* and trying a few brands, but generally the better anchovies are more expensive, and it is easy to see why. Check the label: *qualita selezionata a mano* means they are 'quality hand-picked' rather than machine-processed. If they are preserved in olive oil, the label will say *all' olio di oliva*.

It may be difficult to find anchovies packed in Sicily, but there are some good-quality ones from other parts of Italy, Spain and Portugal. The Spanish white anchovies (also called *boquerones gavros*) are packed in oil and vinegar and more lightly cured – these are much more delicate and less salty.

Pasta chi brocculi arriminata

Pasta rimestata coi cavolfiori

PASTA WITH CAULIFLOWER, SULTANAS, PINE NUTS AND ANCHOVIES

There are many variations on this basic recipe cooked all over Sicily, where coloured cauliflowers are the most common (unfortunately most of the colour fades when they are cooked). As well as the familiar white or cheddar (pale yellow) varieties, there are beautiful purple ones (*cavolfiore viola* in Italian) that range in colour from pink through violet to dark purple. My friend is growing a variety called purple cape cauliflower and one that is light green and pink called *cavolfiore romanesco precoce*. There are also the bright, pale green ones and a sculpted, pointy pale green variety called Roman cauliflower; I have seen these in Rome and throughout Tuscany.

Cauliflowers are called different names in the Sicilian language and in different locations. The Sicilian name for cauliflower is *brocculi* and what the rest of the world (and of mainland Italy) know as broccoli are called often *sparaccedi* – this is also the word for brussels sprouts, which are not very common in Sicily. My relatives' neighbour called his purple one *sciuriddu*, and it was cooked this way, using short fresh pasta (*causanedda*).

Sicilians are also very fond of what they call *cavoli*. Although in Italian it is the word for cabbages, in Sicily, *cavoli* are young kohlrabi always picked with the leaves attached – both parts of the plants are cooked with pasta. There are also different wild greens (mostly brassicas – plants from the mustard family) that are very common in pasta sauces

Some recipes include a little tomato paste for extra colour and flavour, others a little parsley. In some homes the pasta may be served with toasted breadcrumbs, in others with grated cheese. The names of the recipes also change from place to place, capturing the essence of the ingredients.

I have eaten many pasta dishes made with cauli-broc, broccoli, kohlrabi

A tavula si scordanu li trivuli.
(Sicilian proverb)
At the table you forget your troubles.

A ciumi surdi nun cci iri a piscari.
(Sicilian proverb)
Do not go to fish in a silent river.

and the green leaves, with tubular (rigatoni, penne, bucatini, or zite) pasta to trap the sauce. Fresh pasta is also popular in this recipe. I also use this recipe to cook cauliflower as a *contorno*.

METHOD

Soak the sultanas or currants in a cup of warm water.

To prepare the cauliflower, remove the outer green leaves and break the cauliflower into small florets.

In a frying pan large enough to accommodate all the ingredients, sauté the chopped onion in the olive oil. Add the anchovies and let them melt in the oil, stirring with a wooden spoon. Then add the cauliflower florets, bay leaves and the fennel seeds. Stir gently over the heat to colour and coat the vegetable with oil.

Add the pine nuts, the saffron and the sultanas with soaking water, salt and crushed chillies, cover, and allow to cook gently for about 20 minutes, until the florets are soft.

Cook the pasta. Drain and toss with the cauliflower sauce. Coat the pasta evenly and allow to absorb the flavours for about 5 minutes.

Serve with toasted breadcrumbs or grated pecorino cheese.

VARIATIONS

- *N'crostata* (crusted): Place the pasta in an ovenproof dish, cover with grated cheese and bake for 20 minutes in a moderate oven. Cubes or slices of pecorino can be stirred through the pasta before baking.
- *Pasta fritta* (fried pasta): This was a childhood treat. Leftover, dressed pasta is fried in a little hot extra virgin olive oil – it is not stirred so the bottom forms a golden crust. It can then be flipped over like a frittata, allowing a crisp and tasty crust to form on the other side. It is cut like a cake.

INGREDIENTS

600g (1lb 5oz) fresh or 500g (17½oz) dry pasta (see above)

2 tablespoons sultanas or currants

1 medium cauliflower

1 large onion, chopped

½ cup extra virgin olive oil

4–5 anchovies, finely chopped

2 bay leaves

1 tablespoon fennel seeds

2 tablespoons pine nuts

½–1 small teaspoon saffron

grated pecorino or toasted breadcrumbs to taste (see page 57)

salt and crushed dried chillies to taste

Pasta ro' malutempu

Pasta del cattivo tempo

BAD WEATHER PASTA

Pasta ro' malutempu is a dish of necessity and made with ingredients at hand. It was cooked during the times when fishermen could not go out in their boats during bad weather (*malutempu*), hence its fascinating name. With no fresh fish, they had to make do with anchovies and vegetables. Mind you, this is not a bad alternative.

The sauce can be made quickly while the pasta is cooking or it can be made in advance and then reheated – this gives the flavours a better chance to mature. It uses ingredients found in any Italian pantry.

Black olives, anchovies, garlic, usually broccoli, cauliflower or cauli-broc are used. Another choice is romanesco, the cauliflower with yellowish to vivid green colouring and spirals that form multiple pointed heads grouped together. Wild greens and *cime di rape* can be substituted.

INGREDIENTS

500g (17½oz) broccoli,
  cauli-broc or cauliflower,
  divided into flowerets
3 cloves garlic, chopped
about 1 cup extra virgin olive
  oil
5–6 anchovies, finely
  chopped
1 tablespoon fennel seeds
1 cup black olives, stoned
1 cup finely cut parsley
1 tablespoon tomato paste,
½ cup white wine or water
500g (17½oz) short pasta
  or 600g (1lb 5oz) fresh
  pasta
toasted breadcrumbs or
  grated pecorino to serve
salt and freshly ground
  pepper or chilli to taste

BAD WEATHER PASTA FROM PALERMO

METHOD

Steam the broccoli (cauli-broc, cauliflower or *cime di rape*). Sicilians boil the vegetable until soft in plenty of water, drain and reserve the vegetable-flavoured water for cooking the pasta.

Soften the garlic in the extra virgin olive oil, add the anchovies and fennel seeds. Stir the ingredients until the fennel seeds smell fragrant and the anchovies have dissolved. Add the olives, parsley, steamed broccoli, the tomato paste mixed with the wine (or water) and seasoning.

This is where Sicilians and I differ: Sicilians let the sauce continue to cook on low heat until the sauce is creamy and the ingredients are fully amalgamated

INGREDIENTS

¾ cup extra virgin olive oil
3 garlic cloves, crushed
3–4 zucchini, thinly sliced
500g (17½oz) red tomatoes,
*   peeled and chopped,*
¾ cup green olives, chopped
½ cup capers (if using the
*   salted variety ensure that*
*   they have been soaked and*
*   rinsed well)*
red chilli flakes to taste
4–5 anchovies, finely
*   chopped*
1 cup basil leaves, torn into
*   smaller pieces if they are*
*   too large*
500g (17½oz) spaghetti
grated pecorino to taste
salt

– this may require a little more liquid while it is cooking. I like to see and taste the individual ingredients – I combine the ingredients and cook them for a short time, enough to blend the flavours.

Cook the pasta and combine with the sauce. Serve with toasted breadcrumbs or pecorino.

BAD WEATHER PASTA FROM MESSINA

The recipe from Messina must be for the fishermen who experience bad weather in the warmer months because it contains zucchini, which is mostly a summer vegetable. The most common zucchini in Sicily are the round, pale green variety, not the long dark green ones which are more common in the north of Italy. (The round ones are supposed to taste sweeter).

METHOD

In a wide frying pan that will fit all the vegetables, heat the oil and add the garlic; when it is golden discard it. Add the zucchini and toss over a medium-hot flame until golden. Set them aside.

Add the tomatoes and cook uncovered until thick. Add the olives, capers, red chilli flakes, anchovies and basil and cook for 5–7 minutes. Taste for salt and add the zucchini. Heat through.

Cook the pasta, drain and toss back into the saucepan it was cooked in. Add the sauce, toss and serve. Serve with grated pecorino.

Virmiceddi sirausani

Vermicelli alla siracusana

VERMICELLI AS COOKED IN SYRACUSE

Some versions, like this one, contain sautéed eggplants (aubergine). In most versions the ingredients are cooked in one pan. I prefer to cook the eggplants and peppers (capsicum) separately to preserve the individual flavours.

METHOD

For the sauce, in a saucepan place ½ cup of oil, tomatoes, garlic, half the basil, a little salt and pepper. Over gentle heat, reduce, uncovered, to a cream-like consistency. Add olives and capers.

Soak the eggplant in saltwater (if necessary), drain, dry well and fry in very hot oil. Remove. Fry the peppers in the same pan.

Cook the pasta.

Dissolve the anchovies in a pan with a little hot oil. Add to the sauce with the peppers and the eggplants and heat briefly. Combine the pasta and sauce. Sprinkle the remaining basil on top. Serve with grated pecorino.

VARIATIONS

⁊ Instead of pecorino, mix small cubes of fresh *caciocavallo* or *provola* in the pasta just before serving. It melts and makes a very creamy sauce.

⁊ In Salina in the Aeolian islands, the peppers are roasted rather than fried and caperberries (*cucunci*) are substituted for the capers.

INGREDIENTS

1 cup extra virgin olive oil

2–3 red tomatoes, peeled and chopped

2 cloves garlic, crushed, plus 2 whole cloves

about 20 basil leaves

1 cup black olives

½ cup capers, soaked and rinsed

1 eggplant, peeled and cut into small cubes

1 large yellow pepper, cut into thin strips

1 large red pepper, cut into thin strips

500g (17½oz) spaghettini or vermicelli

5–7 anchovy fillets, finely chopped

grated pecorino to taste

salt and freshly ground pepper

Pasta a la palina

Pasta alla paolina

PASTA WITH TOMATOES, ANCHOVIES, CINNAMON AND CLOVES

INGREDIENTS

¾ cup extra virgin olive oil

3–4 red tomatoes, peeled and
chopped

3 cloves garlic, chopped

a handful of basil (I like to
use several small sprigs
with the leaves attached)

600g (1lb 5oz) fresh pasta
or 500g (17½oz) dry
tagliatelle or lasagne ricce

8–10 anchovy fillets, finely
chopped

½ teaspoon ground
cinnamon

¼ teaspoon ground cloves

salt and freshly ground
pepper to taste

This recipe takes its name from the monastery of San Francesco di Paola and originates from Palermo. This Saint Francis was born in Paola, Calabria, and entered a Francisan monastery. And then the miracles began. According to legend, while trying to cross to Sicily from Calabria (across the Strait of Messina) the boatman refused him passage. So he made a boat out of his cloak and his staff, and off he sailed. He and two companions began a movement that become the foundation of a new order of friars, the Hermits of Saint Francis (later the Order of Minims). The friars lived a life of extreme poverty and severity and abstained from meat. One of the monks in the kitchen of the Palermo monastery added cinnamon and cloves to a simple dish of pasta and anchovies.

Wide tagliatelle or *lasagne ricce* (wide flat pasta with a ruffled edge) are commonly used. As you would expect, the recipe has altered over time and there are regional variations. Some use fresh sardines, some add onions, fresh fennel or cauli-broc, but the identifying ingredients for this dish are cloves and cinnamon.

METHOD

Make a sauce with ½ cup olive oil, the tomatoes, garlic and basil.

Cook the pasta while you melt the anchovies to ¼ cup of the oil in a small saucepan. Add to the sauce. Add the spices and mix well.

Combine the pasta with the sauce and serve hot.

Pasta ca buttarga

Pasta con la bottarga

PASTA WITH BOTTARGA

Bottarga, dried tuna roe, is strong tasting and rather salty. It is used to flavour dishes, in the same way as anchovies are, but because it is relatively expensive, even in Sicily, is never used in great quantities. However, substituting anchovies for *bottarga*, would be like using mushrooms to replace truffles.

I have bought *bottarga* in the Ortigia Market in Syracuse in a very special shop filled with herbs, spices and magic products. The shopkeeper Antonio Drago is known as *il mago delle spezie* (the wizard of spices).

As well as the *bottarga*, the shop stocked a range of salted and dried local specialties including *mascione* (made from salted and dried tuna or swordfish fillets) and sausages made from leftover parts of the fish, including the giblets (called *suppizzata*, *sosizzuna*, *ficazza* and *carrubedda*, this last name because it is the colour of carob). There is also *busunagghia* made from the dark meat and *tarantello*, flesh from close to the ribs.

The production of these tuna products (which come mainly from Trapani), especially the practice of locally processing and preserving *bottarga* (in Favignana) is seen as a dying art and worthy of preservation. The products are included in the Slow Food compendium, *The Ark of Taste*, which catalogues thousands of edible species and traditional products that are in danger of extinction. Although these products are made from tuna, presumably Slow Food base their inclusion on the tuna being fished using sustainable practices and the number caught not exceeding the quota (although bluefin tuna is not sustainable). The practice is also favoured because it uses every bit of the tuna – no wastage.

In Ortigia, they produce *lattume di tonno* – tuna testicles that are layered with salt for a month, washed, dried, and served in thin slices with a drizzle of extra virgin olive oil or fried. This was originally regarded as an aphrodisiac. Today it is both a delicacy and curiosity.

Before the *bottarga* is added to pasta, the outer membrane (ovary sacs) are

SUMMER MENU

Olives
Pasta alla norma with *bottarga*
(Pasta a la norma ca bottarga)
Salad of boiled green beans
(Fasulinu vugghiutu) or other
boiled vegetables

removed. The *bottarga* is either grated (using a coarse grater) or shaved very finely and soaked in extra virgin olive oil to soften before use. The other salted tuna products can be used the same way.

Long pasta (spaghetti or spaghettini, linguine, fettuccine or bucatini), is used for this dish. Fresh fettuccine are also very good.

Bottarga is also produced in Sardinia where it is served with fresh pasta made in the shape of *malloreddus* – gnocchetti or small gnocchi (see *gnocculi*, page 49).

INGREDIENTS

500g (17½oz) long pasta
    or 600g (1lb 5oz) fresh
    pasta
1 cup extra virgin olive oil
5 cloves garlic, finely chopped
1 cup finely cut parsley
10–12 basil leaves, to scatter
    on top of finished dish
red chilli, chopped, or chilli
    flakes or freshly ground
    pepper to taste
150g (5oz) bottarga, grated

METHOD

Cook the pasta.

Heat the olive oil and add the garlic, parsley and chilli. Cook over high heat until the garlic is lightly golden and the parsley has wilted. Add the grated *bottarga* (if using sliced *bottarga*, use gentle heat), remove the pan from the heat and toss it into the hot oil.

Add the pasta to the pan and mix with the sauce. Add the basil leaves, stir and serve.

VARIATIONS

- Add grated zest from 1 lemon at the same time as the basil.
- In Syracuse and Trapani the ingredients remain the same, but are mixed together into a paste. When the pasta is cooked, reserve 1 cup of the hot pasta water and stir it into the paste before dressing the pasta.
- Use the sauce to dress pasta made with carob.

PASTA DI FARINA DI CARRUBE CON BOTTARGA DI TONNO

When ground into powder, carob is known as *farina di carrube* (carob flour). This is added to wheat flour to make pasta, in the same way as the Ligurian pasta partly made with chestnut flour. Make the pasta with a ratio of 1 carob to 3 wheat flour. The dough (pasta) will feel heavier. Once rolled, cut the pasta into *maltagliati* (badly cut shapes, see page 49).

Spaghetti ca sarsa murisca

Spaghetti colla salsa moresca

SPAGHETTI WITH MORESCA SAUCE

This dish is eaten in and around the town of Scicli. Its origins are fascinating and complicated. I was interested why it is called *murisca* (*moresca* in Italian, Moorish in English). The combination of sweet and savoury, and some of the flavourings (cinnamon, citrus juice, sugar) mean it could have Moorish origins. But *la moresca* is also the name of a dance, which is still performed in parts of Sicily, especially on feast days. Similar dances are mentioned in Renaissance documents throughout many Catholic areas of Europe. *La moresca* is remarkably like the English Morris dance (or Moorish dance). *La moresca* and the Morris dance are considered to be the oldest European folk dances still performed and inspired by the struggle of Christians against the Moors.

The sauce is not cooked: it is an *impasto*, a paste made with a mortar and pestle. A food processor can be used or stir the ingredients by hand. You can add anchovies dissolved into a paste in a pan with a little hot oil.

METHOD

Pound ingredients together, beginning with *bottarga*, garlic and anchovies. Add sugar, cinnamon, pine nuts, breadcrumbs, parsley, zest and chillies, gradually moistening with oil and citrus juices. Add the vinegar at the end if you wish.

INGREDIENTS

150g (5oz) bottarga, grated
2 cloves garlic, finely chopped
4 anchovies, finely chopped
1 large teaspoonful sugar
½ teaspoon ground
  cinnamon
1 cup pine nuts
1 cup toasted breadcrumbs
  (see page 57)
½ cup finely cut parsley
zest of ½ lemon
1–2 red chilli, chopped
¾ cup extra virgin olive oil
juice of 1 lemon
juice of 1 orange
1 tablespoon vinegar
  (optional)
500g (17½oz) long pasta

Pasta a la norma ca bottarga

Pasta alla norma con la bottarga

PASTA WITH TOMATOES, EGGPLANTS AND BOTTARGA

Pasta alla norma comes from Catania. Many presume it is named after the opera *La Norma* by Vincenzo Bellini, who was born there. But the expression *'a norma'* was used in Catania in the early 1900s by purists to describe food that was conventionally cooked ('as normal', 'as it should be'), according to all the rules and regulations specified in the recipe. It is a classic summer dish, with a sauce of tomatoes and basil and topped with fried eggplant. In this version, *bottarga* is added, replacing *ricotta salata*, which is the usual topping.

INGREDIENTS

3 medium eggplants,
  unpeeled and cubed
1½ cups extra virgin olive oil
3 cloves garlic
1kg (2lb 4oz) ripe tomatoes,
  peeled and chopped
10–15 basil leaves, some
  for the sauce and some for
  decoration
500g (17½oz) casarecci or
  other short pasta
150g (5oz) bottarga, grated
salt (a little) and freshly
  ground pepper

METHOD

Soak the eggplant in salted water if you wish. Dry well and fry in 1 cup of olive oil until golden, turning once. Drain.

For the tomato sauce, sauté the garlic in the olive oil, add the tomatoes and some of the basil and cook, uncovered, until thick.

Cook the pasta. Toss the pasta with the tomato sauce and top with the eggplants and the remaining basil. Add the grated *bottarga* as the finale.

VARIATION

I ate a version of this in a restaurant in San Leone, on the coast near Agrigento. The pasta was served on top of a halved, fried eggplant, along with a few currants, anchovies, thinly sliced *bottarga* and cubes of ricotta salata. If using a large round eggplant, cut it horizontally and take a slice from the centre to make it thinner – the eggplant will cook more evenly.

Comu sacunnu

As second course

THERE ARE AS MANY WAYS TO COOK FISH AS THERE ARE FOR MEAT. UNLIKE MEAT, FISH DOES NOT REQUIRE LONG COOKING TIMES. THE FLESH OF MOST FISH NEEDS TO BE CAREFULLY HANDLED OR IT WILL FALL APART. AS WITH MEAT, WHEN SELECTING FISH SUITED TO PARTICULAR COOKING METHODS, WE ARE BASING OUR PRACTICES ON THE TEXTURE, DEGREE OF OILINESS, FLAVOUR AND THICKNESS OR SIZE OF THE FISH.

Sicilians are more likely to steam or gently simmer a delicate-tasting, soft or flaky-textured fish and braise a dense, meaty one. Whiting is a delicate, fragile fish (called *nasello* in Italian, *merlu* in French, *merluza* in Spanish and hake in Britain and North America). Tuna, swordfish and marlin have a dense texture and firm flesh and therefore can tolerate a greater degree of handling. Frying is more suitable for fillets, cutlets or small whole fish but a whole, large fish may be better baked.

The flavour of fish varies from mild to strong, and usually the darker the flesh, the oilier the flesh and the stronger the taste. White-fleshed fish are mild tasting, cream-fleshed fish are moderately flavourful and dark-fleshed fish (for example sardines, mullet and mackerel) are intensely flavourful. Whole fish and oily fish are more suitable for barbecuing (wrap a less oily fish in foil before placing it on the barbecue to prevent it from drying out and falling apart).

Ascuta a li vecchi cà 'un ci la sgarri. (Sicilian proverb)
Listen to the old and you won't be wrong.

TUNA

In Sicilian cuisine, tuna was regarded as *la carne dei poveri* (meat of the poor), not just because it used to be plentiful and cheaper than meat, but also because it is as versatile. Tuna is cut up in many different ways, sliced vertically and horizontally, allowing it to be cooked in many ways.

I find Sicilian fish markets are amazing. Huge swordfish and tuna

As second course

hang from hooks as if they are carcasses of meat or are exhibited whole. They lie, cut in half and packed on ice on large marble or wooden cutting boards, waiting to be carved into steaks, or they are cut into long fillets or *rota* (round slices cut through the centre of the fish). Some are carved for display. Every part of the tuna is laid out: the head, heart, liver and gills (how else would you be able to gauge the freshness of the fish?). Nothing is wasted and each part is available to fresh, smoked or salted, including the egg and sperm sacs.

Tuna has a medium-to-firm texture and is the most popular fish in Sicily. Recipes make a virtue of its versatility. It is sliced thinly and pounded into steaks, stuffed and rolled and made into *braciole* (like *involtini* or *saltimbocca*). As extravagant as it may seem, Sicilians even mince it and mould it into fish balls.

Tuna are migratory fish and travel long distances during their breeding cycle. There are five major species fished commercially: albacore, bigeye, bluefin, skipjack and yellowfin. As with all fish, specific species may be known by other common and scientific names in different regions and oceans. For instance, skipjack (*Katsuwonus pelamis*), which is the smallest of the tuna family, is also known as striped tuna or arctic bonito.

Albacore tuna (*Thunnus alalunga*) and skipjack are most often used for canned tuna. Unlike bigeye, yellowfin, and bluefin, skipjack stocks have shown greater resistance to commercial fishing, which is why it is viewed as the most sustainable of the tunas.

ALBACORE TUNA

The pale flesh and versatility of albacore tuna is greatly underrated. It is known as the chicken of the sea: its flesh turns white when cooked. Some fishmongers do not stock it, and those who do often sell it containing sections of dark meat. It does not fetch high prices because it is not in demand in Japan (where tuna is preferred eaten raw and red).

For all the Sicilian recipes intended for tuna, swordfish and marlin, I use albacore tuna when I can get it, cut into thick steaks, as a whole fillet, or a round *rota* cut from the centre of the tuna.

Albacore tuna is in the green sustainable category.

YELLOWFIN TUNA AND BIGEYE TUNA

Both these species are wild-caught but because catch rates are declining they are in the orange 'think-twice' category.

Bòn tièmpu e màlu tièmpu nun nùra tutu u tièmpu. (Sicilian proverb)
Good weather, bad weather, neither lasts forever.

Yellowfin tuna is the one most commonly sold fresh in Europe, the USA, Australia and New Zealand. This is the one I buy very occasionally when I cannot find albacore tuna.

Bigeye is the second most popular tuna for sashimi and unfortunately stocks are diminishing fast and so I have not listed it in any of the recipes.

BLUEFIN TUNA

Bluefin tuna always seems to be available for purchase. From a sustainable point of view, it is in the red category and we should say no to the most popular species of tuna because it has been severely over-fished.

The process of catching tuna is sophisticated. Spotter planes are used to locate the them and live sardines (pilchards) are used to entice the tuna into a mass feeding frenzy, making it easier for them (of all sizes) to be fished and killed. Most tuna is snap-frozen on the fishing vessel. Bluefin tuna is Japan's most popular sashimi fish and it fetches very high prices.

Wild-caught tuna is also herded and then fattened in sea-cage aquaculture farms.

SEA-CAGE AQUACULTURE

I used to think that fish such as tuna, ocean trout and salmon produced by sea-cage aquaculture – penned, dense schools of fish in large floating cages moored in bays and estuaries – were sustainable and was surprised to find that conservationists totally oppose sea-cage aquaculture.

There are a number of problems associated with sea-cage aquaculture.

Tuna farming involves herding juvenile tuna from the wild into pens to fatten in cages – it is called fish ranching.

Fish farms are established in bays and estuaries to avoid damage from storms and currents and they need clean and frequent water exchange. Unfortunately, other wild fish and marine life also favour these environs and aquaculture affects their habitat.

Significant amounts of waste are discharged from fish farms back into the ocean: nutrients in unused fish feed, fish faeces and chemicals used to keep the fish healthy and the pens clean. These can be toxic to many aquatic species and impact on the surrounding environment.

There is also the potential for farmed fish to escape. These could spread diseases and can threaten local wild species by competing for food and habitat and interfering with their breeding. Farmed tuna are fed large quantities of

While it takes three tons of wild fish to produce one ton of salmon and five tons of wild fish to produce one ton of cod, it takes a massive 20 tons of wild fish to fatten up just one ton of tuna for market. So it's twenty-to-one. It's a false economy. It's biological nonsense. You're producing less fish from more fish, and it simply doesn't add up.
– Don Staniford, A Stain Upon the Sea: West Coast Salmon Farming

wild, whole fish (pilchards, sardines, herrings and anchovies, chosen for their high oil content and mostly imported). Penned tuna are fed three times a day, whereas in the wild, they may eat once a week.

Imported feed can bring viruses and other diseases. For example, there have been disastrous viral epidemics that affected 5000 kilometres of coastline and killed 75 per cent of the wild adult pilchard population in South Australian waters in 1995 and 1998; it is thought to have been the result of importing pilchards for tuna farms.

Increased numbers of juvenile bluefin tuna are caught each year from an already over-exploited stock – these could have reproduced in the wild and renewed the wild stocks.

Aquaculture farms attract other marine life – wild seals, seabirds especially gulls, and sharks – which can be problematic and often the means taken to eliminate them have detrimental effects on those species.

I cannot believe our government allows us to fish and export a critically endangered species, we would not eat gorilla or bear.
– Prue Barnard, marine conservation campaigner

Agghiotta
Alla ghiotta

The method of cooking *ALLA GHIOTTA* is to prepare food glutton-style, in a manner that satisfies a glutton. This cooking style is particularly common around Messina and the northeastern coast of Sicily. The fish is always cooked *IN UMIDO* (an Italian cooking term – in the damp – that is, simmered or braised in some liquid) and *LA GHIOTTA* is the name of the sauce. Some Sicilians bake the fish in the sauce; others braise it on the stove.

Il siciliano e`un ghiottone di pesce.
(Italian saying)
A person who is un ghiottone is a glutton. It is said that Sicilians are gluttons for fish.

The tomato was introduced to Sicily in the 17th century and fish cooked *alla ghiotta* usually contains this as a principal ingredient. Fresh, ripe tomatoes are always preferable, but canned tomatoes can also be used, especially in the winter months.

As second course

Agghiotta di pisci a missinisa

Pesce alla ghiotta alla messinese

FISH *ALLA GHIOTTA* FROM MESSINA WITH TOMATOES, GREEN OLIVES, CAPERS, PINE NUTS AND CURRANTS

INGREDIENTS

1 cup extra virgin olive oil

6 x 200g (7oz) fish steaks or cutlets

1 celery stalk, finely chopped

1 onion, finely sliced

¾ cup salted capers, soaked and washed

1 cup green olives, pitted and chopped

2 cloves garlic, chopped

½ cup currants, soaked in a little warm water for about 15 minutes

½ cup pine nuts

2–3 bay leaves

500g (17½oz) tomatoes, peeled, seeded, and chopped

salt and freshly ground pepper

There are many variations of this dish. This one contains Sicilian flavours in excess, and it is sure to satisfy the gluttons.

It is intended for *piscispata* (Sicilian for swordfish; *pescespada* is the Italian) but any cutlets or thick fillets of fish are suitable. It is said that the Sicilian fishermen used to talk to the swordfish in Greek to lure them closer to the boats and make them easier to catch. They believed that if Italian or Sicilian were spoken, the fish would not approach – it was a foreign language for the swordfish accustomed to being caught by the ancient Greeks.

Suitable fish

Fish steaks or cutlets of firm, large fish cut into thick slices. The fish I use are: flathead, trevally, kingfish and albacore tuna, snapper, mackerel and barramundi. Other suitable firm-fleshed fish are Pacific or Alaskan halibut or cod, haddock (US hook and line), mahi-mahi (dorado), hoki, sablefish (also called Pacific black cod) turbot (certified farmed), Cape hake and pollock.

METHOD

Heat the extra virgin olive oil in a wide pan, large enough to accommodate the fish in one layer. Shallow-fry the fish for a couple of minutes on both sides over medium-high heat to seal. Remove from the pan and set aside.

For *la ghiotta*, add the celery and onion to the same oil, and cook until softened, about 5 minutes. Stir frequently. Reduce heat to medium, then add the capers, olives, garlic, currants, pine nuts and bay leaves and stir well. Add tomatoes, season, stir, and cook for about 10 minutes until some of the juice from the tomatoes has reduced.

Arrange the fish in the sauce in one layer and spoon some of the sauce over it. Cover and cook on moderate heat until the fish is done.

VARIATIONS

- Add 3 or 4 chopped anchovies at the same time as the capers.
- Omit pine nuts and currants and add cut flat-leaf parsley and/or basil.
- Use black olives instead of green (and be surprised at the differences in taste).
- Potatoes cooked beforehand, then peeled and thickly sliced, can be added at the same time as the fish. Estimate one potato per person.
- In a restaurant in Messina, *pescespada alla ghiotta* was served with slices of thin oven-toasted bread, the same accompaniment as *zuppa di pesce*, and without potatoes.

L'anima mia gustava di quel cibo,
che saziando di se, di se s'asseta.
My soul tasted that heavenly
food, which gave new appetite
while it satiated.
– Dante, from 'Purgatory'
(Purgatorio XXXI, 128)

Agghiotta di tunnu cu pipi e mulinciani

Tonno ala ghiotta con peperoni e melanzane

TUNA ALLA GHIOTTA

INGREDIENTS

1 onion, sliced
1 cup extra virgin olive oil
2 red peppers (capsicum),
   sliced
2 green peppers (capsicum),
   sliced
2 large eggplants
   (aubergine), cubed
½ cup pale celery leaves from
   heart, finely chopped
3 large potatoes, cubed
500g (17½oz) tomatoes,
   peeled, seeded and chopped
flat-leaf parsley and/or basil,
   finely cut
1.2kg (2lb 12oz) tuna, cut
   into large chunks or small
   steaks
salt and freshly ground
   pepper

This is popular in the Catania region. As in most *alla ghiotta* recipes, potatoes can be added to soak up juices. My grandmother Maria simply called it *agghiotta* (Sicilian for *alla ghiotta*). It is traditionally made with tuna.

Suitable fish
See previous recipe.

METHOD

In a pan large enough for all the ingredients, soften the onion in about ½ cup of oil and cook until soft, about 5 minutes, stirring frequently. Reduce heat to medium and add peppers, eggplants, celery and potatoes and sauté for 7–10 minutes until slightly caramelised. Add tomatoes and herbs, season, stir and cook until vegetables are nearly done.

Heat remaining olive oil on medium-high heat and shallow-fry the fish for a few minutes on both sides to seal. Remove. Place the fish in the sauce, cover, and cook for about 10 minutes, until vegetables and fish are done.

Agghiotta di piscistoccu

Stoccafisso alla ghiotta

STOCKFISH *ALLA GHIOTTA* WITH GREEN OLIVES, CAPERS AND POTATOES

Stoccofisso (in Italian, *piscistoccu* in Sicilian) and its counterpart, *baccalà*, are usually associated with *cucina povera*. *Baccalà* is cooked all over Sicily. *Stoccafisso* is the signature dish in Messina.

The differences between stoccafisso and baccalà
Although *stoccafisso* and *baccalà* are used interchangeably in some recipes, they are different. *Stoccafisso* is air-dried, without salt, and cod, haddock or hake may be used. It is dry and hard and usually sold as a whole fish, complete with bones and skin. The Norwegians and Swedes soak it in lye; when cooked in milk and reduced to mush, they call it *lutfisk*. Sicilians never cook it to a pulp; the fish is soaked in water to restore the fresh taste.

    Baccalà is salt-cured cod. In Spanish it is *bacalao*, in Portuguese *bacalhau*, in French *morue*. Different varieties of cod – cod, ling, saithe and tusk – are used. The fish is relatively moist and tender and is usually sold cut in sections. It is skinless, boneless and white. *Baccalà* may seem more appealing, but no ingredients are added to *stoccafisso* and it has a more delicate flavour.

    Stoccafisso and *baccalà* were eaten on days of abstinence when meat was prohibited to Catholics. It is also traditionally served on Christmas Eve all over Italy. Both types of fish were particularly popular inland where fresh fish was difficult to obtain or when *la pesca* (the catch) was poor.

PREPARING *STOCCAFISSO* AND *BACCALÀ*
Stoccafisso and *baccalà* require soaking in cold water before use – *stoccafisso* to rehydrate it and *baccalà* to remove the salt. Italian and Spanish food stores sell it pre-soaked. The pre-soaked *baccalà* is ready for use; the stockfish may need

As second course

cartilage, bones and skin removed. If you are purchasing the fish dry, select a piece of uniform thickness; the flesh should be compact.

To prepare, rinse well and soak in cold water for a minimum of 24 hours (up to 48 hours). The soaking time depends on the quality, thickness and age of the fish, but it will not suffer if soaked for the longer time. Refrigerate it in hot weather and change the water two or three times daily.

Then rinse the fish well. If stockfish, skin it, pick out the bones and cut into large pieces. *Baccalà* takes longer to cook, depending on thickness.

INGREDIENTS

1.2kg (2lb 12oz) stockfish
½ cup extra virgin olive oil
2–3 celery hearts (pale green stalks and leaves), chopped
1 large onion, chopped
1 cup green olives, pitted and chopped
½ cup salted capers, soaked and washed
4 tablespoons parsley, finely cut
500g (17½oz) tomatoes, peeled, seeded and chopped (or 1 cup passata)
500g (17½oz) potatoes, peeled and cut into large chunks
salt and freshly ground pepper

METHOD

Soak the stockfish and prepare it according to instructions above.

For *la ghiotta*, heat the extra virgin olive oil in a pan large enough for all the ingredients, add the celery and onion and cook until softened, about 5 minutes, stirring frequently. Reduce the heat to medium and add the olives, capers and parsley. Stir well. Add the tomatoes, season and cook for about 10 minutes to blend the flavours.

Arrange the fish in the sauce in a single layer and spoon some of the sauce over it. Reduce the heat to very low. Do not stir the fish or it will flake. Cover,and cook for about 20 minutes before adding potatoes. If using *baccalà* instead of *stoccafisso*, cook it at least 15 minutes longer.

Add 1–2 cups of water and leave undisturbed to cook, adding a little more water if it looks as if it is dryng out, until the fish and potatoes are done. It is always served hot; it can easily be reheated.

VARIATIONS

- Some modern recipes also include 1 cup of dry white wine.
- Stockfish *alla ghiotta in bianco* has little seasoning and no tomato. Use the same ingredients but add more parsley and replace the onions with 3–4 cloves of chopped garlic.
- See other recipes for *baccalà* on pages 193 and 376.

A stimpirata
Alla stemperata

ALL THE FOODS COOKED *ALLA STEMPERATA* HAVE DISTINCTIVE, STRONG, FRAGRANT TASTES. APART FROM VINEGAR, THE ESSENTIAL INGREDIENTS ARE CAPERS AND GREEN OLIVES, COMBINED WITH GARLIC OR ONIONS, CELERY AND MINT. THESE ARE COMMON INGREDIENTS IN SICILIAN CUISINE, BUT THE USE OF VINEGAR ENHANCES THEIR FLAVOURS. VINEGAR MAY ONCE HAVE BEEN USED TO PRESERVE THE FOOD OR PERHAPS TO MASK THE TASTE OF THE FISH OR MEAT, WHICH MAY HAVE BEEN SLIGHTLY SPOILED.

Cooking a range of foods *alla stemperata* – vegetables, rabbit, chicken and fish – is very common around the southeastern part of Sicily, near Syracuse and around Ragusa. A s*temperata* sauce can be used as a condiment for boiled root vegetables, especially carrots and young artichokes (see page 266).

It is important that food cooked *alla stemperata* is allowed to rest, to round out the flavours and become better balanced.

WINTER MENU

Fennel tortino (*Turticedda ri finocchiu*)
Pasta with cauliflower, sultanas, pine nuts and anchovies (*Pasta chi brocculi arriminata*)
Tuna *alla stemperata* with onions, vinegar, capers, green olives and mint (*Tunnu `a stimpirata*)
Braised Savoy cabbage (*Cavulu cappucciu a stufateddu*)

Tunnu 'a stimpirata

Tonno alla stemperata

Tuna ALLA STEMPERATA WITH ONIONS, VINEGAR, A FEW CAPERS, GREEN OLIVES AND MINT

I first tasted *tonno alla stemperata* cooked by one of my cousins. Rosetta cuts the tuna into large cubes, so it soaks up the flavours in the sauce and retains moisture. She cooked the fish in the morning and we ate it for lunch (at room temperature) so the flavours had time to develop, with warm, cubed potatoes that had been boiled then fried in extra virgin olive oil and a little rosemary.

Suitable fish
Use firm-fleshed fish with a medium to strong flavour – for example albacore tuna, mackerel, trevally, tropical snappers, red emperor, blue-eye trevella or large flathead. See *pesce alla ghiotta alla messinese* on page 131 for other fish.

METHOD

In a pan large enough to fit all the ingredients, soften the onion and celery in about half the oil, and cook until the onion is golden, about 5 minutes, stirring frequently. Reduce heat and add the tomato paste dissolved in a little water, olives, capers and seasoning. Cook until thickened and check seasoning.

Heat remaining oil in a separate pan and fry fish over medium-high heat until nearly cooked, turning once. Sprinkle over the vinegar, turn up the heat and let it reduce. Arrange the hot fish in the sauce and heat gently to meld the flavours. Serve warm or at room temperature. Add mint just before serving.

VARIATIONS

- Replace the onion with 5–6 cloves garlic.
- The tomato paste is used for colour, not taste, and can be omitted.

INGREDIENTS

3 large white onions, sliced
1 celery heart (pale green stalks and leaves), finely chopped
¾ cup extra virgin olive oil
1 tablespoon tomato paste
½ cup green olives, pitted and chopped
½ cup salted capers, soaked and washed
1.2kg (2lb 12oz) tuna or firm-fleshed fish, cubed or in chunks
½ cup white wine vinegar
½ cup finely cut mint leaves
salt
red chilli flakes to taste

Bracioli

Braciole or involtini

A BRACIOLA (SINGULAR) GENERALLY IS A CUTLET BUT IN
THE SOUTH AND IN SICILY IT IS ALSO A SLICE OF FISH OR
MEAT ROLLED AROUND A STUFFING.

Small *bracioli* (Sicilian) are also referred to as *braciulini* and *braciulittini*. To
complicate matters, in some parts of Sicily they are called *bammughiati* or
abbuttunati. In the rest of Italy stuffed rolls of meat or fish are commonly
known as *involtini* – usually made with veal and stuffed with cheese, ham and
sage and then fried in a little butter or oil. You may know them as *saltimbocca*
or *salti in bocca* ('jump in the mouth') and sometimes *ucelletti* or *ucellini* ('little
birds'). In French, rolled beef with a stuffing are known as *oiseax sans têtes*
('headless birds'). *Braciole* are versatile and can be braised, sautéed, baked,
grilled or poached.

Suitable fish
Braciole are usually made with tuna or swordfish. The flesh of both is firm and
meaty; finding a sustainable fish to substitute is not always easy. I use fillets
(with or without skin) from a variety of sustainable fish with a medium to firm
texture: albacore tuna, flathead, bream, trevally, whiting, tailor and dory.

METHOD

Albacore tuna is commonly sold skinless and in steaks. Cut into slices (4cm/
1½in thick) and flatten to about 10 x 10cm (4 x 4in) and 5–10mm (¼–½in)
thick between sheets of plastic wrap. Fish fillets should be skinned (but if
the skin is soft, it can be left on). Flatten fish fillets into rectangular shapes,
following their natural contours.

*Siragusa, terra amurusa, cu cincu
grana si mancia, vivi e campa la
carusa. (Sicilian saying)*
*Siracusa terra amorosa, con
cinque grani, vive e si diverte la
ragazza. (Italian)*
*Syracuse, a lovely place, on next to
nothing, a girl can live and have a
good time.*

The fish slices are stuffed, then rolled and secured by:

- using toothpicks
- tieing into a parcel with twine, or sew using a trussing needle (for larger rolls)
- fitting on a skewer (3 or 4 per stick, like kebabs, with a fresh bay leaf between each) or inserted onto stems of rosemary and bay
- flexible netting, especially for larger *braciole* (netting is available from specialist stores or butchers).

DIFFERENT COOKING METHODS

Cooking times depend on the size of each fish roll. Cook on both sides, turning over only once, to eliminate chance of breaking. There are regional variations in the stuffings. The same stuffings used for *braciole* can be used for small calamari. The following recipes provide enough scope to be adventurous. For alternative stuffings see s*ardi a beccafico*, page 150.

Sautéed

Sauté in extra virgin olive oil. Add seasoning and (if you wish) herbs (rosemary, bay, oregano) or whole garlic cloves or 1 finely sliced onion. A few minutes before the end of cooking, add about ½ cup white wine and reduce. Remove herbs and garlic and serve.

Baked

Place on a well-oiled oven tray and cook in a preheated oven (200°C/400°F) for about 10–20 minutes, depending on size. Pour a little more oil on each and bake. Serve baked (and grilled) *braicole* with lemon juice or with a simple sauce or dressing (see chapter 4, pages 252–73).

Grilled

Cook on an oiled barbecue plate or grill over charcoal on moderate heat.

Poached in a tomato sauce

Sauté 2 cloves garlic in ½ cup extra virgin olive oil and toss around before adding 3 ripe peeled and chopped tomatoes, 1 tablespoon of fresh chopped oregano, seasoning and 1 tablespoon of wine vinegar. Stir frequently. Reduce the heat to low and cook for about 10 minutes. Poach the *braciole* in the sauce for 7–20 minutes, depending on their size.

Cavaddi rausani, muli spaccafurnari e scecchi muricani. (Sicilian popular saying, written by proud people from Ragusa) *Horses from Ragusa, mules from Spaccaforno and donkeys from Modica.*

Braciulittini

Braciolini o involtini

SMALL BRACIOLE STUFFED WITH HERBS

INGREDIENTS

750g (1lb 12oz) fish fillets
fresh herbs (rosemary, flat-
leaf parsley and oregano)
garlic, finely chopped
fresh red chilli, deseeded and
sliced (optional)
about ½ cup extra virgin
olive oil
salt and freshly ground
pepper

These make wonderful little morsels on an antipasto platter. Because these are small *braciole* and the stuffing is light – only herbs and garlic are used – fillets of small fish (with skin on) are suitable: anything from mild-flavoured whiting, stronger tasting flathead or gunard to even stronger oilier fish such as mullet or sardines.

METHOD

Flatten each fillet; if using steaks, cut into small pieces.

Mix the herbs, garlic, chilli and seasoning with the olive oil. Place a little of the stuffing at one end of each fillet and roll up. If using chilli, use about 1 slice per roll in the herb stuffing.

Secure each roll and cook using one of the suggested methods (page 141).

Braciole di tonno

TUNA BRACIOLE WITH EMMENTHAL CHEESE, ANCHOVIES AND CITRUS

This recipe is for swordfish or tuna and, once again, albacore tuna is excellent for this purpose. This is a rather sweet stuffing and the citrus juices are used for sharpness and moisture.

Instead of pecorino, Emmenthal or Gruyére cheese is used – both cheeses are appreciated by Italians. In my family, they were used as table cheeses and sliced thinly for stuffings. My mother still uses these cheeses in preference to parmesan or pecorino for any rolled meat or fish.

METHOD

Cut the tuna into slices, reserving any trimmings for the stuffing, or flatten each fillet or steak.

Soak the sultanas in warm water for 20 minutes.

Finely chop 1 onion and sauté it a pan with ¼ cup of olive oil. Cut tuna trimmings into very small pieces and add, along with the drained raisins, then sauté for about 5 minutes. Add half the breadcrumbs and cook over a very gentle flame for a few minutes. Remove from the heat. Add citrus zest and juice. Season and stir well. The result should be a thick paste.

Smear the paste on one side of the fish slices. Add the cheese. Roll up and moisten the rolls with a little extra virgin olive oil and sprinkle with the remaining breadcrumbs. Slice the remaining onion. Thread the rolls onto metal skewers, with a slice of onion and a bay leaf between each.

Grill the skewers on a barbecue hotplate for about 15 minutes or bake.

VARIATION

  In a restaurant in San Leone on the coast off Agrigento, I ate *braciole* stuffed with a mixture of breadcrumbs, cooked puréed eggplant, anchovies, currants, pistachio nuts and grated *bottarga*. They were served

INGREDIENTS

700g (1lb 9oz) tuna, sliced
½ cup sultanas or raisins
2 large onions
½ cup extra virgin olive oil
1 cup breadcrumbs, made
* from good-quality day-old*
* bread, very finely ground*
2 lemons (juice of 2 and the
* grated peel of 1)*
juice of 2 oranges
100g (3½oz) Emmenthal or
* Swiss cheese, finely sliced*
about 10 bay leaves
salt and freshly ground
* pepper to taste*

As second course

with what I have always called a *crosta di formaggio* (a crust of cheese). My father grilled slices of pecorino or parmesan held on a fork directly on our electric hot plate. My mother complained about the smell, but then again she used to char peppers the same way. Now with non-stick frying pans, all you need do is place thin slices of the cheese in a lightly oiled pan until it melts and forms a wafer. It will harden when you switch off the heat and it cools in the pan.

Chini

Ripieni

STUFFING MEAT, FISH AND VEGETABLES IS A POPULAR CULINARY METHOD IN ALL OF ITALY. *RIPIENI* IS ONE OF THE WORDS MEANING 'STUFFED' IN ITALIAN. ANOTHER IS *FARCITI*. IN SICILIAN, THE CULINARY TERM IS *CHINI*, OR *ABBUTTUNATI*, WHICH IS NOTHING LIKE THE ITALIAN WORD. YOU CAN SEE WHY I HAD PROBLEMS SPEAKING TO MY PATERNAL GRANDMOTHER WHEN I WAS A CHILD! INSTEAD OF RICE BINDING THE STUFFING (POPULAR IN OTHER CULTURES), FRESH BREADCRUMBS ARE GENERALLY USED.

As second course

Cozzuli chini

Cozze ripiene con besciamella

STUFFED MUSSELS WITH BESCIAMELLE

Stuffed mussels are popular in most Sicilian restaurants as an antipasto. The mussels are steamed open and then filled with a mixture of fresh breadcrumbs, parsley and garlic, dribbled with extra virgin olive oil and baked till the bread is crisp and fragrant (called *cozze gratinate* or *cozze al forno*). This unusual stuffing does not include breadcrumbs – the mussel meat is removed from the shells and mixed with a little *besciamella* (*besciamelle* or béchamel sauce) and a tomato sauce.

METHOD

Clean and pull off beards from the mussels. Place mussels in a large saucepan with about a cup of water, cover, and place over high heat to steam – they should open in 2–3 minutes. Drain, reserving the liquid. Traditionally this dish is made with small mussels – if they are large, chop up the meat.

For the sauce, place the tomatoes, garlic, basil, salt, olive oil and mussel liquid in a saucepan over moderate heat and reduce to about 1 cup. Cool.

To make the *besciamella*, melt the butter in a saucepan over a moderate heat and add the flour. Cook the flour, stirring, for 1–2 minutes. Add the milk gradually over a low heat, continuing to stir. When all the milk is added continue cooking and stirring until the mixture thickens (it should be quite thick). Season and add nutmeg. Let it cool.

Heat oven to 230°C (440°F). Mix together the tomato sauce, *besciamella*, ground pepper, mussel meat and cheese. Spoon the mixture back into the shells. Sprinkle each with extra virgin olive oil and place in the oven for 4–5 minutes until they are coloured on top.

INGREDIENTS

2kg (4lb 6oz) mussels
50g (1¾oz) pecorino cheese, grated
salt and freshly ground pepper

TOMATO SAUCE
500g (17½oz) tomatoes
2 cloves garlic
basil leaves,
¼ cup extra virgin olive oil
salt

BESCIAMELLA
2 tablespoons butter
2 tablespoons flour
500ml (16fl oz) milk
¼ teaspoon freshly grated nutmeg
salt to taste

Calamaricchi chini ca' marsala e mennuli

Calamaretti ripieni con marsala e mandorle

STUFFED CALAMARI WITH FRESH CHEESE, ALMONDS AND NUTMEG BRAISED IN MARSALA

Calamaretti are small squid, the *-etti*, signifying the diminutive. The smaller they are, the more tender they will be. Any of the *braciole* stuffings are suitable. This one is very delicate. The stuffed *calamaretti* can be sautéed or baked and will be brown on the outside and white and moist on the inside. An essential ingredient is *marsala secca* or *fina* (dry) – not the more common sweet or *all'uovo* varieties. Marsala is the fortified wine of Sicily and originally was made with grapes grown around the city of Marsala. Like sherry, there are various blends, some aged in wood for longer than ten years (called *marsala stravecchia*).

INGREDIENTS

6 medium squid (or 12 small squid)

1 cup breadcrumbs, made from good-quality day-old bread, toasted in a little oil

2 tablespoons flat-leaf parsley, finely cut

¼–½ teaspoon nutmeg

150g (5oz) fresh cheese (tuma, pecorino fresco, mozzarella, fior di latte or bocconcini), cut into small cubes

1 cup dry marsala

½ cup almonds, blanched and chopped

3 tablespoons extra virgin olive oil

salt and freshly ground pepper to taste

METHOD

Clean the squid: pull off the head and the inside of the squid and discard. Cut off tentacles and save them for another time.

Mix the remaining ingredients except the oil together; check the seasoning. Stuff the squid and secure each end with a toothpick.

Sauté each squid in olive oil – when the juice escapes it caramelises – turning once only during cooking. Alternatively, cover with foil and bake in a 200°C (400°F) oven for about 10 minutes. The squid will produce its own juice. To caramelise, remove foil and bake the squid for an extra 10 minutes.

VARIATION

 Add chopped pistachio rather than almonds.

Sardi a beccafico

Sarde a beccafico

SARDINES A *BECCAFICO*, STUFFED WITH CURRANTS, PINE NUTS, SUGAR AND NUTMEG

When friends come for a meal I like to serve something they may not have tasted before – such as sardines. Some weekends I used to invite friends on both Saturday and Sunday. I must have been mad – or overcome with youthful enthusiasm – and to economise on time and effort I would double quantities and serve the same meal, with some variations, on both days. *Sarde a beccafico* was one such dish, served hot on Saturday as a main course and cold on the Sunday as an antipasto.

The *beccafico* (*Sylvia borin*) is a small migratory, fig-eating bird that nests in mainland Italy and flies over to Sicily when the figs are in season (*becca* means peck and *fico* is fig). When the sardines are stuffed they resemble a *beccafico* and *sarde a beccafico* is a homage to this little bird, a gourmand that stuffs itself on fresh figs. Tomaso D'Alba, in *La Cucina Siciliana di Derivazione Araba*, says that the *beccafichi* are stuffed and cooked in the same way as sardines – if this bird still exists in Sicily. Italians fancy themselves as great hunters and love to shoot. No matter how small the bird, it is fair game. In Trieste we used to eat small birds with polenta and they were succulent. I was too young to know better.

There are local variations in the stuffing, the method of cooking and the names of the dish. In Sciacca, a city on the west coast, they are called *sardi a chiappa* and two sardines are used to hold the stuffing. In other parts of Sicily these are called *sardi fritti a cutuletta*. I have selected my favourite ingredients for this dish from a number of local recipes.

SARDINES OR PILCHARDS

Sardines are very common in Sicilian cuisine – and highly esteemed. These small, saltwater, oily silvery fish are soft-boned and are from the herring family (Clupeidae). There are more than 20 varieties of fish sold as sardines throughout the world. They are also known as pilchards, herring and sprats. They have a strong taste and are very versatile. They are ideal barbecued, stuffed, fried or baked and can be eaten marinated and raw (see page 217).

Sardines are caught in large numbers. Purse seine nets are used to catch fish in schools, which are located by sonar or echo sounders. The word 'purse' is used because of the bag-like shape of the net; seine because the net hangs vertically, with floats at the top and weights at the bottom. Although this method of fishing sardines is very efficient, with the target species often comprising at least 95 per cent of the catch, it also makes them particularly vulnerable to overfishing. The sustainability of the current catch is being re-examined. Sardines are a significant part of the diet of seabirds and large fish, so they are a key link in a food chain. They are also used to feed fish on aquaculture farms, especially tuna.

As an alternative to sardines, I have often used mullet. Both are oily and strong tasting and, like sardines and herrings, mullet can be butterflied.

INGREDIENTS

1kg (2lb 4oz) sardine fillets
1 cup breadcrumbs, made from good-quality day-old bread
¾ cup extra virgin olive oil
½ cup pine nuts
½ cup currants
5–8 anchovy fillets, finely chopped
juice and zest of 1 lemon
2 cloves garlic, chopped
¾ cup finely cut parsley
½ teaspoon nutmeg
10 bay leaves
1 tablespoon sugar
salt and freshly ground pepper to taste

METHOD

Scale, gut, butterfly and clean sardines, leaving the tail on. Fillets are sometimes sold without tails – when the sardine is closed around the stuffing, the tail is flicked upright to resemble a bird. Wipe the sardines dry.

Preheat the oven to 190°C (375°F). For the stuffing, in a non-stick frying pan, toast the breadcrumbs until golden in 2 tablespoons of olive oil over a low flame. Take off heat and cool. Then stir in pine nuts, currants, anchovies, lemon zest, garlic, parsley, nutmeg, salt and pepper. Add a little more olive oil if the mixture is dry.

Place a spoonful of stuffing on each sardine and fold it over itself to resemble a fat bird. Arrange the sardines side by side in an oiled baking dish with tails sticking up with a bay leaf between each. Sprinkle with lemon juice and any leftover stuffing, the sugar and remaining oil. Bake for 20–30 minutes.

VARIATIONS

- Omit or vary the amounts of any of the following: nutmeg, pine nuts, currants and anchovies.
- Add about 2 tablespoons of pecorino cheese to the stuffing.

- In eastern Sicily *sarde a beccafico* usually consist of two open sardines, with the filling sandwiched in the middle.
- In Palermo cheese is usually not included, but anchovies are added to the stuffing and the breadcrumbs are browned in oil – this has stronger and more complex flavours and is the best version for eating cold.
- In some recipes the sardines are first soaked in wine vinegar for about an hour before they are stuffed. All my relatives do this to soften the strong flavours of the sardines (I always omit this step. It is also a common practice to soak rabbit or game in vinegar, to remove the gaminess and to tenderise.)
- Nonna Maria from Catania used the same stuffing for artichokes and tomatoes: breadcrumbs, grated pecorino, parsley, garlic and a little olive oil. This seems to be a common variation in Catania. She always fried the sardines rather than baked them. To fry sardines, place the stuffing between pairs of butterflied sardines, dip the sardines lightly in flour, then in beaten eggs and fry in very hot extra virgin olive oil. If you are concerned about the stuffing holding together, add 1 egg to the mixture.

Pisci d'ovu (Fish made of egg)

My mother always mixed any leftover stuffing with egg to form a batter, which was fried in the oil remaining in the pan when the fish had been fried. One always gives the best of everything to children and it was offered to me. She called it a *frittatina* (a small frittata). I have discovered that there is a traditional recipe for this called *pisci d'ovu*. A spatula is used to manipulate the batter into the shape of a fish as it fries.

Mix 8 eggs, 150g (5oz) each of grated pecorino and fresh breadcrumbs, ½ cup of cut parsley and seasoning to form a batter. Drop spoonfuls of the batter into hot extra virgin olive oil and fry until crisp. When you first drop the batter into the oil, use the spoon to pull it into the shape of a fish. A variation is to add a little sautéed onion to the batter.

CLASSIC SICILIAN SPECIALTIES

These menus include some of the signature dishes of Sicily. Although desserts are not included in this book, cassata and cannoli are compulsary.

MENU 1
Caponata made with eggplants or with eggplants and peppers
Pasta with sardines from Palermo (*Pasta chi sardi*)
Grilled fish (*Pisci 'nta braci*) with *salmoriglio* dressing
Green leaf salad (*'Nzalata virdi*)

MENU 2
Pasta with tomatoes, eggplants and *bottarga* (*Pasta a la norma ca bottarga*)
Sardines *a beccafico* (*Sardi a beccaficu*)

Zuppa

A *ZUPPA* IN SICILIAN AND ITALIAN IS A SOUP (THE WORD COMES FROM THE MIDDLE ENGLISH AND FRENCH *SOUPE*). A *ZUPPA DI PESCE* IS USUALLY SERVED OVER SLICES OF BREAD LIKE A BOUILLABAISSE. SOMETIMES IT IS ALSO CALLED A *GHIOTTA DI PESCE*.

The line dividing a fish stew from a *zuppa di pesce* is blurry. Generally, a *zuppa* contains more liquid and a stew involves cooking in a small amount of liquid that is reduced and concentrated.

Originally, *zuppa di pesce* may have been *cucina povera*. In medieval times in some cities, when fish markets closed for the day, the poor were sold the leftover or damaged fish at reduced prices. There were laws directing vendors to dispose of all their merchandise to prevent them from selling produce the next day when it was no longer fresh. The fish would have been added to water, a little oil and parsley and, after the Spaniards arrived in the 17th century, a little tomato. Bread would have been used to mop up the broth.

A mixed catch of inexpensive fish is still commonly used for *zuppa di pesce* and for making the fish broth for couscous. I have seen boxes of fish especially labelled for *zuppa* in fish markets in Sicily. This cheaper and/or less popular fish is more difficult to find in some parts of the world.

Zuppa ri pisci
Zuppa di pesce

FISH SOUP WITH A *SOFFRITTO* OF GARLIC AND PARSLEY

I once ate a very simple fish soup in a trattoria in the Catania fish market. It was served with very little liquid – what there was, was strong and concentrated – and with a couple of chunks of grilled bread rubbed with oil and garlic.

A *soffritto* made of olive oil, garlic and parsley is poured over the hot *zuppa* just before serving. *Soffritto* is one of the building blocks for Italian cooking (*sotto* means 'under' or base, and *fritto* 'fried'): chopped onions and/or other vegetables softened in olive oil before other ingredients are added. Although in this case it is added last, it is still known as a *soffritto* and is a common way to introduce a new depth of flavour. I generally pour a *soffritto* made with extra virgin olive oil, garlic and finely chopped parsley over pulses and thick vegetable soups.

Suitable fish

A variety of seafood is preferable, but avoid oily fish such as sardines and mackerel.

Select at least two different types of fleshy fish, either firm or flaky (I use combinations of: flathead, leatherjacket, albacore tuna, all types of whiting, snapper and blue-eye trevalla, red emperor, coral trout, ling); some green (uncooked) crustaceans – prawns (shrimp), lobster or crabs; cephalopods – cuttlefish, octopus or squid; and molluscs – such as mussels and cockles (also known as vongole or pipis). Porgy, kob, kingklip or monk (all from South Africa) are also suitable.

METHOD

Prepare the fish and seafood. Cut the fish into chunks. Clean the shellfish, molluscs and squid. Cut the squid into mouth-sized pieces.

Acqua, cunsigghiu e sali, a cu 'unn'addumanna 'un ci nni dari. (Sicilian proverb)
Acqua, consiglio e sale, non darne a chi non te ne chiede. (Italian)
Water, advice and salt, do not give these to those who do not ask for them.

Heat ½ cup of extra virgin olive oil in a deep pan large enough to fit all the ingredients. Add 2 cloves of garlic and the tomatoes and cook for 5 minutes. Add the olives, capers, bay leaves, ¼ cup of parsley and about 4 cups of water and bring to the boil.

Add the fish and bring back to the boil, then cover and simmer for 10–30 minutes (according to taste, Italians cook it for the longer time). Add pine nuts when the fish has finished cooking.

For the *soffritto*, heat the remaining olive oil in a wide frying pan until it is very hot. Add 3 finely chopped cloves of garlic and parsley, then allow it to sizzle. Pour the *soffritto* onto the hot *zuppa* before serving.

To make oven-toasted bread, cut slices of bread as thinly and evenly as possible and remove crusts. Place the bread on a wire tray in a 180°C (350°F) oven and leave it to dry out for 5–10 minutes; take it out before it colours.

Place 1–2 slices of bread in the bottom of each plate and then spoon some of the fish and its juices over them. Alternatively, bread can be served separately.

VARIATION

🌿 For additional flavour use fish stock rather than water.

INGREDIENTS

2kg (4lb 6oz) mixed seafood
1 cup extra virgin olive oil
5 cloves garlic, chopped
500g (17½oz) tomatoes,
*   peeled, seeded and chopped*
100g (3½oz) green olives
½ cup salted capers, soaked
*   and washed*
3–4 bay leaves
1 cup finely cut flat-leaf
*   parsley*
1 cup pine nuts, toasted
*   (optional)*
good-quality white bread
salt and freshly ground
*   pepper*

Making fish stock

UNLIKE MAKING A MEAT-BASED STOCK, FISH STOCK
REQUIRES LITTLE COOKING: ABOUT 15–20 MINUTES.
THE SHORT COOKING TIME AVOIDS THE BITTER TASTE
OF THE BLOOD LEACHING OUT FROM THE FISH BONES.

INGREDIENTS

2 medium onions, thinly
    sliced
2 stalks celery, very thinly
    sliced
2 carrots thinly sliced
2 bay leaves
a handful flat-leaf parsley
    stems (not leaves), roughly
    chopped
herbs – 1 or more of the
    following: garlic cloves,
    the outside parts of fennel
    bulbs or fennel seeds
1 tablespoon peppercorns
½ cup dry white wine
    (optional)
about 1kg (2lb 4oz) fish
    bones and heads, from firm
    white-fleshed fish, cleaned
    of blood

I have been making fish stock inspired by an article by the food writer Terry
Durak published in a weekend paper in 2003. Durak says that 20 minutes is
barely enough time to get the flavour from the vegetables and recommends
making a vegetable stock first. He uses two pots – one for the vegetable stock,
the other for the fish. I always use cold water for any stock. My mother said
that if you want to eat the solids (meat, vegetables or fish) place them in hot
liquid, which will seal in the flavour.; if you want to savour the liquid, place
the solid ingredients in cold liquid to extract the flavour.

METHOD

Place the vegetables, herbs, peppercorns and wine in a large saucepan with
6 cups of cold water. Bring to the boil and then simmer for 30 minutes.

In the second saucepan, cover the fish carcass with 2 cups of cold water
and bring it slowly to the boil. Then add the fish and its water to the vegetable
stock and simmer for 15 minutes. Pass the liquid through a fine-mesh strainer,
pressing the solids firmly with a wooden spoon to extract the flavours. If you
are not using the stock within the hour, chill it as quickly as possible. Cover
after it has cooled and refrigerate for up to 3 days, or freeze.

Zuppa ri pisci a sirausana o furnu

Zuppa di pesce alla siracusana

RICH FISH SOUP FROM SYRACUSE COOKED IN THE OVEN

INGREDIENTS

2kg (4lb 6oz) mixed seafood

1 cup dry white wine

2 cups fish stock

500g (17½oz) tomatoes, peeled, seeded and chopped

½ cup extra virgin olive oil

2–3 celery hearts (pale green stalks and leaves), chopped

3–4 bay leaves

10 cloves garlic, finely chopped

2 tablespoons finely cut flat-leaf parsley

fronds for fennel, finely cut

1 tablespoon fennel seeds, crushed

zest of 1 orange, peeled thinly and cut into large pieces

salt and freshly ground pepper

Zuppa di pesce from Syracuse is reputed to be the best in Sicily. It is made with prime fish, contains powerful flavours and is very aromatic. Here the *zuppa* is baked, leaving the fish undisturbed so it does not break up. The use of wine and fish stock made separately suggests a modern recipe.

Suitable fish

See previous *zuppa* recipe, page 157, but use a greater variety of fish.

You need large chunks of boneless fish – either buy a whole fish, fillet it yourself and use the heads and bones for the stock, or make the stock from fish carcasses (ask what type of fish it is).

METHOD

Cut the boneless fish into chunks. Clean shellfish, molluscs and squid and cut the squid into mouth-sized pieces.

Arrange the fish in an ovenproof pan that will fit all the ingredients. Add the wine and cover the fish with the strained stock. Add all the other ingredients. Cover the pan (use foil if you do not have a lid) and place in a 200°C (400°F) oven for 30 minutes.

Serve with oven-toasted bread.

Pisci chi chiappareddi

Pesce e capperi

FISH POACHED IN BROTH WITH CAPERS

Here are two very different soupy recipes from two very different parts of Sicily. Both recipes can be served with potatoes or oven-toasted bread.

My relatives, Salvo and Sally, took me to their favourite seaside restaurant in Marina di Ragusa on the south coast of Sicily. On the menu was a poached fish dish, served *in brodetto* (cooked in broth). It is one of the restaurant's signature dishes. It is very simple to prepare and the fish should just fall off the bones. Chunks of fish, potatoes and stock are served on individual plates like a *zuppa di pesce*.

I found a very similar recipe from the Aeolian Islands where the fish is poached in a vegetable-based stock and, once cooked, the broth is thickened with a little butter, flour and egg yolk.

Suitable fish
This is usually made with a large delicate fish caught locally. I use large fleshy fish (either firm or flaky) such as large flathead, King George whiting and garfish. Use firm white fish if you prefer fillets and leave the fillets whole.

METHOD

Scale, gut and wipe the fish dry. Use a sharp knife to make shallow slashes on the outside of the fish.

Place the oil and garlic in a pan on moderate heat. Stir for 1 minute before adding the capers and heating through. Place the fish in the pan, turn up the heat, add the wine and let it reduce.

Add the potatoes, parsley, seasoning and half of the stock. Cover and cook on a gentle heat for about 30–35 minutes. Test every 10 minutes to make sure the fish is not overcooked and add more stock as necessary.

INGREDIENTS

1.5kg (3lb 5oz) fish
½ cup extra virgin olive oil
1 large head garlic, cloves roughly chopped
½ cup salted capers, soaked and washed
1 cup white wine
1–3 potatoes per person, cut into medium-sized cubes (optional)
¾ cup finely cut flat-leaf parsley
1–1.5 litres (32–48fl oz) fish stock (see page 159)
good-quality extra virgin olive oil to drizzle over the cooked fish when serving
salt and freshly ground pepper or chilli flakes

To serve, lift the flesh off the bone – it should come off easily. Make sure that each person has some potato, chunks of boneless fish and a little stock. Drizzle over some of your best extra virgin olive oil and grind black pepper on top.

VARIATION

PESCE CON I CAPPERI DALLE ISOLE EOLIE (FISH WITH CAPERS FROM THE AEOLIAN ISLANDS)

The butter and egg yolk used to thicken the soup (probably French-influenced) makes this *zuppa* quite different from the above recipe. Use the same types of fish as in the previous recipe but whole fish is preferable.

Place all the stock ingredients in a pot (I use a fish kettle) with 2 litres (64fl oz) of cold water. Cook uncovered on moderate heat for about 20 minutes. Add the fish, cover and poach gently until it is cooked, 10–20 minutes. Take it off the heat. Drain off about three-quarters of the stock; set aside.

Melt the butter in a separate saucepan, add the flour, stir quickly for about 30 seconds and then gradually add the drained stock. Cook until thickened for about 7 minutes. Stir the egg yolk in a little cold water and add to the thickened stock (on gentle heat). Stir through the capers.

Serve the fish whole or take the flesh off the bone. Add the fish and leftover stock to the egg-enriched stock. Season with some freshly ground pepper. Ladle into soup bowls. Serve with oven-toasted bread or young boiled potatoes drizzled with a little extra virgin olive oil as a side dish.

INGREDIENTS

1.5kg (3lb 5oz) fish
50g (1¾oz) butter
1 tablespoon plain flour
1 egg yolk
¾ cup salted capers, soaked, washed and finely chopped
salt and freshly ground pepper

THE STOCK
1 onion, halved
1 stalk celery, halved
1 carrot, halved, lengthways
salt
3–5 black peppercorns
3 cloves
3 tablespoons white wine vinegar
herbs – select 1 or all: bay leaves, parsley, fennel fronds

Polpettine in brodo di pesce

SMALL FISH BALLS IN FISH BROTH

Some immigrants from the Aeolian Islands settled in Melbourne before World War I and they founded the Societa' Mutuo Soccorso Isole Eolie in 1926. In 1969, the society changed its name to Societa' Isole Eolie. This is one of their recipes.

The fish is first poached in water or stock. The fish is then drained and the flesh is used to make *polpettine*, small fish balls. These are then returned to the stock and the soup is eaten with oven-toasted bread.

Suitable fish
Use any kind of white-fleshed, mild-tasting fish (flaky or firm textured).

INGREDIENTS

fish stock (see page 159)
500g (17½oz) white-fleshed
    fish, skin and sinews
    removed
1 cup breadcrumbs, made
    from good-quality day-old
    bread
2 eggs, lightly beaten
½–¾ cup pecorino grated,
    to taste
½ cup finely cut parsley
flour to coat the fish balls
2 red tomatoes, in very small
    cubes
2 tablespoons fennel fronds,
    parsley or basil, finely cut
salt and freshly ground
    pepper

METHOD

Place the fish in a saucepan with 1.5 litres (48fl oz) stock or water and poach for 20 minutes. Drain the fish, reserving the stock. Remove bones and skin from the fish and discard.

Use the flesh for the fish balls. Add breadcrumbs, eggs, pecorino, parsley and seasoning. Add more breadcrumbs if the mixture is too sloppy. Shape into mouth-sized balls and roll each ball in a little flour; shake off excess.

Drain the stock of solids and bring to the boil. Poach the balls in the stock for 5–7 minutes. Add tomatoes and herbs and allow to soften for a few minutes before serving.

Stufatu

In umido

In umido is an Italian culinary term for braising in a small amount of liquid (it literallly means 'in humid' or 'wet'). Cooking fish or meat *in umido* is a very common technique in Italian cooking, producing food that is moist and with concentrated flavours. I had difficulty finding an equivalent word in Sicilian – the closest I can find was in a very old publication of Sicilian recipes. There I found a recipe for a *stufatu*, which means to cook slowly, with a little liquid on a *stufa* (the Italian word for stove). Interestingly, the Greeks use the term *stuffato*. Vegetables, such as potatoes, peas, fennel or peppers, are often added to foods cooked *in umido*.

Ancidda in brouet

Anguilla in brouet

EEL *IN BROUET* WITH SAFFRON, CINNAMON, NUTMEG AND GINGER

**MENU FOR
ALESSANDRO
SCARLATTI**

*Born in Palermo, Scarlatti
(1660–1725) is credited with
being the father of Neapolitan
opera and admired for the
psychological nature of his scores.
His operas were performed in
theatres in Florence, Venice and
Rome.*

*Small fish balls in fish broth
(Polpettine in brodo di pesce)
Eel in brouet
Pesto made with potatoes,
almonds and garlic (Scurdalia)
Braised broad beans*

This is an ancient recipe with French origins. The eel is cooked *in brouet*, the French word meaning in broth. Eels are common in Italian cuisine and are traditionally eaten on Good Friday and Christmas Eve (much the same as *stoccafisso* and *baccalà*). In parts of Italy, usually near rivers, they are sold on the roadside threaded on a metal wire in the shape of a necklace.

Eel may soon win the popularity it deserves and those who have tasted it, either smoked or fresh, know that the meat is sweet and succulent.

Eels are eaten all over Italy. In Trieste, when I was a child, we used to buy them at the Ponte Rosso fish market and I was always horrified to see the fishmonger chop it into portions while the eel was still alive. Of course, it kept on wriggling. My mother cooked eel *alla cipollata* – with onions, bay leaves and vinegar, all suitable ingredients because it is an oily fish. Our relatives in Augusta, south of Catania, grilled it over charcoal on skewers, alternating the flesh with bay leaves, and basting it with oil and lemon juice.

The Italians of the Middle Ages were fond of freshly ground pepper and saffron; the French favoured ginger and cinnamon. This recipe contains all these spices – plus cloves – but because ginger is difficult to find in some parts of Sicily, it is often omitted. Saffron is also very ancient: it is said that Persephone was collecting the crocus flowers when she was snatched into Hades.

Suitable fish
Although this recipe is for eel, the combination of spices is also worth trying with other species. Use thick fillets or steaks of firm-textured fish.

PREPARING EEL
The eel has to be skinned, which is relatively easy. The worst part is the similarity between eels and snakes.

Hold the head on a solid work surface with a cloth (to prevent slipping) and, using a sharp knife, make an incision around the neck, just behind the head. The skin is thick and will come away quite easily. Grip the skin (some people use a pair of pliers), and pull it down the length of the eel to the tail. Rip it off. As when cleaning fish, make a slit down the length of the fish and pull out the innards. Wipe or rinse the eel with cold water. Cut off the head and slice the body into portions (about 6cm/2½in thick).

METHOD

Dip the eel in flour (optional) and fry in very hot extra virgin olive oil. Add the wine, seasoning and the spices. Cover and braise over low heat until the eel is soft and the flesh is coming away from the bones.

This dish is like a *zuppa di pesce*, and can be served with thin slices of oven-toasted bread, broken up, in the liquid. I prefer it with a *purea di patate* (a potato purée made with butter, a little milk and seasoning).

VARIATIONS

- Add fresh bay leaves.
- Add 2 chopped onions before you add the eel and sauté until golden. Then add the eel and seal before adding the wine and spices.

INGREDIENTS

1kg (2lb 4oz) eel, skinned, cleaned and cut into slices
flour to coat eel (optional)
½ cup or more extra virgin olive oil
1 cup white wine
1 teaspoon ground ginger
6–10 cloves
3 pinches of saffron
1 stick cinnamon
salt and freshly ground pepper to taste

As second course

Tunnu chê pipi

Tonno con peperoni

TUNA WITH PEPPERS (CAPSICUM)

My cousins Lidia and Giacomo and Silvana often cook tuna braised with peppers. I have also eaten grilled or pan-fried fish served with *peperonata* as a *contorno*. The peppers are the long sweet, thin variety used for frying. The red and yellow ones are sweeter than the light green ones. For the peppers, the cooking process is begun in water and some extra virgin olive oil; they finish up being fried.

Suitable fish
Use albacore tuna or other thick fillets or fish steaks of firm-textured fish.

INGREDIENTS

6 long thin peppers (red, yellow and light green), deseeded and cut in strips
¾ cup extra virgin olive oil
4–6 cloves garlic, peeled and flattened, or/and 2 onions, chopped
a splash of red wine vinegar
1–1.2kg (2lb 4oz–2lb 12oz) tuna, thick fillets or steaks cut into large chunks
salt and freshly ground pepper to taste
mint sprigs to serve

METHOD

Place the peppers in a frying pan with a lid, add half the oil, the garlic (and/ or onions), a little salt and ½ cup water. Cover and cook until the water has evaporated and the peppers are frying in the oil. When they have coloured, add the vinegar and reduce. Remove and set aside.

Add a little extra virgin oil to the same pan and fry the fish. When nearly cooked, add the peppers. Allow the flavours to penetrate the fish by tossing it around for about 5 minutes. Remove the garlic and serve with mint.

VARIATION

- Use bulb fennel instead of peppers. Cut 2 fennel bulbs lengthways into thin slices. Heat ¾ cup extra virgin olive oil in a pan, add the fennel and sauté for 5–10 minutes, then 1 cup wine (or water) and seasoning. Cover and cook on low to medium heat for about 20 minutes, until the fennel is soft. Increase the heat to reduce any liquid left – the fennel will turn deep gold.

Pisci chè favi

Pesce con le fave

FISH WITH BROAD BEANS

You may have seen the film *Stromboli, terra di Dio* directed by Roberto Rossellini and starring Ingrid Bergman. The film was set on the island of Stromboli, one of the Isole Eolie (Aeolian Islands), an archipelago of unique rock formations and volcanoes. Rosselini's portrayal of Stromboli combines earth, fire and water: the harshness of the land, the fury of the volcano and, the only kindly element, the sea, provider of food. This recipe for *pisci chi favi* is from Lipari, the main island of the archipelago.

I have served *pisci chi favi* as a pasta sauce in a very non-Italian way of serving pasta – lots of sauce with little pasta – and as a main meal.

Suitable fish
Traditionally the recipe uses swordfish which is not sustainable. The alternative is any thick fillets or steaks of firm-textured fish.

METHOD

Sauté the onion in hot extra virgin olive oil. Add the broad beans, celery and flat-leaf parsley and lightly toss in the hot oil for about 5 minutes. Add the pieces of fish and cook until they caramelise slightly.

Pour over the wine and let it reduce. Add seasoning and some of the stock and braise the contents over a low heat for 7–10 minutes, until the fish is cooked to your liking. Add extra stock or water during the cooking process if necessary.

Serve with the grated pecorino.

INGREDIENTS

1 onion, chopped
1 cup extra virgin olive oil
1.5kg (3lb 5oz; before shelled) broad beans
1 celery heart (pale centres and leaves), chopped
1 cup flat-leaf parsley, cut
1–1.2kg (2lb 4oz–2lb 12oz) thick fish fillets or steaks, cut into chunks
1 cup white wine
about 1 cup fish stock or water
1 cup pecorino cheese, freshly grated
salt and freshly ground pepper to taste

Purpi' no sucu

Polpi in sugo

OCTOPUS BRAISED WITH TOMATOES

As a young child, one morning in Sicily my father took me for a walk along a rocky beach where we saw fishermen beating an octopus on the rocks. My father said it was done to tenderise it. Some Spanish recipes recommend freezing it for two weeks. Other recipes suggest beating it with a hammer or banging it repeatedly on a marble slab. An Italian fisherman in Australia told me he tenderises it in an old top-loading washing machine.

Octopus can grow to 3kg (6lb 10oz) in weight, but small and medium-sized ones are more tender. Italians remove most of the skin and suckers. But the suckers come off easily when octopus is cooked and I do not worry about the skin, especially in dishes using red wine or tomato or when the octopus is chargrilled. The skin of live octopus is generally brown, but their colour can vary according to their emotions – fascinating.

I treat octopus like squid, cooking it very quickly or for a long time on a low heat. Here it is braised slowly in oil, garlic and tomatoes. The recipe includes a lot of garlic: it melts into the dish and becomes sweet. This dish is of Arabic origins, originally cooked in a *quartara*, a well-sealed pot made of clay and buried in hot coals. I make this with large local octopus.

INGREDIENTS

3kg (6lb 10oz) octopus, cut
   into bite-sized pieces
1 cup extra virgin olive oil
1 cup tomatoes (about 4),
   peeled and chopped
15 cloves garlic, chopped
1 cup finely cut parsley
salt and freshly ground
   pepper

METHOD

Cut the octopus into large bite-sized pieces. Place it in a pan, add the oil, tomatoes, garlic and parsley, cover, and simmer gently for 1–1½ hours. Do not season until it has cooked for about 1 hour or it will toughen. Remove the octopus from the pan; remove and discard any big suckers. Reduce the sauce, return the octopus to the pan and serve.

Pesce spada con agrumi e pistacchi

SWORDFISH WITH CITRUS AND PISTACHIOS

This recipe is adapted from *Ricette di Osterie e Genti di Sicilia, Slow Food Editore* as cooked by Ristorante Metro in Catania. I have not provided the Sicilian name for the dish because this is what it is called on their menu.

This dish may not be very traditional, or very old, but I particularly like it because it makes use of local ingredients: swordfish caught in the straits of Messina, citrus (70 per cent of Italian oranges are grown in Sicily) and pistachio from Bronte (inland from Catania). The other ingredients are also local Sicilian produce.

PISTACHIOS IN BRONTE

Bronte is a town and province of Catania near Mount Etna. It is famous for its links with Admiral Nelson who was given an estate there by Ferdinand III (king of Sicily, of Naples, of Two Sicilies), as a reward for having helped save the king and his family during the 1798 revolution of Naples. Nelson died before seeing the estate. Probably just as well, because he was never considered a hero in Bronte – the Sicilians wanted to overthrow Ferdinand and his unpopular regime and Nelson prevented it.

More than its anti-monarchist tendencies, Bronte is renowned for the production of pistachios and for its links with the Slow Food Movement. Pistachio is an important ingredient of Sicilian cuisine. It originated in the eastern Mediterranean basin, in Persia and Turkey. The nuts are harvested by hand and in small quantities but although they are superior in quality – taste, colour and fragrance – the Bronte pistachios struggle to compete with less expensive, inferior quality pistachios from Iran, Asia and America. The pistachio from Bronte is intensively coloured: rich red on the outside and an extraordinary green on the inside. It is called *rosso di Bronte* and is highly prized by pastry and gelato makers – no artificial colouring is needed.

Cu voli manciari pisci di puortu, nun voli aviri lu vurzuni strittu.
(Sicilian proverb)
Chi vuole mangiare pesce del porto, non vuole avere il portafoglio stretto. (Italian)
He who wants to eat freshly caught fish, should not have a tight purse.

Sicily is the only Italian region where pistachio nuts are produced and Bronte grows 80 per cent of them. It is also the main economic resource of the territory. They grow only in the hilly volcanic soil of Bronte and are one endangered food that may survive.

Pesce spada con agrumi e pistacchi is cooked with citrus juice and wine. The tuna in the original recipe is fried in butter so the use of extra virgin olive oil is optional. Butter is rarely used in Sicilian cooking and is either a modern addition or a leftover from the *monzù* type of cooking (see page 16). As in most recipes, the fish is lightly floured beforehand, but I have never been a great lover of this practice so have made this optional too.

Ingredients

butter or extra virgin olive oil
* for frying*
3–4 cloves garlic, peeled
6 tuna fillets or steaks
1–1½ cups white wine
6 tablespoons sultanas
3 oranges
wild fennel or the green
* feathery part of 1 fennel*
*   bulb (or 1 teaspoon of*
*   crushed fennel seeds)*
juice of 1 lemon
12 tablespoons pistachio nuts
flour to coat fish (optional)
1 red chilli or freshly ground
* pepper*
salt to taste

Suitable fish

The alternative to swordfish is any thick fillets or steaks of firm-textured fish.

Method

Heat butter or oil in a frying pan, add the garlic cloves and discard when they are golden. Add the fish and fry on both sides. Add the wine and sultanas, grated orange zest (to taste) and fennel. Reduce the wine, add the juice of 3 oranges, the lemon juice, some of the pistachio nuts and seasoning.

Cover and braise until the fish is cooked to your liking. Add more juice if necessary.

Remove the fish, place on a platter. If there is too much liquid, reduce the sauce. Pour over the fish and serve sprinkled with more pistachios.

Ammuttunatu e o'rau

Steccato e in ragù

THE FISH IS AMMUTTUNATU (A SICILIAN TERM FOR STUDDED) BEFORE IT IS BRAISED SLOWLY. THE WORD DERIVES FROM AMMUTTUNARE (THE PROCESS OF GENTLY INSERTING FLAVOURS INTO THE FLESH OF MEAT OR FISH – LIKE LARDING). THE ITALIAN TERM FOR THIS PROCESS IS STECCARE, HENCE STECCATO, STUDDED.

Once studded it is cooked *in ragù* (Sicilian is *o'rau*). This method is particularly popular in the northwest coast of Sicily for large pieces of tuna.

Ragú is a corruption of the French word *ragout*, the culinary term for a slow-cooked stew. This method of cooking is associated with meat, but tuna can also be cooked slowly without falling apart. Cooking *ragú* became popular in Italy during the Renaissance and in Sicily with the *monzù* (French-trained chefs) who cooked in aristocratic and well-to-do households.

A *ragú* of fish or meat will go extremely well with *purea di patate*, mashed potato made with a fair amount of butter and a little milk or cream (very French). I also like mashed potato with oil and garlic, which is not traditional.

Tunnu ammuttunatu

Pesce steccato e con marsala

TUNA STUDDED WITH FLAVOURS AND BRAISED IN MARSALA

I like to use a whole fillet of fish, which I estimate will feed no more than four people when cut into portions. For more people, I buy two fillets – long fillets will not cook evenly. Individual portions of large fish can also be studded and cooked in this manner. I like to serve this very pink in the centre, but it will not suffer if it is cooked longer, as done in Sicily.

Stud the flesh with one or more flavours – garlic (halved), cloves, a cinnamon stick (broken into small pieces) – and a herb, (mint, rosemary or oregano).

Suitable fish
Mackerel or kingfish can also be used.

METHOD

Use a knife with a long thin blade and make a number of deep, regularly spaced slits in the fillet. Insert flavourings (see above) into each slit. When you cut the fillet into portions, each portion should have four slits.

Heat oil in a pan and seal the fish on all sides. Add marsala and bay leaves and reduce slightly, cover and braise over low heat. Add more marsala (or water) if the dish is drying out. A fillet of four portions cooks in about 15–20 minutes. To test, insert a metal skewer into the centre – if it is done the skewer will be just warm to the touch. If it feels cool, cook for a little longer. Place the fish on a large platter, pour over the sauce and scatter with mint.

INGREDIENTS

1–1.2kg (2lb 4oz–2lb 12oz) tuna fillet
1 cup dry marsala
flavourings (see intro)
½–¾ cup extra virgin olive oil
salt and freshly ground pepper to taste
3 fresh bay leaves
mint leaves for serving

Tunnu a' rau` ca cannedda

Tonno in ragu, con cannella

TUNA RAGOUT WITH CINNAMON

MENU FOR THE INCORRUPTIBLES

The magistrate Rocco Chinnici (1925–83) formed an anti-mafia pool of magistrates and investigators. He was killed by a car bomb shortly after forming this group. Giovanni Falcone (1939–92) and Paolo Borsellino (1940–92) carried on his work and both were killed by car bombs two months apart. These strong men of character were very appreciative of the cuisine of Palermo and there is a sense of balance in what they are eating.

❦

Spaghetti with fried crab
(*Spaghetti cu granciu frittu*)
Orange and fennel salad
Tuna ragout with cinnamon
(*Tunnu a' raù ca cannedà*)
Sautéed wild greens (*Verdura verde saltata*)

This recipe seems to be a culinary dish of mixed origins – the slow braise and the terminology can be attributed to the French, but spices were first used by the Roman upper classes, and later made popular by the Saracens. This is not a dish where the tuna can be cooked rare – the flesh will be succulent and white (like chicken). When the tuna is cooked, it is flaky like canned tuna.

The fish is marinated beforehand. The ingredients include garlic and onions, which are not used together as a rule, but because the garlic is in the stuffing and the onions are in the sauce, the combination is acceptable.

This recipe is from the area around Milazzo on the northwest coast. It is similar to my grandmother's way of cooking *a rota* (*ruota* in Italian, meaning wheel) of tuna but contains cinnamon. I also add cloves. I love combining and contrasting flavours and in this recipe I use bay leaves as well as rosemary. There is also a little tomato paste, mainly to add colour rather than taste to the braising liquid, but this can be omitted.

Milazzo was named Mylae by the ancient Greeks, who settled there around 700 BCE. In one of the great sea battles of the First Punic War, the Romans defeated the Carthaginians, driving them out of the port. Milazzo is also where, during the Risorgimento, Garibaldi's army defeated the Bourbons in July 1860, a victory that led to the unification of Italy.

Suitable fish and cuts

Large pieces of tuna or swordfish are the traditional fish, usually a *rota* cut into a large, thick, round slice from the centre of the fish. If you are unable

to buy this cut of albacore tuna, yellowfin or mackerel, use a whole fillet (not a steak) or the largest pieces of firm-fleshed fish you can find. The *rota* is cooked in one piece and is sliced when it is ready to serve. I remember my grandmother Maria in Catania cooking a very large tuna *rota*, which must have weighed about 2 kilograms (4lb 6oz) and fitted very tightly into a shallow frying pan.

INGREDIENTS

1.2kg (2lb 12oz) tuna
2 cups white wine or water
½ teaspoon sugar
6 cloves or 4–5 cloves garlic, halved, or 1 sprig rosemary per portion
¾ cup extra virgin olive oil
2 onions, sliced
1 tablespoon tomato paste, diluted in 1 cup of water
2 cinnamon sticks
3 bay leaves
salt and freshly ground pepper to taste

METHOD

Marinate the fish in the white wine, salt and sugar and freshly ground pepper for about 1 hour.

Use a thin sharp knife with a long blade and make a number of deep, regularly spaced slits in each piece of fish. Into each slit, insert a clove, or half a garlic clove or sprigs of rosemary. If I am using a whole piece of tuna rather than portions, I estimate where I will carve the fish and insert the flavouring so that each portion has a balance of tastes. More rosemary can be added to the braising liquid.

Heat ¼ cup of extra virgin olive oil in a pan large enough to fit the fish in one layer. Sauté the onions until they are a pale golden colour.

Remove the fish from the marinade and dry, reserving the marinade. Add the fish to the pan with the onions and brown it. Add the diluted tomato paste, cinnamon sticks, bay leaves and a little of the marinade. Cover and cook on low heat, adding more marinade a little at a time to keep the dish moist. It will take between 20–40 minutes to cook, depending on the size of the fish. I always test the fish as it is cooking, most importantly about 10 minutes before the end of my estimated cooking time.

When it is cooked, separate the fish into portions and serve with its sauce.

VARIATIONS

  When in season, I like to add 2 cups of shelled peas after browning the fish, or replace the wine with dry marsala.

Vivi e lascia vivere. (Italian proverb)
Live and let live.

'O furnu
Al forno

FURNU (OR *FUORNU*) MEANS OVEN IN SICILIAN; *FORNO*
IS THE ITALIAN WORD. *AL FORNO* OR *INFORNATO* IS THE
ITALIAN CULINARY TERM FOR BAKED OR ROASTED AND
'O *FURNU* IS THE SICILIAN. I ALWAYS FEEL THAT I HAVE
GREATER CONTROL OF REGULATING TEMPERATURES
AND ESTIMATING COOKING TIMES WHEN I USE A
HOTPLATE, BUT MAYBE THIS IS BECAUSE I GREW UP IN
AN ENVIRONMENT WHERE THE OVEN WAS RARELY USED.

As second course

Pisci che' patati 'nfurnatu

Pesce infornato con patate

BAKED FISH WITH POTATOES, VINEGAR AND ANCHOVIES

This is very easy: the fish is marinated for about an hour and then baked with potatoes. Anchovies are often added to fish in Sicilian cooking. They are either stuffed in the slashes or sometimes gently melted with a little oil and poured over the fish while it is baking. They change the taste of the dish completely.

Suitable fish
Any whole fish or large fillets of medium to firm fish, preferably with the skin on. The fish is cooked whole and carved like meat at the table.

INGREDIENTS

1–1.5kg (2lb 4oz–3lb 5oz) whole fish, or large pieces
½ cup extra virgin olive oil
3 tablespoons red wine vinegar
2 onions, finely chopped
a small bunch parsley, finely chopped
250g (9oz) potatoes, thinly sliced
3–6 anchovies, finely chopped (see above)
juice of 2 lemons, plus grated zest of 1 lemon
salt and freshly ground pepper to taste

METHOD

If using whole fish or fillets with skin, make a series of slashes in the skin. Mix the oil with the vinegar, onions and parsley. Add seasoning and marinate the fish for about an hour, turning frequently.

Place the fish in an ovenproof dish, spoon half of the marinade over it, and bake for 10 minutes in a 200°C (400°F) oven. Arrange the sliced potatoes around the fish. Sprinkle the potatoes and the fish with more marinade, the anchovies, lemon juice and grated zest. Bake for another 20–35 minutes, depending on the type of fish. Serve hot.

VARIATION

Place rosemary and bay leaves underneath the fish in the baking pan.

Pisci o' furnu co bruoru ri carni

Pesce al forno con brodo di carne

BAKED FISH WITH MEAT BROTH

My mother always said that meat and fish are like *il diavolo e l'aqua santa* (the devil and holy water) and the two should never be mixed. This would exclude numerous Asian dishes and paella. When I told her about this traditional recipe, she would not accept that it could possibly be Sicilian and decided it must have been an Arab dish. I have found versions in several sources and it is unusual because the fish is basted with a chicken or veal stock – the meat stock makes the fish taste sweeter. The herbs are thyme and rosemary. As a rule, thyme is not found in Sicilian cooking, but is used in Greek and French food.

This method of cooking fish is popular around Agrigento, which had a large Greek settlement in ancient times and was supplanted by the Saracens (so my mother might be right after all). Several people in Agrigento told me that some of the elderly may still cook it.

Suitable fish
In Sicily, the recipe is made with dentice, a delicate, white-fleshed fish, but any firm- to medium-textured fish is suitable.

METHOD

Make some slashes in the fish and insert some of the rosemary and thyme. Sauté the onion and chilli in the olive oil and stir until they begin to soften. Add the potatoes, the remaining rosemary and thyme and salt. Sauté for about 5 minutes, then add the capers. Transfer the mixture into

INGREDIENTS

1 x 1.5–2kg (3lb 5oz–4lb 6oz) fish
a small mixed handful rosemary and thyme
2 onions, finely chopped
chilli flakes or 1 fresh red chilli
500g (17½oz) potatoes, cubed
2 tablespoons salted capers, soaked and washed
½ cup extra virgin olive oil
1–3 litres (32–100fl oz) chicken or veal stock (preferably homemade)
2 tablespoons red wine vinegar or lemon juice
salt

Bruoru ri iaddina e carni di
puddascia. (Sicilian proverb)
Brodo di gallina e carne di
pollastra. (Italian)
Broth from the chicken and meat
from the pullet.

a well-oiled baking dish. Place the fish on top and moisten with about 1 cup of the stock.

Place the baking dish into a preheated 200°C (400°F) oven and bake for about 10–15 minutes. Add more stock. Repeat this process every 10 minutes until the fish and potatoes are cooked to your liking. Pour over the vinegar or lemon juice and serve.

VARIATIONS

- Add cleaned green prawns (shrimp) with their tails left on about 10 minutes before the fish is cooked. Place the prawns under the potatoes in some of the liquid in the base of the baking dish.
- Replace the capers with green olives.

Gallina vecchia fa` buon brodo.
(Ancient Italian proverb)
An old chicken makes good broth.

Pesce al cartoccio

FISH IN A BAG

I have eaten this in a restaurant in Sciacca, plain and unadulterated so that the taste of the sea and the freshness of the fish is best appreciated. Adding seawater to fish dishes is a common practice in Sicily – the restaurant called their version *pesce in acqua di mare*. In a restaurant in Mazara del Vallo, my fish in *cartoccio* contained some whole prawns and small mussels in their shells. A few cockles or clams can be used instead.

Suitable fish
Small to medium-sized whole fish. Portions or fillets of fish can also be used, of any texture or level of oiliness.

METHOD

To prepare the packages, use two layers of baking paper or aluminium foil, leaving extra for folding.; if using foil, lay baking paper on top. Coat the paper with olive oil.

Preheat the oven to 220°C (420F).

Make some shallow cuts on the outside of the whole fish. Place the fish in the centre of the prepared paper. Add the other ingredients. Fold the edges of the foil together to make a neat, tightly sealed package.

The estimated cooking time for portions or small whole fish is 10 minutes. A fish weighing 1–1.5kg (36–53oz) will take 30–35 minutes; check it after this time and cook it longer if necessary. Once you take the fish out of the oven, it will continue to cook – either serve it immediately, or make a hole in the parcel to allow some of the heat and steam to escape.

Serve the packages at the table. Once the package has been cut, lemon juice and a drizzle of your best extra virgin olive oil added to the cooking juices will make it even more aromatic.

For a different dressing, see recipes in chapter 4, pages 252–73.

INGREDIENTS

6 whole fish or portions
12 prawns (shrimp; shelled or whole), mussels in their shells or cockles (vongole)
1–3 cloves garlic, chopped
24–30 cherry tomatoes
½ cup extra virgin olive oil
½–1 cup flat-leaf parsley, finely cut
salt or 1 tablespoon of seawater (optional)

As second course

Baccalaru 'o furnu

Baccalà al forno

BAKED BACCALÀ

Baccalà has to soak for a couple of days before it is cooked, so begin preparations early (see page 134). According to my relatives, only Sicilians know how to cook *baccalà*. Coming from Trieste, I was familiar with northern Italian recipes and I tried, unsuccessfully, to introduce them to *baccalà mantecato* (cod fish boiled and then whipped with oil and garlic).

This recipe is probably my favourite for *baccalà*. It is full of flavours and colours that can only be Sicilian. Leftovers make a great antipasto.

INGREDIENTS

1–1.2 kg (2lb 4oz–2lb
    12oz) baccalà, soaked
1 cup extra virgin olive oil
1 large onion, finely sliced
2 cloves garlic, chopped
1 cup finely cut parsley
500g (17½oz) tomatoes,
    peeled, seeded and chopped
    (or canned)
2 tablespoons tomato paste
    mixed with ½ cup water
flour for coating
½ cup salted capers, soaked
    and washed
½ cup sultanas or currants
½ cup pine nuts
1 cup white wine
½ cup black olives, pitted and
    chopped
salt and freshly ground
    pepper

METHOD

Cut the *baccalà* into square portions and leave to dry on a paper towel.

Heat ½ cup of oil in an ovenproof casserole. Add the onion, garlic and parsley and cook until the onion is pale golden. Add the tomatoes, the tomato paste and seasoning and cook until thickened.

Lightly coat the *baccalà* with flour and fry in hot oil.

Arrange the *baccalà* in the casserole with the capers, sultanas, pine nuts and ½ cup of wine. Bake in a preheated 180°C (350°F) oven for 30–45 minutes. Add the rest of the wine and the olives and bake for another 15–30 minutes until cooked (the fish should flake). During cooking, check to see if it is dry and either add more wine or water.

VARIATION

- Sprinkle with fresh basil leaves or extra pine nuts and serve with chopped chilli and a dribble of extra virgin olive oil.
- Cook any firm-fleshed fish this way. Large thick pieces are best.

Pesce incrostato di sale

SALT-CRUSTED FISH

I first ate whole fish encased in rock salt in a restaurant called Al delfino, just outside Palermo, near Sferacavalli and Isola delle Fimmine (Island of Women). The restaurant was not what we would call elegant, but was near one of Sicily's most beautiful beaches and had a reputation for being unpretentious, expertly run, and for serving very fresh fish and not much else. This is where the locals ate. This is where we wanted to be. And so did every one else. Every chair and table was occupied and the floor space was crammed to capacity. Busy waiters sidestepped around the room and performed balancing acts with platters piled with food. All good signs.

The fish encrusted in salt was one of many dishes we ate. The crust was cracked at our table and the skilled waiter quickly dismembered the fish. There were no distracting flavours – just fish on a clean white plate.

Replicating the dish was rather scary. I had once cooked chicken in a flour and water casing and it had been very successful. This was the same principle, but with so much sea salt! What if it seeped into the flesh? But the salt bakes hard like pottery, and the fish retains the succulent juices and sweet natural flavours. It looks pretty impressive too.

To enhance the delicacy of the fish, a sprinkle of your best extra virgin olive oil, a squeeze of lemon juice and pepper are sufficient.

Suitable fish
My relatives thought that the fish we ate was *spiegola*, called *branzino* in the north of Italy, sea bass in Britain and North America. This fish is not common in the Pacific but the dish can be cooked with any whole fish that is not too oily: bream, mulloway, kingfish, barramundi, snapper, coral trout, dory, red emperor and perch. I sometimes buy smaller fish (estimate half fish per person) and reduce the cooking time.

INGREDIENTS

*1 x 1.5–2kg (3lb 5oz–4lb
6oz) whole fish (about
350–400g/12–14oz flesh
per person), cleaned, gutted
and scaled*

extra virgin olive oil

*2kg (4lb 6oz) coarse sea
(rock) salt for every 1kg
(2lb 4oz) of fish*

*1 egg or egg white, lightly
beaten (optional)*

*best-quality extra virgin olive
oil for serving*

lemon juice for serving

freshly ground pepper

METHOD

Dry the fish. Season the cavity with pepper and a little extra virgin olive oil.

Grind the salt with a food processor until it resembles coarse sand. Splash a very little water on the salt and squeeze it together (like moist sand). Adding an egg or egg white to the salt will make the crust harder.

To encase the fish, put about one-third of the salt mixture on the bottom of the baking tray (about 1cm/½in thick). Place the fish on top, and pack the rest of the salt around the fish to cover and seal it. Cover with foil, shiny side down to reflect the heat.

In a 220°C (420°F) oven, bake the fish for about 30 minutes (or less if smaller), take out and leave to rest for another 10–15 minutes. It will keep on cooking. To test the fish is cooked, prick the thickest part with a metal skewer, hold it there for 30 seconds, then pull it out quickly; if the skewer feels warm the fish is cooked.

Serve the fish at the table, breaking open the salt crust in front of your guests. Watch the steam, smell the aroma and extract the fish gently. Serve accompanied by some extra virgin olive oil, a grind of black pepper and a squeeze of lemon.

VARIATIONS

- Serve with *salmoriglio* dressing, which is common throughout Sicily and probably of Greek origin (see page 256).
- At a cooking demonstration in Melbourne, a chef cooked a large 2kg (4lb 6oz) wild-caught barramundi in a salt crust. It tasted marvellous. He served the flesh and part of the skin separately so that the gelatinous nature and unique taste of the barramundi could be appreciated. He accompanied it with a light citrus sauce (he called it citrus oil): cut all the skin and pith off 1 lemon, 1 orange, 1 ruby grapefruit and 1 blood orange. Section the citrus, flesh from the membranes. Mash the fruit and slowly add 100ml extra virgin olive oil, salt and pepper to taste.

'Nfurnatu cà muddica

Infornato colla mollica

FOOD WHICH IS 'NFURNATU IS BAKED. MOLLICA IS
THE SOFT PART OF THE BREAD AND USED TO MAKE
BREADCRUMBS (MULLICA IS SICILIAN). ITALIANS – AND
THAT INCLUDES SICILIANS – LOVE TO EAT FRESH BREAD,
PREFERABLY WHEN IT IS STILL WARM. ITALIAN (AND
FRENCH) BAKERS USUALLY BAKE TWICE A DAY. AS FAR
AS SICILIANS ARE CONCERNED, A DISH WITHOUT BREAD
DOES NOT QUALIFY AS A MEAL.

*A tàvula s'havi 'a manciari sinu
all'ultimu tozzu dû so' pani: cu'
'u lassa, lassa l'anni so'.* (Sicilian
saying)
*A tavola bisogna mangiare sino
all'ultimo boccone del proprio
pane: chi lo lascia perde i suoi
anni.* (Italian)
*At the table one has to eat his/her
own bread to the last mouthful:
he or she who leaves some, puts
his/her life on the line.*

Bread is sacred and blessed in religious ceremonies. It is never wasted and
never discarded. Not so long ago, if you dropped a piece of bread, you picked
it up and kissed it, and then you either ate it or gave it to an animal to eat
(some of the old people still do this). Wasting bread is tempting fate.

There is always leftover bread to be used up. Often it is baked hard and
broken into milk and coffee for breakfast, or into soups. Breadcrumbs are
frequently used for stuffings, to thicken sauces, toasted and sprinkled over
food, and also used to seal baked ingredients.

Here small fish are placed in layers, topped with breadcrumbs and then
baked. The breadcrumbs are added towards the end of cooking and form a
golden crust when baked. The oven temperatures need to be high so that a
delicious *crosta* forms on top of the baked food – set the oven to 220–230°C
(420–450°F).

Crostata di sarde

BAKED SARDINES WITH CHEESE, BREADCRUMBS AND EGGS

A *crostata* is a tart with a crust on top or underneath. This is a layered dish made with sardines and topped with breadcrumbs. It's great as a lunch dish with a simple salad or as an antipasto. Leftovers are good eaten cold.

Sicilians do wonderful things with sardines and this is one of them. I cooked this for my parents on a Good Friday and my mother was very moved because she had not eaten this type of dish for a very long time.

INGREDIENTS

700g (1lb 9oz) sardine fillets
3 eggs
1½ cups dry breadcrumbs
   (medium to fine ground)
¾ cup grated pecorino cheese
3 cloves garlic, chopped
juice and grated zest of
   1 lemon or orange
1 cup flat-leaf parsley, finely
   cut
¾ cup extra virgin olive oil
flour to coat the sardines
salt and freshly ground
   pepper

METHOD

Prepare the ingredients for the separate layers. Wipe the sardines dry. Beat the eggs with a fork, and add a little salt and freshly ground pepper. Mix the breadcrumbs with grated cheese, garlic, lemon zest and parsley. Mix the oil and lemon juice together.

Heat some of the oil in a frying pan. Coat the sardines lightly with flour and fry quickly in the very hot oil, just enough to crisp the skin. Do not overcrowd the fish in the pan or they will poach rather than fry. Drain on paper towels and set aside.

Oil an ovenproof dish that will fit all the ingredients. Begin with a layer of the breadcrumb mixture, then sardines (not overlapping). Cover the sardines with a sprinkling of breadcrumbs and follow with half the olive oil and lemon juice. Top with the remaining sardines, then the rest of the breadcrumbs, oil and lemon and finally the eggs. Bake in a preheated 200°C (400°F) oven until a crust forms on top, about 30 minutes.

VARIATIONS

- Add ¾ cup of chopped green olives, blanched almonds or pine nuts.
- Serve with an orange salad (I like the look and taste of blood oranges and when fennel is in season I add some).

Pisci a la matalotta

Pesce alla matalotta

FISH *ALLA MATALOTTA* WITH TOMATOES, CAPERS AND BREADCRUMBS

Alla matalotta is nothing like the French *matelote* from the Loire, which is made with river fish, red wine and mushrooms and served with croutons.

Pesce alla matalotta is common in the northwestern coast of Sicily around Palermo. Two cooking styles are often used interchangeably with *alla matalotta*. *Alla marinara* is a generic term, which encompasses all things associated with the Mediterranean: tomatoes, aromatic herbs like oregano and basil and sometimes, anchovies, olives, capers and garlic. *Alla pescatora* should contain a mix of seafood, including prawns (shrimp) and/or mussels.

Suitable fish
Use any fish with a medium to firm texture.

METHOD

Arrange the fish and tomatoes in a heatproof ovenproof pan large enough to fit the fish in one layer. Add ½ cup olive oil, garlic, capers and seasoning. Add water to just cover the fish. Cook over a brisk heat until the liquid has almost evaporated. Avoid stirring or turning the fish to prevent breaking.

Sprinkle the breadcrumbs and herbs on top of the fish. Dribble with a little extra virgin olive oil. Place the fish in a preheated 180°C (350°F) oven and bake for about 10 minutes, until a golden crust has formed.

VARIATIONS

- Add basil to the tomatoes, oregano to the herbs. Omit the mint.
- Seal the fish in hot oil before adding it to the pan with the tomatoes. Bake the fish for a shorter time than in the main recipe.

INGREDIENTS

1–1.2kg (2lb 4oz–2lb 12oz) tuna or fish fillets, in large slices

500g (17½oz) tomatoes, peeled, seeded and chopped (or canned)

¾ cup extra virgin olive oil

4 cloves garlic, finely chopped

½ cup salted capers, soaked and washed

1 cup dry breadcrumbs

4 tablespoons flat-leaf parsley and/or mint, finely cut

salt and freshly ground pepper

As second course

In biancu

In bianco

IF YOU AREN'T FEELING WELL, ESPECIALLY IF YOU HAVE AN UPSET STOMACH (ITALIANS SAY THAT YOU ARE *DEBOLE DI STOMACO*), THE HOME CURE IS TO EAT *IN BIANCO*, LITERALLY 'WHITE FOOD'. *IN BIANCO* IS A DISH THAT IS SERVED PLAIN WITH LITTLE SEASONING. BUT EVEN SICK ITALIANS COULD NOT IMAGINE EATING SOMETHING COMPLETELY NAKED, SO LEMON, SALT AND A LITTLE EXTRA VIRGIN OLIVE OIL ARE ALLOWED.

In Sicily, food cooked *in bianco* can be called *vogghiutu* (boiled or steamed). *Bollito* or *lesso* is the Italian culinary term. Food cooked *a bagniomaria* (in a bain-marie) is also considered *in bianco*. Broth, boiled rice, boiled chicken, certain boiled vegetables, steamed white fish, *bistecca di vitello a bagnio maria* (veal steak cooked in a bain-marie), *latte di mandorla* (almond milk) and *bianco mangiare* (dessert made with almond milk) are some of the foods considered to be *mangiare in bianco*.

Even if you are in perfect health, you will enjoy fish *in bianco* because this method of cooking enhances the delicate, fresh taste of the fish but does not overpower it. An excellent accompanying sauce can be made with a little finely chopped flat-leaf parsley, chopped garlic, lemon juice, seasoning and your finest olive oil. Another more modern accompaniment is a light egg mayonnaise (but not for the weak).

Ogghiu comuni sana ogni duluri.
(Sicilian proverb)
Olio comune cura ogni dolore.
(Italian)
Plain oil cures every pain.

Pisci a bagnumaria

Pesce a bagnomaria

FISH IN A BAIN-MARIE

Bagnomaria is Italian for bain-marie, the method of steaming food in a double boiler or bain-marie (or bowl over a pan of simmering water). The food is cooked in a *bagno*, bath, in a gentle way. Food cooked *a bagnomaria* is *leggero* (light). This dish contains tomato so is considered *leggero* (light) but not *in bianco*. I love meat or fish cooked *a bagnomaria*: a thin slice of yearling steak or fish with a little extra virgin oil, sage and oregano. Herbs add a subtle flavour and the juices are concentrated and delicious.

Because the fish needs to fit in the pan in one layer, I generally cook *pesce a bagniomaria* for two people at the most – the quantities given are for two.

Suitable fish
Use non-oily, white fish – whole fish or fillets. Flat fish such as sole and turbot are ideal: soft textured and delicate tasting.

INGREDIENTS

*2 x 200–220g (7–8oz)
    white-fleshed fish fillets*
*2 spring onions (scallions),
    white part only (left
    whole)*
*a little flat-leaf parsley or
    celery leaves*
2 bay leaves
extra virgin olive oil
*salt and freshly ground
    pepper to taste*

METHOD

Fill a large saucepan with hot water and heat it to simmering. Place the spring onions, herbs and a little olive oil in the inner container. Arrange the fish on top, add a little seasoning and sprinkle with about 1 teaspoon of water. Cover and allow it to cook gently over the pan of simmering water.

To serve, drizzle it with your finest extra virgin olive oil. Heavenly!

VARIATIONS

- Add very small amounts of chopped tomato and basil.
- Omit the bay leaves, parsley or celery. Add 1 small peeled and chopped tomato per person and sprigs of basil at the same time as the onions.

Ammarinatu cu acitu

Marinato con aceto

AMMARINATU MEANS MARINADED. THE SICILIAN WORD FOR VINEGAR IS *ACITU*. *PISCI AMMARINATU* (MARINATED OR SOUSED FISH) IS A VERY FAVOURITE WAY TO SERVE FISH IN THE LEONE FAMILY (MY MOTHER'S SIDE). WHOLE SMALL FISH OR FILLETS ARE FIRST FRIED IN HOT OIL AND THEN SOUSED OR PICKLED IN VINEGAR. THE VINEGAR IS ALWAYS REDUCED BEFORE BEING ADDED AS THE MARINADE.

Saturating foods with acid – vinegar in this case – and salt was a way of short-term preservation of food before refrigeration. Fish was the staple protein in Nonna Maria's kitchen. I remember always smelling soused fish in her house. If there was any spare fish around, it was soused and kept in pottery terrines covered with plates in her Sicilian kitchen. Whenever she visited us in Trieste, she filled our fridge with *pisci ammarinatu*.

The smell and taste of things remain poised a long time, like souls, ready to remind us, waiting and hoping for their moment, amid the ruins of all the rest.
– Marcel Proust remembers petites madeleines in Remembrance of Things Past.

Pisci all' agghiata

Pesce all' agliata

SOUSED FISH WITH VINEGAR, GARLIC AND MINT

Aglio is the Italian word for garlic (*agghiu* in Sicilian), so it is easy to guess what ingredient is the defined flavour – in Sicily, the soused fish is flavoured with garlic or onions. I really began to appreciate soused fish as a young adult when I wanted to impress dinner guests. It is a good dish to serve as a starter or main course, especially in summer. The fish can be kept in the fridge for a few days and the flavour improves with time. I like to serve one or two small whole fish to each guest.

Fish cooked in this manner is not uncommon and it can be found with other names, and not just in Italy. In Trieste and in Venice it is called *pesse in saor* and is often made with sardines and eaten with white polenta. *Pesce alla scapace* is cooked in central and southern Italy and *escabeche* is the Spanish and Portuguese versions.

Traditionally the fish is lightly dusted with flour before being fried in very hot olive oil. Although the flour helps to hold the fish together, the frying oil will need to be discarded (the sediment taints it) and the flour coating often comes away in the marinade. I don't think it is necessary.

Suitable fish
Mackerel, sardines and tuna are used traditionally, but any firm-fleshed, white or oily fish is good. Fillets of fish are also suitable but are more difficult to handle.

METHOD

Coat the fish lightly in flour with a little salt (optional).

Fry the fish in extra virgin olive oil until golden on all sides. Drain on paper towels. Heat the same oil (or replace it if you have coated the fish with

MENU FOR VINCENZO BELLINI

Born into a musical family in Catania, Bellini (1801–35) was a musical sensation. The undoubted master of bel canto opera, his most famous works are Norma, La Sonnambula *and* I Puritani. *This menu includes* Pasta alla norma – *some believe it was named in his honour.*

≈

Whitebait fritters (*Crispeddi di nunnata*)
Pasta with tomatoes, eggplants and *bottarga* (*Pasta a la norma ca bottarga*)
Soused fish with vinegar, garlic and mint (*Agghiata*)
Fried zucchini

INGREDIENTS

1–3kg (2lb 4oz–6lb 10oz)
   fish
flour for coating (optional)
6–10 cloves garlic, halved
1 cup whole mint leaves
   (leave on stems, these are
   replaced with fresh mint
   when the fish is ready to
   present)
¾ cup white wine vinegar
¾ cup extra virgin olive oil

flour) and fry the garlic until it turns golden, then add the vinegar and reduce for a few minutes.

Place the fish in a deep bowl. Scatter the mint leaves through the fish. Pour over the marinade. Cool it, cover and let the fish rest for several hours before serving at room temperature (or store in the fridge until ready to serve, and remove it about an hour beforehand).

To serve, decorate with fresh mint leaves.

VARIATION

  For *Pisci ca cipuddata* (Soused fish with vinegar, onions, sugar and bay leaves) follow the main recipe, but use *cippolata* (see page 265) instead of garlic and replace mint with 8–10 bay leaves. Decorate with bay leaves.

Crudo e cunzato

Crudo e condito

WHEN I WAS LITTLE MY FATHER USED TO PREPARE
BISTECCA ALLA TARTARA (WHICH MEANS 'HOW TARTARS
PREPARED STEAK') OR AS WE KNOW IT STEAK TARTARE.
STEAK TARTARE IS USUALLY RAW FILLET OF BEEF, FINELY
CHOPPED WITH A KNIFE, TOPPED WITH A RAW EGG YOLK,
AND SERVED WITH CHOPPED ONIONS, CONDIMENTS AND
CAPERS.

My father's *bistecca alla tartara* was different. It was a thin slice of raw meat
that was left to marinate overnight in lemon juice and oregano. It was served
with a dressing of capers, extra virgin olive oil and a little finely chopped
celery heart.

Most Italians call this *crudo* but, really, the acid in the vinegar or lemon
in the marinade has done the cooking. *Crudo* means raw, *condito is* dressed –
but it can also mean marinated. Raw fish (*pesce crudo*) is treated in the same
manner as steak tartare except that the fish only needs to marinate very briefly,
so its fresh flavour is not diminished.

When marinating, avoid using salt as this draws out the moisture from
both the fish and the meat. Once the fish has been marinated, it is then *condito*
– you can see similarities with the word condiment.

A testa a na patedda e la cura a
mari. (Sicilian proverb)
La testa e in padella e la coda nel
mare. (Italian)
The head is in the frypan and
the tail is in the sea.

Tonno cunzato

RAW MARINATED TUNA

The fish needs to be fresh and of excellent quality and sliced thinly. Keep it in the fridge while it is in the marinade. The recipes for marinating tuna suggest using a mixture of 7 parts vinegar to 3 parts lemon juice. I prefer to use just lemon juice, or 9 parts lemon juice to 1 part vinegar. You may wish to experiment.

This dish is usually served as an antipasto.

Suitable fish

The recipe is intended for bluefin tuna, which is not sustainable. Any skinless fillet cut thinly can be marinated the same way.

INGREDIENTS

500g (17½oz) tuna or other
   thinly cut, skinless fish
juice of 4 lemons
¼–½ cup white wine vinegar
dried oregano to taste
2 spring onions (scallions),
   finely chopped
2–3 stalks celery (pale green
   stalks and leaves from
   heart), finely chopped
½ cup capers
¼ cup finely cut parsley
¾ cup extra virgin olive oil
salt and freshly ground
   pepper

METHOD

Marinate the fish in the lemon juice and vinegar, making sure that the fish is covered with the marinade. Add oregano and place in the fridge for 30 minutes.

For the dressing, mix together the spring onions, celery, capers, parsley, olive oil and seasoning. When ready to serve, remove the fish from the marinade and pour the dressing on top.

Calamaricchi crudi e cunzati

Calamaretti crudi e conditi

RAW MARINATED SMALL CALAMARI

Here the marinade is also the dressing. This recipe is intended for young small squid. If they are unavailable, very fresh squid sliced thinly can be treated in this way. I ate raw marinated prawns (shrimp) as a starter in a trattoria in Sciacca (which also served scampi prepared in the same manner): use 4–6 prawns for each person using the following recipe.

METHOD

Mix the lemon juice, garlic, parsley, olive oil and seasoning together for the marinade. Add the squid, ensuring that it is completely covered by the marinade. Place in the fridge for at least 60 minutes before serving.

INGREDIENTS

500g (17½oz) squid, cleaned
juice of 2 lemons
2–3 cloves garlic, finely chopped
¾ cup parsley, finely chopped
¾ cup extra virgin olive oil
salt and freshly ground pepper

As second course

Anciovi cunzati

Acciughe condite

RAW MARINATED SARDINES

Alici are also known as *acciugghe* and *anciovi*. In some countries, anchovies are labelled as sardines and sold interchangeably. Begin your preparations a day ahead – these are marinated for a longer period because of their stronger fishy taste. The sardines must be freshly cleaned and filleted with no head, central spine or innards.

INGREDIENTS

1–3 sardines, cleaned, per person
juice of 3–4 lemons
3 cloves garlic, chopped
½ cup finely cut parsley
¼ cup finely cut fresh oregano
extra virgin olive oil
salt and freshly ground pepper

METHOD

Arrange the fish in one layer on a plate and pour over the lemon juice. Cover with plastic wrap and refrigerate for 3–6 hours. They are ready when they have turned almost white.

Drain the sardines in a colander, then quickly dry with paper towels.

Arrange the fillets in a single layer on a large plate. Sprinkle with garlic, herbs and salt and pepper. Dress with extra virgin olive oil, cover with plastic wrap and refrigerate again for about an hour until ready to serve.

VARIATIONS

- For rolled anchovies or sardines (*alici arrotolate*), wrap the drained, dried fillet around a piece of *giardiniera* (pickled vegetable), a pitted green olive or a piece of roasted pepper, and secure with a toothpick.

- When we first came to Australia, fresh sardines or anchovies were unobtainable, but we could get anchovies packed in sea salt. My father would marinate them for snacks or as an antipasto and we'd eat them with bread. Brush the salt off the anchovies, rinse and dry. Place on a plate, sprinkle with a little vinegar or lemon juice, dress with olive oil and season with chilli flakes. Keep in the fridge for up to 1 week.

'Nzalata ri mari

Insalata di mare

'NZALATA IS THE SICILIAN FOR SALAD. SEAFOOD SALADS
ARE POPULAR ALL OVER ITALY, ALL YEAR ROUND AND
ARE BASED ON WHAT IS LOCALLY AVAILABLE. THEY ARE
USUALLY SERVED AS AN ANTIPASTO.

As second course

Nzalata ri mari

Insalata di mare

MIXED SEAFOOD SALAD

Use very fresh produce, a variety of seafood and small specimens – small octopus, squid or cuttlefish, with most of it served whole. I mix the salad and store it in a large glass jar in the fridge until ready to use. This allows me to shake the dressing through the salad. The squid and octopus will shrink when cooked. Freeze cooking juices for stock.

METHOD

Clean the seafood: clean and cut calamari into thin rings or strips; clean and cut octopus into bite-sized pieces; de-vein the prawns; de-beard and scrub the mussels; and wash the cockles.

Cook the calamari, octopus and prawns separately, in batches, for only a few minutes by plunging them into boiling salted water. Drain, reserving the juice for stock.

Steam the mussels and cockles in a large covered pan in a little water – they cook in 2–5 minutes. Remove them from the shells, saving a few in their shells for serving. Reserve the juice for stock.

Place the mussels and cockles in a serving bowl. Add the calamari, octopus and prawns. Add the sliced celery, parsley and lemon slices.

For the dressing, combine the lemon juice, extra virgin olive oil, garlic and seasoning.

Toss the ingredients together, cover and keep in fridge. Remove from the fridge about 1 hour before serving and add the black olives.

INGREDIENTS

250g (9oz) calamari
250g (9oz) octopus
200g (7oz) small prawns (shrimp)
200g (7oz) large prawns (shrimp; I prefer green, shelled)
6 unshelled prawns for decoration (optional)
500g (17½oz) mussels
500g (17½oz) cockles
2 celery hearts (pale green stalks and leaves from heart), sliced
1 cup finely cut parsley
1 lemon, finely sliced, plus the juice of 2 lemons
¾ cup extra virgin olive oil
1–3 cloves garlic, chopped
about 20 black olives, pitted
salt and freshly ground pepper or chilli flakes

As second course

Tunnu vugghiutu d'u capu rais

Tonno lesso del capo rais

BOILED TUNA AS THE CAPO RIAS ATE IT

Sicilians are permanently nostalgic for the dishes of yesteryear. They love recipes that have changed very little over time. This is from around Trapani and the Egadi Islands. The largest of the three islands is Favignana from where the Capu Rais leads the tuna fishing ritual, the *tonnara*, and directs the *mattanza* (see page 17). The Capu Rais likes to eat his tuna *vogghiutu* (boiled or steamed), *lesso* in Italian. The large fillet is poached in water with milk and lemon, which keep the flesh white. *Lattume* (tuna testicles) are a delicacy on the northwest coast (crumbed and pan-fried), and a few were added to keep the men virile. They are sliced and dressed with the same sauce.

Suitable fish
Albacore tuna works well and is white when cooked. Buy two whole fillets, 500–800g (18–29oz) each. Other firm-fleshed fish also works well.

INGREDIENTS

½ cup milk
2 lemon, peeled, seeded and quartered
1–1.6kg (2lb 4oz–3lb 12oz) piece of tuna
salt to taste
1 cup finely cut parsley
juice of 1 lemon
¾ cup extra virgin olive oil
salt and freshly ground pepper to taste

METHOD

Combine the milk, lemon and seasoning and add water to cover the fish. Bring to the boil, add the fish, reduce the heat and simmer gently until cooked. Leave in the poaching liquid until ready to serve (for up to three days). For rare tuna, gently poach for 15 minutes. Turn off the heat and leave in the poaching liquid for about 20 minutes. Drain the fish and carve into 2–3cm (1in) slices. Place on a serving platter and cover with the dressing.

For the dressing, mix the parsley, lemon juice and olive oil together, season, and allow it to rest for about 10 minutes to allow the flavours to develop.

Purpu vugghiutu

Insalata di polpo

OCTOPUS SALAD WITH CELERY, CARROTS, GREEN OLIVES AND MINT

No Sicilian cookbook is complete without an octopus salad. Octopus is a popular street food in parts of Sicily, especially in Palermo. It is boiled in large cauldrons, sold dressed with a little oil, parsley, salt and pepper and eaten warm. In restaurants it is often served as a starter.

For most salads, boiled octopus is marinated in the dressing for a few hours and a few ingredient are added for colour: red pepper flakes, parsley or mint, spring onions (scallions), celery, tomatoes. My cousin Lidia who lives in Augusta makes a different *insalata di polpo* and this is her recipe. It contains generous amounts of salad ingredients and is served warm, shortly after it is made. I like the contrasts of textures and flavours.

INGREDIENTS

*about 3kg (6lb 10oz)
octopus, cleaned (I prefer
the large ones to baby
octopus)*
2–3 carrots, in thin rounds
*4 celery hearts (pale green
stalks and leaves), sliced*
small bunch mint, chopped
*2 lemons, finely sliced, plus
juice of 2 lemons for the
dressing (or use a dash of
wine vinegar)*
¾ cup extra virgin olive oil
1–3 cloves garlic, chopped
*salt and freshly ground
pepper*

METHOD

Place the octopus in a saucepan with sufficient cold water to cover it. Bring slowly to the boil, add salt and simmer for 5–10 minutes. Turn off the heat and leave the octopus in the water for another 15 minutes to finish cooking. Drain, remove any dark skin and large suckers and slice into chunks.

Arrange the carrots, celery, mint, lemon slices and olives in a serving bowl and add the octopus.

For the dressing, combine the lemon juice, olive oil and garlic and season to taste. Pour over the salad and toss, then leave to infuse the flavours for at least 10 minutes. Serve at room temperature.

VARIATION

🍃 I like to include 6–10 cherry tomatoes and/or about 20 green olives.

Sutt'ogghiu
Sott'olio

CANNED TUNA IS CALLED *TONNO SOTT'OLIO* (LITERALLY, 'TUNA UNDER OIL'). IN THESE RECIPES THE FISH IS COOKED THEN PLACED IN JARS AND PRESERVED UNDER OLIVE OIL.

The Romans and the Greeks boiled tuna to preserve it, thus contributing to recipes for *la vugghiata* (Sicilian for *bollita*, meaning boiled). I am not advocating you preserve tuna (and risk botulism), but it is an interesting way to keep cooked tuna moist. Keep it in a wide-mouthed jar and remove small quantities (with a clean fork). The contents need to be submerged in the oil and kept in the fridge at all times. I have kept *tuna sott'olio* in the fridge for up to a week; if it is left for longer, the amount of salt needs to be increased and the cooked tuna must be placed in preserving jars and processed in a water bath.

In the traditional recipes the tuna is soaked prior to cooking. This is to remove any blood from the raw fish, which may have been a problem with using bluefin tuna hooked by a gaffe. Although soaking is not necessary with albacore tuna (its flesh is paler), soaking partly precooks the fish and helps keep it moist when it is cooking. Most recipes say to soak the tuna for about 4 hours, but if I soak it at all 1 hour is sufficient. There are three ways of making *tonno sott'olio*. It can be poached: in the oven with wine and lemon, with oil and vinegar, or in olive oil.

Suitable fish
I use albacore tuna. Buy two whole fillets, about 500–800g (18–29oz) each. Any firm-fleshed fish, thickly sliced, is also suitable.

Funnu sutt' ogghiu o furnu

Tonno sott'olio cucinato nel forno

TUNA POACHED IN THE OVEN WITH WINE AND LEMON

INGREDIENTS

2 x 550–800g (20–29oz)
  tuna fillets
500ml (16fl oz) white wine
1 lemon, sliced
5 bay leaves
1 cup or more extra virgin
  olive oil
salt

METHOD

Trim the tuna so that it will fit into a large, wide-mouthed glass jar. The pieces should fit comfortably but not overlap, and be kept large to prevent breakage. If soaking, place the tuna in a container and cover with water; place in the fridge for 1–4 hours and change the water at least twice.

Drain the fish, wipe it dry and place it in a deep baking tray which fits the fish comfortably with no overlapping but with little room to spare. Add the wine, lemon slices, bay leaves, olive oil and salt. All the tuna should be covered with liquid. Cover with foil and bake in a preheated 160°C (325°F) oven for 30 minutes.

Allow to cool completely before removing the fish from the liquid. Drain, remove the lemon and pour off the oil – this can be used to cover the fish. The bay leaves can be added to the jar or use fresh ones.

Place the fish in a sterilised jar and completely cover with the oil, adding fresh oil if needed – there should be at least 2cm (¾in) of oil covering the ingredients. Make sure that there are no air bubbles rising to the surface, then cover the jar with a lid. Store in the fridge until ready to use.

To use, drain the tuna. The usual dressing is a dribble of extra virgin olive oil and some fresh lemon juice. Or you could use mayonnaise and *salsa verde*, which are more modern sauces and are excellent. Serve with some hard-boiled eggs, a little chopped parsley and black olives around the tuna.

Tunnu sutt' ogghiu vugghiutu cu acitu

Tonno sott'olio lesso con aceto

TUNA POACHED IN OIL AND VINEGAR

The tuna can be soaked in water as in the previous recipe before it is cooked. The vinegar and wine used in the recipe will also assist to keep the flesh pale.

INGREDIENTS

1 cup white wine
¼ cup white wine vinegar
1 onion, peeled and left whole
8–10 cloves garlic
5–8 bay leaves
2 x 1kg (2lb 4oz) whole fillets of tuna
10 peppercorns, freshly ground
2 cups extra virgin olive oil

METHOD

Place the wine, vinegar, onion, 4 cloves of garlic and 4 bay leaves in a large saucepan with 3 litres (12 cups) of water. Bring to a simmer and reduce by one-third. Add the tuna – make sure that the liquid covers the tuna and that the tuna fits tightly in the pan – and continue to simmer on very low heat for 30 minutes.

Drain the tuna and place in a sterilised jar, add freshly ground peppercorns and the remaining cloves of garlic and bay leaves.

Cover the contents completely with the extra virgin olive oil – there should be at least 2cm (¾in) of oil covering the ingredients. Make sure that there are no air bubbles rising to the surface, then cover the jar with a lid. Store in the fridge until ready to use. (When raw garlic is stored in oil, the oil's oxygen-free environment is perfect for growing bacteria, so make sure that it is well refrigerated and use within 5 days).

Drain and serve with some of the oil, lemon juice and freshly ground pepper or a dressing of your choice.

If you have any tuna left over, return it to the oil.

Na paddeda

In padella

FOOD COOKED *IN PADELLA*, ('N OR 'NA *PADEDDA* IN
SICILIAN) IS COOKED IN A FRYING PAN. THIS IS THE
CULINARY TERM USED FOR SAUTÉED, SHALLOW FRIED
AND PAN FRIED. THERE DOES NOT SEEM TO BE A
CULINARY TERM FOR DEEP FRYING. FOOD, WHICH IS
FRIED IN EITHER A LITTLE OIL OR IN A CONSIDERABLE
AMOUNT OF OIL IS SIMPLY *FRITTO* (FRIED).

This cooking method is relatively fast and the medium to high heat required is
easily controlled. I find that when I use a heavy-based frying pan rather than a
non-stick pan the cooking is faster, the fish is crisper and the juices left in the
pan are more caramelised and tastier.

In padella suits almost any whole fish (river or sea), fillets or cutlets.
The two recipes here are for trout, but any fish can be cooked in this manner
and will benefit from the flavours of these two recipes. Cooking times will
vary, depending on the thickness of the fish and whether you prefer it to be
cooked through.

*Cci dissi a la padedda la
gradigghia: ju` pisci grossu
vugghiu no fragagghia.* (Sicilian
proverb)
*Disse la padella alla graticola: io
pesci grossi voglio, non fragaglia
[miscuglio di pesciolini].* (Italian)
*The frypan said to the grill: I
want large fish, not small fry.*

As second course

Trotta d'u manghisi

Trota del manghisi

TROUT FROM THE MANGHISI RIVER WITH GARLIC, TOMATOES, MYRTLE AND CROUTONS

Here the trout is treated much more boldly with stronger flavours. This is a dish from the Manghisi River area around Noto. It is flavoured with myrtle, which was considered sacred to the ancients. The glossy, green leaves or berries are aromatic when crushed and are a suitable alternative to bay leaves in cooking (I have used native Australian myrtle in this dish, which is an interesting flavour, but is definitely not the same). In Ragusa myrtle is often used with pork and pan-fried fish also benefits from the strong taste.

In Sardinia *digestivi* are made with myrtle. My aunt, Zia Niluzza, often adds myrtle instead of bay to the liqueur she makes.

Other suitable fish
Use any firm- to medium-fleshed fish, whole small fish, fillets or cutlets.

INGREDIENTS

6 large cloves garlic (or more)
6 generous tablespoons extra
    virgin olive oil
6 x 350g (12oz) whole trout
1 red chilli, chopped
6 medium tomatoes, peeled
    and chopped into large
    pieces
6 tablespoons salted capers,
    soaked and washed
6 myrtle or bay leaves
croutons (fried in lard)
salt to taste

METHOD

Clean the trout and check that it has been scaled. Wipe each trout clean.

Use the garlic to flavour the oil – add it to hot olive oil in a frying pan; when it is brown, discard it. Add the fish and chopped chilli and pan-fry the fish on both sides.

Add the tomatoes, capers, myrtle and seasoning and simmer until reduced to a sauce-like consistency. If the fish is not cooked sufficiently, add a little water, cover and allow it to braise until cooked.

FOR CROUTONS

Cut slices of good-quality bread into small cubes and fry in hot lard. Or fry the bread in duck fat (*magnifico!*) – but definitely not traditional.

Trota in padella con olive e finocchio selvatico

TROUT WITH OLIVES AND WILD FENNEL

INGREDIENTS

6 x 350g whole trout
   (or 3 x 450–600g/
   16–21oz trout)
6 generous tablespoons extra
   virgin olive oil
up to 1 cup feathery wild
   fennel (or green feathery
   part of fennel bulb, finely
   sliced and ½ teaspoon
   fennel seeds)
60g (2oz) green olives, pitted
   and sliced
60g (2oz) black olives, pitted
   and sliced
2 lemons, finely sliced
   (2 slices per fish)
salt to taste

Trout is rare in Sicilian restaurants and I have only occasionally seen it in the fish markets, but it is caught in the island streams. Sicilians prefer marine fish, which is not surprising since the island is surrounded by ocean. I had difficulty finding many Sicilian recipes for trout, which is seen as a delicate fish and is mostly cooked *in bianco* (steamed or lightly poached) and presented with boiled vegetables and a dressing of flat-leaf parsley, oil and lemon and sometimes a little cut mint. Trout is also served *fritta*, lightly coated with flour, fried in olive oil and served with lemon.

This is my favourite recipe for trout – with wild fennel (the green feathery part), green and black olives and thin slices of lemon. Wild fennel bushes grow along riverbanks or vacant land. Alternatively, use the green feathery part from the top of the cultivated bulb fennel and ½ teaspoon of fennel seeds.

Other suitable fish
Use any firm- to medium-fleshed fish, whole small fish, fillets or cutlets.

METHOD

Clean the trout and check that it has been scaled. Wipe each trout clean.

Heat the extra virgin olive oil in a frying pan and pan-fry the fish. Add a little salt and set aside.

Add the fennel (and fennel seeds if using cultivated fennel) to the pan and sauté until caramelised. Add olives and lemon slices and heat through.

Return the fish to the pan (fillet the larger fish) and toss around in the hot ingredients for 1 minute and serve.

Frittu

Fritto

PESCE FRITTO IS VERY COMMON ALL OVER ITALY, INCLUDING IN SICILY, AND IT IS USUALLY SERVED HOT. COOKED WELL, IT IS FULL OF FLAVOUR, ESPECIALLY WHEN EATEN WITH AN INTERESTING SAUCE AND A TASTY CONTORNO. MINT PESTO IS A VERY SUITABLE ACCOMPANIMENT – THE REFRESHING TASTE OF THE MINT COMPLEMENTS THE SWEETNESS OF THE FISH. SEE CHAPTER 4 , PAGES 252–73, FOR OTHER SUITABLE SAUCES.

Hot oil is essential for frying – wait until the oil begins to wobble in the pan and smoke before putting the fish in. This seals the fish and keeps it moist. It is best to coat the fish very lightly with flour (and a little salt) before frying.

As with all fried foods, it is advisable to cook the fish in batches and not to overcrowd the pan – the oil maintains its temperature and the fish has room to sizzle rather than poach.

As second course

Fritto misto di pesce

MIXED FRIED FISH

Misto means mixed in Italian. *Fritto misto* is often served in restaurants as an antipasto as well as a main course.

Suitable fish

Use whole small fish. In Sicily, *neonata* are used – and you know my feelings about that. Sicilians love to eat little fish cooked whole, head and bones included. Fillets can be substituted but have little visual impact. Small fish such as red mullet, mullet, whiting, sardines, herrings, gunard, flathead, garfish and small trout are perfect.

GENERAL INSTRUCTIONS

There are no set times for *pesce fritto*. It is cooked *all'occhio* (by eye – in other words, intuition).

Cook fish of the same species and of similar size together.

Dry the fish before you dip it into flour seasoned with a little salt. Shake off the excess flour.

It is a good idea to score the fish to allow the heat to penetrate.

Use clean extra virgin olive oil (at least 1 cup) in a heavy-based frying pan. The oil must be hot (about 180°C/350°F or smoking) before you add the fish. Fry fish a few at a time. If you are concerned about keeping the fish hot (which Italians aren't) use more than one frying pan.

As the fish is cooked, place it on absorbent paper towels. Add more oil to the frying pan as necessary and allow the oil to return to the correct heat before adding the next batch.

If the fish is in plenty of oil it may not need to be turned, but if you need to turn it, do this only once to prevent breakage.

The fish will cook very quickly (in a few minutes). To test, poke the thickest part of the fish with the tip of a knife – if the flesh pulls away from the bone, it's ready to serve.

As second course

SERVING

The fish is usually served with quartered lemons.

It is quite common to serve fried fish with either:

- a little tomato salad, made with tomatoes (not too ripe), some young pale leaves from the heart of the celery and red onion sliced thinly (called *cipolla calabrese* in Italy), and dressed with extra virgin olive oil, salt and dried oregano or fresh basil.

- mint pesto (see recipe, page 268).

Crispeddi di nunnata

Fritelle di neonata o bianchetti

WHITEBAIT FRITTERS

Fritelle are fritters made with very small fish mixed in a batter and dropped by the spoonful into hot oil: they are served hot and with slices of lemon.

In Australia and New Zealand whitebait is available for a limited season. This refers to the juvenile stage of several species of predominantly *galaxias*

(small freshwater fish) fished in the marine phase of their lifecycle. The larvae hatch in a river but are washed downstream to the ocean where they develop and return to rivers as juveniles and further develop and remain as adults.

In Britain and the USA, the term 'whitebait' usually refers to smelt, which are much bigger. The smaller the whitebait, the better. If the fish are less than 4cm (1½in) long, they don't need to be gutted or cleaned; anything over 4cm is too big to be whitebait.

Whitebait fritters are common all along the Sicilian coast as a starter. There are slight variations in recipes, the main differences being the use of flour rather than breadcrumbs and the consistency of the mixture – whether it shaped into patties with moist hands or dropped into hot oil by the spoonful. I prefer to make bite-sized morsels and slide the not-too-stiff mixture off the spoon into the hot oil. For a lighter texture, I use breadcrumbs rather than flour.

In various parts of the island the fritters made with miniscule fish are called *sciabbacchieddu*, from *sciabbacuni* or *sciabbica* (the net used to catch the small fish).

INGREDIENTS

800g (1lb 13oz) whitebait, rinsed and drained well
breadcrumbs (fresh) or plain flour, as much as the ingredients will absorb
100g (3½oz) grated pecorino
½ cup finely cut parsley
1 egg
olive oil for frying
salt and pepper

METHOD

Clean and drain the whitebait – dry them with a paper towel. Mix together the breadcrumbs or flour, pecorino, parsley and seasoning in a bowl. Fold in the egg and then the whitebait. If the mixture is too thin, add more breadcrumbs or flour.

Heat the oil in a heavy-based frying pan until very hot. Drop in spoonfuls of the batter and fry until golden on all sides. Turn them once if necessary. Drain the *fritelle* on paper towels and eat with a squeeze of lemon juice.

VARIATION

🌿 Add a little chopped wild fennel (or the green top of bulb fennel or some crushed fennel seeds) and/or 1–3 cloves of finely chopped garlic to the batter.

'Nta braci

Alla brace

ALLA BRACE (ITALIAN) IS ONE OF THE TERMS USED TO DESCRIBE FOOD COOKED OVER COALS AND EMBERS, BUT THERE ARE OTHER COMMON EXPRESSIONS USED INTERCHANGEABLY. IN ITALIAN MENUS YOU MAY SEE *ARROSTITO IN GRATICOLA* – FOOD COOKED ON A GRATE; *SULLA PIASTRA* – ON THE BARBECUE PLATE RATHER THAN THE GRILL; OR *AI FERRI*, WHICH CAN ALSO MEAN COOKING IN A GRILL PAN (*A FERRO*) – FROM THE LATIN *FERRUM* (IRON) REFERRING TO THE GRATE OF AN IRON GRILL.

Cuisine is when things taste like themselves ... In cooking, as in all the arts, simplicity is the sign of perfection.
– Maurice Curnonsky, The Prince of Gastronomes

All Italian kitchens have a *ferro*. When we came to Australia we couldn't buy one so got a blacksmith to make one. It sat on top of our electric hotplate. Explaining what we wanted was very difficult and he must have thought that it was a very strange request.

Italian grilling is remarkably rustic and simple compared with other traditions – they are nothing like the elaborate, huge gas or coal barbecues in Australia or the USA. In my cousin Lidia's *casa in campagna*, she has set up a *ferro* on which she cooks all types of meats, vegetables and fish *alla brace* (the Sicilian is *'nta braci*). I have been too embarrassed to tell her about the size and sophistication of ones in our country.

As second course

Pisci 'nta braci

Pesce alla brace

GRILLED FISH

It is hard to beat the flavour of fresh grilled fish and this is probably the way Sicilians prefer to eat fish.

Suitable fish
Any oily, firm or flaky fish is suitable, small or medium sized whole fish or filleted fish, squid or crustaceans.

GENERAL INSTRUCTIONS

Let the fire burn down to coals that have a little ash on them first.

Always season the fish with salt before it is grilled and leave to rest for about 15 minutes. This makes it less likely to stick to the bars (the salt removes water from the skin – my parents and relatives also do this with meat) and helps with the process of caramelising the juices. Score the fish to allow the flavours and the heat to penetrate.

Brush extra virgin olive oil on the grill before cooking and on the fish during cooking. Lidia flavours the oil with oregano or uses rosemary stems as a brush. Some cooks add small branches of herbs, especially oregano or rosemary, to the coals as the fish cooks.

If you are using different sized fish or a mixture of fish, cook the larger ones first. Turn whole fish and fillets only once to prevent breakage.

Fish fillets cook quickly. Start whole fish off on a hot heat but finish over a milder heat. To see if it's cooked, prick the thickest part of the fish with the tip of a knife – when the flesh pulls away from bone it's ready to be served.

Squid and octopus taste marvellous chargrilled, but some people do not like the chewy texture. Both can be precooked (see pages 173 and 223; it is done when the flesh can be pierced easily with a knife – with octopus this

SUMMER MENU

Roasted or grilled peppers
(*Pipi arrustuti*)
Grilled fish (*Pisci 'nta braci*)
Tomato salad (*'Nzalata ri pumaroru*)

could take 45 minutes) and once cooled, brushed with olive oil, salt and a pinch of dried oregano and then grilled to lightly caramelise.

Octopus can cook in its own juices on the grill wrapped in foil. Splash the arms with a little extra virgin olive oil and cook it slowly for 30–40 minutes, then slit the parcel with a knife, remove the octopus, smear it with more oil and grill.

Variations

- Small or delicate-textured fish can be wrapped *in cartoccio* (in a parcel – use foil) and grilled on coals. Dress the fish with a little extra virgin olive oil and a squeeze of lemon juice. In each parcel, place a few crushed fennel seeds, a little chopped parsley; in modern recipes, a slice of pancetta, chopped is added. Seal and grill over moderate heat for 8–12 minutes, depending on its size. Turn once. Allow to rest for a few minutes before opening.

Ammaru 'nta brace

Gamberi alla brace

Grilled prawns (shrimp)

In a seafood restaurant in Cefalu, I was served a platter of grilled prawns – with a bowl of strongly flavoured black olives, dried in salt and dressed with fennel seeds, garlic, orange peel and extra virgin olive oil, compliments of the house. It made a wonderful impromptu accompaniment to the prawns.

I prefer grilled prawns as a *primo* and guests can peel their own. For a *secondo*, I feel compelled to peel them – and as I like to serve them with a *contorno* and hold my cutlery with clean hands, I assume guests do too.

The Sicilian words for prawns are unrecognisable: *ammari* or *jammari* and *gamureddu* (for small prawns). When I first heard the words yelled out in Palermo's Vucciria market, I had no idea what they were talking about.

La Vucciria is an astonishing, noisy market: the textures, tastes, colours and smells, the vendors' shouting, are, like a Fellini film, thick with bizarre characters. Its name originates from the French *boucherie*, mispronounced by the Sicilians as *bocceria* and transformed over time to *vucciria*. Originally, the market mainly sold meat, hence *boucherie* (a butcher's shop in French). Sicily's markets date from Saracen rule in the 9th century. La Vucciria, once the favourite, has shrunk. The Ballarò now has the best selection of fresh produce. The Capo market sells increasing amounts of cheap clothing and hardware and less food.

Method

Cut the shell down the middle of the back (tail segment) with scissors, but leave the shell on while cooking. Grill on a hot plate or grill for 1–3 minutes each side, basting with a little extra virgin olive oil. For more flavour, use a strong sprig of rosemary or oregano to baste.

Serve on a large platter and top with simple dressing of oil, lemon, parsley, or one of the sauces in chapter 4, see pages 252–73.

Ingredients

large green prawns (shrimp)
extra virgin olive oil

Tonnu rigatanu
Tonno alla griglia con origano

GRILLED TUNA WITH OREGANO

Tuna is often sold in thick steaks. Tuna steaks in Sicily tend to be cut thinly, about 1cm (½in) thick, probably because Italians prefer their fish not to be pink in the middle. I like tuna seared so that the outer is crisp and the inner left rare.

The tuna steaks are usually marinated in oil, lemon and oregano before being grilled. Swordfish, also a firm meaty fish, is prepared the same way. Not all grilled fish is marinated beforehand, but it is always salted and brushed with extra virgin olive oil before and during cooking – usually with a large sprig of rosemary or oregano as a brush.

Other suitable fish
I use albacore tuna, kingfish or mackerel, but any large, fish steak or cutlet of firm-fleshed fish can be marinaded and cooked by this method.

INGREDIENTS

6 x tuna steaks

THE MARINADE
1½ cup extra virgin olive oil
4 large cloves garlic, peeled,
*   left whole and squashed*
2 teaspoons dried or
*   3 teaspoons finely chopped*
*   fresh oregano*
3 bay leaves
juice of 2–3 lemons
salt to taste
peppercorns, crushed or
*   ground, to taste*

METHOD

Make the marinade by mixing all of the ingredients together. Place three-quarters of it in a container large enough to fit the fish. Reserve the rest of the marinade.

Wipe the fish and place in the marinade for about 30 minutes. If you marinate it longer, the fish will start to cook. Turn the fish half-way through. Drain, reserving the marinade to baste the fish while it is cooking.

Grill the tuna steaks, turning them once and basting them.

Serve with the reserved marinade. (It is quite usual to pour over the marinade in which the fish was seeped; some of us may feel a little uneasy about the taste, health and safety features of doing this.)

Purpetti e sasizzeddi

Polpette e salsicciette

TUNA IS OFTEN TREATED AS MEAT AND THESE TWO RECIPES ARE A REFLECTION OF THIS. *PURPETTI* IS SICILIAN FOR MEATBALLS. THE WORD IS DERIVED FROM THE ITALIAN *POLPA*, MEANING FLESH. *PURPETTI* IS SOMETIMES USED FOR PATTIES MADE FROM FISH OR VEGETABLES. *SASIZZEDDI* IS THE SICILIAN WORD FOR SMALL SAUSAGES.

The flesh of albacore tuna is pale in colour and perfect in texture for fish balls and fish sausages. However, any firm skinless, non-oily fish can also be used. You will need a mincer or a food processor to mince the tuna for the fish balls but, if you are up to it, the tuna can be coarsely chopped by hand for the sausages.

AUTUMN MENU

Sautéed mushrooms (*Funci trifulati*)
Pasta with swordfish and mint (*Pasta con spada e menta*)
Tuna balls (*Purpetti di tunnu*), pan fried
Christmas caponata (*Caponata di natale*)

As second course

Purpetti di tunnu ca sarsa

Polpette di tonno con la salsa

TUNA BALLS IN SALSA

Purpetti di tunnu are made with as many combinations of flavours as meatballs and cooked in as many ways. They can be fried and eaten plain with a squeeze of lemon juice or poached in a tomato or an *agro dolce* sauce (see variation). These *purpetti* are from around Favignana and Trapani, on the northwest coast.

METHOD

Cut the tuna into chunks, remove any dark flesh and mince using a meat grinder or food processor.

Soak the breadcrumbs in milk and squeeze dry.

To make the fish balls, combine the tuna, breadcrumbs, eggs, parsley, seasoning and 1 tablespoon each of the currants and pine nuts. Form into balls, roll each lightly in flour and shake off excess.

Heat ¾ cup of extra virgin olive oil in a frying pan and, using a slotted spoon, carefully lower the balls into the hot oil and cook until they are a light golden, about 2 minutes. Do not overcrowd – it is better to cook them in batches. Remove with a slotted spoon and drain on paper towels.

For the tomato sauce, heat ¼ cup of extra virgin olive oil in a separate pan which is large enough to fit the *polpette* and cook the garlic until it is light golden. Add the tomatoes, rosemary, the rest of the currants, pine nuts and seasoning. Add the *polpette* and braise for 8–10 minutes. Add the white wine and basil leaves and leave uncovered until the sauce is thick and the *polpette* are cooked. Serve hot.

INGREDIENTS

600g (1lb 5oz) tuna, skin and sinews removed
1 cup fresh breadcrumbs
¼ cup milk
2 eggs, lightly beaten
2 tablespoons parsley, finely chopped
2 tablespoons currants
2 tablespoons pine nuts
flour or fine toasted breadcrumbs for coating
about 1 cup extra virgin olive oil
2 cloves garlic
500g (17½oz) tomatoes, peeled and chopped
½ teaspoon rosemary, finely cut
1 cup white wine
8–10 large basil leaves
salt and freshly ground pepper

VARIATIONS

🍂 Omit the tomato sauce and replace the pine nuts and currants with one or more of the following: grated pecorino, lemon zest and/or cinnamon. Fry the balls a little longer and serve as a starter.

🍂 Fish balls *in agro dolce*: Fry the fishballs in some oil, drain and return to the frying pan. Add 2 tablespoons of sugar and ½ cup of vinegar. Mix ingredients well, allow the vinegar to reduce completely and serve.

🍂 In Trapani *sardi a purpetti* (fish balls made with sardines) are common. Mix finely minced sardines, breadcrumbs, chopped parsley, egg and grated pecorino cheese. Add a little oil to soften the paste and shape into balls.

Sasizzeddi du tunnu

Salsicette di tonno

TUNA SAUSAGES

Rather than minced, the tuna is chopped finely with a sharp knife and, as in homemade pork sausages, the size of the mince is irregular. I cheat a little and mince half of the tuna flesh and chop the rest by hand to get the right consistency. I have a food processor with a mincer and a sausage nozzle attachments, so making sausages is easy. But I think how all of those *nonne* and *mamme* stuffed the casings by hand. You can use a funnel with a wide hole and push the mince through with the handle of a wooden spoon. It is important to have moist hands so the fish does not stick to your fingers – have a bowl of water (or wine) nearby. The mixture needs to rest before it is put into the casing, so begin preparations early.

Other suitable fish
You can substitute any other firm-fleshed fish.

CASINGS

Order sausage casings from a butcher. There are two kinds of casings. Natural casings are the intestines of animals, specifically those of cows, pigs and sheep. Manufactured casings are synthetic (cellulose, starch, collagen) and need little preparation other than soaking before use.

Natural casings are packed in brine or salt and need to be washed. Place them in a large bowl, fill with water, let them soak for a few minutes then drain and refill; repeat a few times. Then place a few inches of water in a sink and add the casings. Take a casing, open one end and fill the with water from the tap. Do it for one whole length, then drop it back into the sink and move to the next one.

Meat sausages are often made into a long continuous cord and cooked coiled, and you can make the fish ones in this shape. The coiled sausage can

Camina chi pantofuli finu a quannu non hai i scarpi. (Sicilian proverb)
Cammina con pantofole fino a che non hai le scarpe. (Italian)
Walk with your slippers on until you can find your shoes.

As second course

INGREDIENTS

1kg (2lb 4oz) tuna, skin and
    sinews removed
200g (7oz) fresh
    breadcrumbs
salt
freshly ground pepper or red
    chilli flakes
1 cup or more extra virgin
    olive oil
50g (1¾oz) grated pecorino
½ cup parsley
3 cloves garlic, finely chopped
6–8 whole cloves or
    ¾ teaspoon ground cloves
125ml (4fl oz) white wine
1 metre (39in) sausage
    casing

TOMATO-BASED SAUCE
½ cup extra virgin olive oil
3 onions, finely sliced
500g (17½oz) tomatoes,
    peeled and chopped
    (or 1 can)
2 tablespoons parsley
oregano or basil to taste
1 cup white wine
salt to taste

*Burdens become light when
cheerfully borne.*
– Ovid

be baked, or pan-fried (with a little water or white wine added towards the end of cooking and evaporated to make a sauce). The long sausage is a *sasizza* (Sicilian for sausage) rather than *sasizzedi* (small sausages).

METHOD

Cut tuna into chunks, remove any dark flesh and chop coarsely using a very sharp knife (or mince the tuna).

Combine all the ingredients, reserving some wine to moisten your hands while you are making the sausages. Leave to rest for about an hour.

Prepare the casings (see above). Using a funnel as a nozzle, stuff the fish mixture into the casings, using your palms and fingers moistened with water or wine. If you have a sausage attachment for a food mixer, stuff the casings following the manufacturer's instructions. Tie the ends with string at regular intervals to make individual sausages or make links by twisting the sausages; it can also be made into a continuous length and coiled to cook. Remove air pockets by pricking the sausages with the tip of a sewing needle or thin knife.

The sausages can be pan-fried or poached in a tomato-based sauce.

PAN-FRIED SAUSAGES

Seal the sausages and pan-fry in a little extra virgin olive oil. Add wine and reduce to deglaze the pan.

POACHED SAUSAGES IN A TOMATO-BASED SAUCE

Heat the extra virgin olive oil in a frying pan and add the onions. Cook until the onions have softened and turned golden. Add the tomatoes and herbs and reduce until thickened.

Add the sausages (kept together in sets of 2 or coiled in the pan like a snake) and wine. Braise until cooked, about 15–20 minutes.

Come fare una bella figura

How to make a good impression

MOST OF THE FISH RECIPES INCLUDE THEIR OWN SAUCES, BUT THERE MAY BE TIMES WHEN AN ACCOMPANYING SAUCE OR A PESTO IS NEEDED TO ADD THAT INDEFINABLE EXTRA TO A STEAMED, BAKED, GRILLED OR FRIED FISH. AS WELL AS ENHANCING THE FLAVOUR OF THE FISH, YOU WILL HAVE MADE A *BELLA FIGURA*.

Fare una bella figura, putting on a good face, is the central tenet of Italian life. It is what Sicilians live and die by. You must always play the part and look your best. The opposite of making a good impression is *fare una brutta figura*, a loss of face that can never be forgotten or forgiven by Sicilians.

In the Italian language there is a distinction between the words commonly used for sauces: *condimento, sugo, salsa, salsetta* and *pesto*.

Condimento means a condiment, seasoning, flavouring and dressing. When a green salad is dressed with a simple extra virgin oil and vinegar, it is *condita* (dressed) with the vinaigrette.

A *sugo* is a sauce simmered and made with meat (*un sugo di carne*) or fish (*un sugo di pesce*) and then reduced.

A *salsa* is lighter than a *sugo* as it usually does not contain meat or fish. It may be cooked (for example, *salsa di pomodoro*, a simple sauce of tomato, extra virgin olive oil and basil) or uncooked (*salsa verde*).

A *salsetta* (literally, 'a little *salsa*') is less dense than a *salsa* or *sugo*. It may contain chopped ingredients suspended in liquid, such as oil and/or the juices from the ingredients.

For a *pesto* the ingredients are pounded to a paste-like consistency in a mortar and pestle. The word pesto refers to the process (from *pestare*, 'to pound') as well as the product. Pesto is usually associated with the one made in Genoa in Liguria of basil, pine nuts, garlic, extra virgin olive oil and pecorino, which combine to make the fragrant sauce used to dress pasta.

The mortar and pestle have been used since antiquity and are still widely used in Sicily. The textures and consistencies obtained using them are very different from those that are processed or blended. I find herbs chopped in a food processor taste grassy rather than fragrant – if you use a food processor, add any finely chopped herbs last of all and pulse them for a very short time.

Au caru 'cattaci, au mercatu pensaci. (Sicilian proverb)
Compra cose di qualità e diffida da ciò che viene offerto a buon prezzo. (Italian)
Buy quality goods and think again about what is offered at a bargain price.

MENU FOR TWO HONORARY SICILIANS

I have two heroes who deserve to be honoured as Sicilians and one day I hope to have them together in my house for a meal (or two).

Peter Robb spent 15 years living the material that became Midnight in Sicily. *American-born Mary Taylor Simeti has lived in Sicily for a long time and is an authority on its food and history.*

❧

SUMMER MENU

Caponata made with eggplants and *bottarga (Pasta a la norma ca bottarga)*

Bad weather pasta from Palermo *(Pasta ro' malutempu)*

Fried sardines with *sarsa a friddu*

Green leaf salad *('Nzalata virdi)* with fennel

❧

SPRING MENU

Grilled eggplants, zucchini and mushrooms *(Mulinciani, cucuzzeddi e funci 'nta braci)* with *salmoriglio rosso*

Pasta with artichokes and tuna *(Maccarruna che caccocciuli)*

Baked fish with potatoes, vinegar and anchovies *(Pisci che' patati 'nfurnatu)*

Braised peas

ABOUT THE RECIPES

Here is a range of Sicilian sauces traditionally served with fish. Some are also suitable for simply cooked meat or for grilled vegetables; where this applies, I have stated this in the recipe.

There are regional and local variations for the names of the sauces, but many are known by their principal ingredients (*aglio e olio*, oil and garlic), their origins (where it is from – for example, *pesto trapanese*, pesto from Trapani) or what it is for (*sarsa ppi' pisci co pumarorú*, tomato sauce for fish). I have provided the English translation when applicable.

I've stayed faithful to preserving the genuine Sicilian flavours and aromas. There are no set weights and measures – the measures are purely an estimation of the ratio or balance of ingredients and flavours.

I usually prepare sauces well in advance and sometimes make double quantities of the more versatile ones to store in the fridge sealed with a thin layer of extra virgin olive oil.

INGREDIENTS

Oily fish suits a strong-tasting sauce, often containing vinegar and spices. The lighter sauces made with fresh herbs and lemon go better with white and delicate varieties of fish.

As for all the dishes, using good-quality fresh ingredients is essential. All the herbs are fresh, except when dried oregano is preferred (it is more aromatic when dried).

It is most important to use the best-quality extra virgin olive, especially for cold sauces. When the cold sauce hits the hot food, the fragrance of the oil will be obvious.

Pumarori is the Sicilian word for tomatoes (*pomodoro* in Italian). The fresh tomato-based sauces are summer condiments and most appropriate for grilled fish. Use sun-ripened tomatoes, organic if possible.

Garlic is a common ingredient and using seasonal, preferably local, garlic is best. Sometimes you may need to use imported garlic (but I never buy the chemically bleached, tasteless variety).

Salamurrigghiu

Salmoriglio

DRESSING MADE WITH OIL, LEMON AND OREGANO

This is the most common of the Sicilian dressings. *Salmoriglio* is made with salt (*sale*), lemon (*limone*), oregano (*origano*), hence sal + mo + riglio. It is also called salmorigano. In Sicilian, there are many variations to the spelling of the sauce – *sammurigghiu, sarmurigghiu, sarmuriggiu*.

The origins of *salmoriglio* are Greek and traditionally the cold dressing is poured over hot grilled meat, fish or vegetables. The heat releases the aromas and stimulates the appetite. It is also a marinade or a basting liquid for grilled meat or fish.

METHOD

Use a fork to whip all the ingredients together in a glass or narrow jug.

VARIATIONS

- Add a little hot water to the dressing and heat in a bain-marie for about 5 minutes. Heating the sauce accentuates the fragrances of the ingredients.
- I have seen a recipe where fresh oregano (4 tablespoons) is pounded with salt (1 tablespoon) in a mortar and pestle. Add 2 tablespoons of lemon juice, 8 of oil and some black pepper.
- My family always adds ½ cup of parsley and 1 finely chopped garlic clove.

INGREDIENTS

2 tablespoon fresh oregano,
  finely chopped, or
  1 teaspoon dry oregano
1 cup extra virgin olive oil
juice of 2 lemons
salt
pepper or chilli flakes, to taste

How to make a good impression

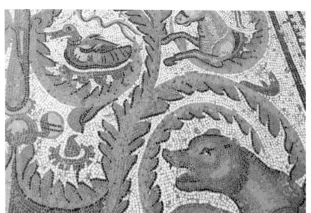

Sarsa a friddu

Salsa fatta a freddo

UNCOOKED SAUCE MADE WITH TOMATOES, HERBS AND GARLIC

Friddu means cold in Sicilian but it also means that it is made with raw ingredients. The ingredients are finely chopped and stirred and the sauce has the consistency of a runny tomato salad. The sauce should be made in advance so the flavours develop. Italians generally prefer firm orange-green tinged tomatoes for salads. There is no need to add lemon or vinegar to this sauce, as the tomatoes provide the required acidity.

As well as using this sauce for fish, I particularly like this as a dressing for *bocconcini* (not traditional). It is suitable for all grilled foods.

METHOD

Peel and deseed the tomatoes and chop very finely. Place them in a bowl and add extra virgin olive oil. Add the garlic, herbs and the seasoning.

Mix the ingredients together and allow this to rest for at least an hour before using.

INGREDIENTS

500g (17½oz) tomatoes
1 cup extra virgin olive oil
4 cloves garlic, chopped
½ cup finely cut parsley
oregano or basil leaves, finely cut
salt
1 fresh red chilli, finely chopped

How to make a good impression

Salamurrighiu russu

Salmoriglio rosso

DRESSING MADE WITH COOKED TOMATOES AND CHILLI

This sauce is a more flavourful variation of *sarsa a friddu* and is a sister to *salmoriglio*. The sauce contains grilled ripe tomatoes – *russu* means red in Sicilian – which make it richer and sweeter.

It you are grilling fish (or meat or vegetables), put the tomatoes on the hot grill rather than bake them in the oven.

Salamurrighiu russu should be the consistency of a thick mayonnaise. The ingredients are very finely chopped and then stirred together in a deep narrow bowl or a jug. A food processor can be used, but it really is not worth the bother of washing it.

INGREDIENTS

100g (3½oz) roma
  tomatoes
5–6 cloves garlic, finely
  chopped or minced
½ cup finely cut parsley
2 tablespoons oregano, finely
  chopped
juice of 1 lemon
salt and chilli flakes to taste
¾ cup extra virgin olive oil

METHOD

If grilling the tomatoes, put them on a hot grill and turn them until the skins are charred and they feel soft to the touch. If baking, depending on the size, keep them whole or halve them; place in a baking pan with a little extra virgin olive oil and cook in a preheated oven (180°C/350°F).

Peel the cooked tomatoes and drain in a colander for about 30 minutes. Chop them and place in a deep narrow bowl with the rest of the ingredients and, using a wooden spoon, stir and pound the ingredients together. Slowly add a little oil and, stirring in the same direction, amalgamate the oil a little at a time until the sauce has the consistency of mayonnaise.

VARIATIONS

- Replace the oregano with fresh basil (½ cup, leaves only).
- Use roasted garlic (baked with the tomatoes) – it has a different, more mellow taste.

Sarsa di chiappareddi

Salsa di capperi

SAUCE MADE WITH CAPERS AND ANCHOVIES

I particularly like this sauce with delicate-tasting fish (and boiled meats).

METHOD

Place the ingredients in a narrow jug or jar and whip together with a fork.

For a stronger tasting, more fragrant sauce, heat a little extra virgin olive oil before adding the anchovies and capers. Stir these ingredients in the hot oil to release their flavours. Add the parsley and juice of a lemon (instead of the vinegar) just before serving, poured over the hot fish.

VARIATIONS

- Add 2 finely chopped cloves of garlic and/or 1 tablespoon finely chopped oregano leaves.

INGREDIENTS

1 cup extra virgin olive oil
1 tablespoon wine vinegar (or the juice of 1 lemon for the hot version)
2–3 anchovies, finely chopped
1 cup capers, if salted, rinse well and soak
½ cup finely cut parsley
salt
pepper or chilli flakes to taste

How to make a good impression

Sarsa virdi siciliana

Salsa verde siciliana

SICILIAN GREEN SAUCE

One of my tasks as a teenager was to make *salsa verde*. We always kept a jar in our fridge to eat with *pesce lesso* (poached or steamed fish) and *carne bollita* (boiled meat – my mother made *brodo* once a week and we always ate the meat).

I have come across different (non-Italian) recipes for *salsa verde* that include basil, mint and even rocket. I am a purist and insist that it is predominantly a parsley sauce. 'Once Sicilian, always Sicilian' my mother-in-law always said. Traditionally, the sauce is fairly liquid so it can be poured over the fish. However, you can add larger quantities of the solid ingredients, and serve it in spoonfuls on the side of the meat or fish.

INGREDIENTS

1 slice bread, crusts removed
1½ tablespoon wine vinegar
1 cup finely cut parsley
3–4 anchovies, finely chopped
½ cup capers, if salted, rinse and soak
¾ cup extra virgin olive oil
1 hardboiled egg, finely chopped
2 cloves garlic, chopped
½ cup chopped green olives
salt to taste

METHOD

Soak the bread briefly in 1 tablespoon of the vinegar and squeeze dry.

Combine it with the remaining ingredients in a wide-mouthed jar or jug and stir gently. The anchovies generally provide sufficient salt, but check the seasoning. Allow to rest for at least an hour so the flavours develop.

VARIATIONS

- Add a couple of small finely chopped pieces of turnip (the white root) or gherkins (green) from Italian mixed garden pickles (*sotto aceti* or *giardiniera*).
- Add more or less anchovies and/or capers.
- I sometimes replace the vinegar with lemon juice and zest (not traditional).

Sarsa ppi'i pisci

Salsa per i pesci

COOKED SAUCE MADE WITH ALMONDS, GREEN OLIVES, CAPERS AND TOMATOES

Ppi'i pisci in Sicilian means 'for fish'. In some parts of Sicily this sauce is also known as *sarsa di miennuli* (or *mennuli*), *mandorle* in Italian and almonds in English. It is a rather a grand *salsa* made by blending two different sauces, both cooked. It is particularly good with large baked whole fish.

METHOD

For the first sauce, sauté the onion in ½ cup of olive oil until soft. Once it has turned golden, add the tomatoes or passata and reduce until thickened. Add the olives and capers and simmer slowly for 2–4 minutes.

For the second sauce, heat the remaining olive oil in a different saucepan, add the anchovies and dissolve. Then add the sugar, almonds and vinegar.

Add the two sauces together in one pan, stir and heat through.

Fillet the baked fish, pour a little of the sauce on the bottom of each serving plate and a little over the top of the hot fish and serve.

VARIATION

  Add ½ cup finely chopped parsley to the first sauce.

INGREDIENTS

1 onion, very finely chopped
about 1 cup extra virgin olive oil
¾ cup tomato passata or 2 ripe tomatoes, peeled and chopped
1 cup green olives, pitted and finely chopped
¾ cup capers, if salted, rinse and soak
4 tablespoons wine vinegar
2–3 anchovies, finely chopped
1 teaspoon sugar
1 cup almonds, blanched, toasted and finely chopped
salt and freshly ground pepper

How to make a good impression

Sarsa saracina d'alvi janchi

Salsa saracina di olive bianche

SARACEN GREEN OLIVE SAUCE

This sauce is good with poached or baked fish or white meats prepared in the same way. It is a cooked sauce and has the ingredients that are so common in Sicilian food: olives, pine nuts and sultanas.

In the early period of the Roman Empire the Saracens were a nomadic Arab tribe. Later the Greek-speaking subjects of the Empire called all Arabs, particularly those in Sicily, Saracens. After the rise of Islam, and especially at the time of the crusades, the term was extended to Muslims. The sauce contains sugar and saffron, which are Saracen ingredients and particularly popular in foods from the northwestern side of Palermo.

ABOUT GREEN OLIVES

There are many varieties of pickled green olives and in this particular recipe it is important to use either home-made pickled olives or *schiacciate* (green olives that have been cracked and seeped in oil and brine; they are sold in jars and are always from the south of Italy). *Schiacciate* means squashed and these olives retain some of the bitter olive taste. Some commercially pickled ones (usually Spanish) have a medicinal taste.

INGREDIENTS

½ cup extra virgin olive oil
2–3 anchovies, finely chopped
1 cup green olives, pitted and
   finely chopped
1 teaspoon sugar
¾ cup pine nuts or blanched
   almonds, toasted and finely
   chopped
½ cup sultanas, finely chopped
1 tablespoon fresh oregano,
   finely chopped, or
   ½ teaspoon dry
2 good pinches saffron
   (depending on the potency
   of the saffron – you need to
   be able to taste it and see
   some yellow tinge)
salt and freshly ground pepper

METHOD

Heat the oil in a saucepan, add anchovies and stir to dissolve. Add the olives and the rest of the ingredients and stir to amalgamate the flavours.

Add the saffron mixed in a little warm water and heat through.

Cippudata

Cipollata

THICK SAUCE MADE WITH ONIONS, SUGAR AND VINEGAR

Cipollata is very similar to onion jam and in Sicily it is regarded as a condiment for fish, especially fried fish. It also goes well with baked fish or meat, and cold fish or meats.

Allow the flavours to develop for a few hours before serving. It is used in the recipe for fish soused in vinegar and onions (see page 208).

INGREDIENTS

1kg (2lb 4oz) onions, finely sliced
½ cup extra virgin olive oil
about 3 teaspoons sugar to taste
3 tablespoons white wine vinegar
salt to taste

METHOD

Place the onions in a saucepan with 125ml (4fl oz) of water and cook until the water has evaporated.

Add the oil and continue to cook, stirring often until the onions are golden. Add the sugar, salt and the vinegar and cook for 1–2 minutes.

Serve the sauce cold.

VARIATION

❧ Use red onions (called *cipolla calabrese* in Italian) and red wine vinegar.

Stimpirata

THICK SAUCE MADE WITH GREEN OLIVES, CAPERS, CARROTS AND VINEGAR

This sauce is very common around Ragusa and Siracusa and is traditionally used with cold fish or meat. It also enhances the taste of boiled vegetables. I generally make large quantities: it tastes better as it matures and will keep for a week.

The recipe gives an idea of the proportions, but my method in the kitchen has always been if a handful is not enough, add more.

METHOD

Heat the olive oil and then add the garlic. After 2–3 minutes of gently stirring, add the carrots, celery, olives, capers, olives, mint and seasoning.

Continue to toss for another 5 minutes over moderate heat until the vegetables are slightly softened. If necessary, add a little water to prevent it sticking.

Turn the heat up to high, add the vinegar and let it reduce.

Cool and store it in the fridge.

INGREDIENTS

1 cup extra virgin olive oil
4 cloves garlic, finely chopped
2–4 medium carrots, cooked to taste, finely sliced
2–3 stalks from celery heart, plus the pale green leaves, finely chopped
400g (14oz) large green olives, pitted and chopped
200g (7oz) capers
¾ cup mint leaves, finely chopped
1 cup white wine vinegar
salt and freshly ground pepper to taste

How to make a good impression

Scurdalia

PESTO MADE WITH POTATOES, ALMONDS AND GARLIC

There are two versions of this sauce – one with almonds and the other, more unusual one, is made with poppy seeds.

I am familiar with the Greek *skorthaliá* or *skordalia* (originally called *scoradalme*, from *scoradon*, Greek for garlic). The modern versions are made mainly with potatoes, oil and garlic. In various parts of Greece, walnuts or almonds are included and it is sometimes made with bread instead of potatoes.

Scurdalia, the Sicilian version, is made with bread, potatoes and almonds. Its origins may be Greek, although *picada* (Catalan garlic sauce) and *ajo blanco* (from southern Spain) are very similar.

This sauce is particularly suitable for poached, sweet freshwater fish. I have used it with steamed or baked fish. Pino Correnti's version in *Il Libro d'Oro della Cucina e dei Vini di Sicilia* is made with poppy seeds, but tell your guests what is in the sauce – the black colour can be a little alarming.

I use a mortar and pestle to make the sauce. I use a food processor to almost pulverise the almonds and crush the poppy seeds lightly.

INGREDIENTS

6 cloves garlic
1 red chilli
100g (3½oz) blanched almonds, finely chopped
1 cooked potato, peeled and cubed
30g (1oz) white bread, crusts removed, soaked briefly in tepid water and squeezed dry
1 cup parsley, finely chopped
½ cup wine vinegar
1 cup extra virgin olive oil
1 tablespoon poppy seeds (optional)
salt to taste

METHOD

Begin by pounding the garlic and fresh chilli with salt in the mortar and pestle. Gradually add small amounts of almonds, potato, bread and parsley. Continue to pound and at the same time add some of the oil and vinegar (and the poppy seeds if using) until all the ingredients are finished and you have a smooth paste.

VARIATION

  Omit the bread and double the quantity of potatoes.

Zogghiu

PESTO MADE WITH GARLIC, PARSLEY AND MINT

This pesto is an ancient recipe, thought to be Arab-Maltese in origins (*zogghiu* comes from *zejjet*, to dress with oil) and is traditionally made in a mortar and pestle. Although it is said to have originated in Palermo, used by fishermen with grilled fish, some of my father's relatives in Ragusa use it for all grilled food – fish, meat, grilled or fried slices of zucchini and eggplants. But they call it after its ingredients: *agghiu* (garlic), *pitrisinu* (parsley), *ougghiu* (oil) *e minta* (and mint). The Sicilian language is so very different to the Italian: *aglio, prezzemolo, olio e menta*.

METHOD

Pound the garlic with a little salt. Add some herbs and pound some more. Continue to add the ingredients (but not the vinegar) a few at a time until they have all been used and you have a homogenous sauce.

Add the vinegar and more oil if you prefer a runnier dressing.

VARIATIONS

꙳ There are variations from all over Sicily. Add one of the following: a ripe tomato (chopped, peeled and deseeded) at the same time as the herbs, or 3–4 anchovies, or 1–3 cloves of garlic or 1 teaspoon of sugar.

INGREDIENTS

3 cloves garlic
1 cup finely cut parsley
¾ cup mint leaves, finely chopped
¾ cup extra virgin olive oil
1 tablespoon wine vinegar
salt
freshly ground pepper or chilli flakes to taste

How to make a good impression

Ammogghia e Mataroccu

PESTO MADE WITH TOMATOES, BASIL, PINE NUTS OR ALMONDS

The most popular Sicilian pesto is called *ammogghia* or *mataroccu* and is used with pasta (sometimes topped with whole, fried small fish in Favignana; see recipe, page 63). It is also served with fried or grilled fish. *Ammogghia* and *mataroccu* are different regional versions of the same *pistu* (Sicilian for pesto). There is also pesto *pantesco* (from the island of Pantelleria in the southwest).

Like pesto *genovese* (from Genova), the sauce contains pine nuts, garlic, oil and basil, but the Sicilian pesto also includes ripe tomatoes. In Trapani this pesto is usually made with almonds.

One wonders who made pesto first: the Sicilians or the Genovese? There were strong trade links between Genova and the northern coast of Sicily, where pesto is popular, especially the cities on the coast – Marsala, Trapani, Castelmare del Golfo – and the Egadi Islands.

If using a food processor, add the finely chopped herbs last and blend them for a very short time.

INGREDIENTS

8–10 cloves garlic
2–3 ripe tomatoes (about 400g/14oz), peeled, deseeded and chopped
200g (7oz) pine nuts or blanched almonds
1½ cup basil leaves, finely chopped
½ cup parsley, finely chopped
about 1 cup extra virgin olive oil (your most fragrant)
salt and freshly ground pepper to taste

METHOD

Pound the garlic with a little salt to obtain a paste. Add some of the tomatoes, pine nuts, herbs and a little oil and pound some more. Keep on adding a few ingredients at a time until they have all been used and you have a smooth homogenous sauce.

VARIATIONS

- Use pale green leaves from the heart of the celery, finely chopped.
- Or add 2 tablespoons of capers (this is popular in Marsala).

Maionese

MAYONNAISE

My mother always told me that Italian women had strong arms because they kneaded pasta and bread and made mayonnaise by hand.

Mayonnaise is fabulous with simply cooked fish. Although Italians do not tend to add anything to the mayonnaise, when I serve it with fish I sometimes add finely chopped capers or green olives or herbs such as finely chopped fennel (or the non-Sicilian herbs chervil or tarragon). I also like a Spanish-influenced mayonnaise flavoured with roasted garlic (2–3 cloves) and saffron soaked in a little hot water – add after the mayonnaise is made.

Mayonnaise can be stored in the fridge for up to two weeks.

THE STRONG-ARMED ITALIAN WOMEN'S METHOD

Place 2 egg yolks in a mixing bowl with a pinch of salt. Use a wooden spoon and stir, in a clockwise direction, drizzling a little extra virgin olive oil slowly into the yolks until the mixture is creamy. Make sure that all the oil has been incorporated before adding more. The mayonnaise will absorb about 1 cup of oil. Once all of the oil has been incorporated, add 1 tablespoon of lemon juice.

THE MODERN METHOD

Modern cooks make mayonnaise using a blender or food processor or electric wand. Mix 1 egg (sometimes I use an extra egg yolk with a little salt) in the blender, food processor or wand jar. Slowly add 1–1½ cups of extra virgin olive oil in a thin, steady stream through the feed tube while the blender or processor is running. Make sure that all the oil has been incorporated before adding more. When the mayonnaise is creamy add 1 tablespoon of lemon juice. (Non-Italian versions often use vinegar instead of lemon juice plus 1 teaspoon of Dijon mustard.)

TROUBLESHOOTING

If the eggs are not fresh, or too much oil is added too quickly, the mayonnaise will not set (the yolks separate from the oil and the eggs curdle). The mayonnaise can be saved.

Place it in a jug. Wash the mixing bowl and dry it carefully. Add another yolk. Blend the yolk with a little oil, as if beginning to make mayonnaise, then slowly incorporate the mixture (as you would the oil, dribble by dribble) into the new mayonnaise.

How to make a good impression

Festa

Feast

'Mpanata
Imapanata

AN ELABORATE SWORDFISH PIE (CALLED *IMPANATA*)
AND A COUSCOUS FEAST ARE TWO DISHES REMINISCENT
OF DAYS GONE BY. SIMPLER VERSIONS OF THESE RECIPES
ARE STILL PREPARED IN RESTAURANTS OR BY SOME
SICILIANS IN HOME KITCHENS, PARTICULARLY ON
SPECIAL OCCASIONS.

These two recipes are made of fish. The first imapanata is an elaborate dish, a recipe which reached the heights of sophistication during Sicily's period of haute cuisine in the mid-19th century. There are wonderful descriptions of this cuisine in *The Leopard* (*Il Gattopardo*) by Giuseppe Tomasi di Lampadusa. During this time, the aristocracy cultivated opulent tastes. Driven by the imperative to *fare una bella figura* (impress and outdo others), their chefs transformed some simple traditional recipes into elaborate dishes. With *impanate*, the plain bread dough used to envelop savoury fillings was replaced with a rich *pasta frolla* (short pastry) and the fillings became more elaborate, with more costly ingredients. The chefs were called *monzù*, the professional cooks of the Sicilian aristocracy in the 18th and 19th centuries (see page 16).

    The other festive recipe is for making couscous. This was not necessarily the food of the rich, but it is very labour intensive. Couscous is still enjoyed in some Sicilian homes – but now there are instant versions available.

*'Nda casa du patruni è festa ogni
jornu.* (Sicilian proverb)
*Nella casa del padrone è festa
ogni giorno.* (Italian)
*In the master's house every
day is a holiday.*

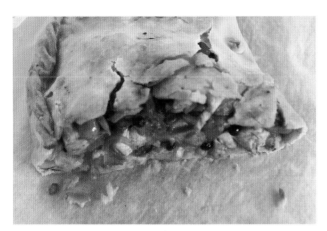

'Mpanata
Impanata

My relatives in Ragusa celebrate Easter in a big way, so I am very familiar with *'mpanata ri agnieddu*, a focaccia-style pie made with very young lamb (complete with bones) and encased in a bread dough crust – the traditional dish eaten at lunch on Easter Sunday. The juices from the meat and herbs soak into the bottom pastry crust and are as delicious as the filling.

There are other *'mpanate* from elsewhere in Sicily made with pork or beef, vegetables or fish. They come in various shapes and sizes. The most common shapes have the filling sandwiched between two circular layers of bread dough or short pastry. They are baked either in a dish or without one. Another variation is the crescent moon shape (like a calzone) made by folding a circular or oval-shaped dough over the filling.

Some smaller *'mpanate* – known as *'mpanatigghia* – look like a Cornish pasty: the filling may be a slice of fish placed in the centre of a circle of pastry, which is folded over the filling and pinched together on top. In Modica, about 20 minutes' drive from Ragusa, the specialty is *'mpanatiggha* with a filling of minced beef, almonds, honey, cloves, cinnamon and chocolate, suggesting both Spanish and Arabic origins.

The word *'mpanata* (*impanata* in Italian) appears in a Sicilian lexicon published in 1785. It probably comes from the Spanish *empanada*, from *empanar*, meaning to wrap or coat with bread. They are the semi-circular stuffed wheat-flour pastries common all over the Spanish-speaking world, including the Caribbean, South America and the Philippines. It is likely that they were brought to Sicily by the Spaniards, probably a legacy of the Moors who occupied Spain for 800 years. It is also possible that *'mpanate* may have been adaptations of the breads of ancient civilisations.

Simpler versions of *impanata* can be found all over Sicily: stuffed breads with a variety of fillings called by different names, including *nfigghiulata*, *fuazza, pastizzu, ravazzata, scacciata, scaccie* and *sfinciuni*.

The most notable is made with swordfish and called *'mpanata di pisci spata* (*impanata di pesce spada*). It is one of the elaborate, moulded and baked dishes made with sweet short pastry. Just how short the pastry is up to you – in the most traditional recipes a combination of lard and butter is used. Some recipes specify only using egg yolks and shortening for binding the flour, but I prefer to add a little white wine. This makes the pastry pliable and cuts the fat a little. I also like to add citrus peel to the pastry – a baronial touch. In other recipes there are three layers of pastry, one in the middle of the pie, but this is not my preference.

The second recipe is for the less opulent, more common version of *impanata* with a plain bread dough enriched with a little oil. Either filling can be used with either pastry.

Ingredients vary – some recipes use black olives rather than green ones; in other versions the combination of pine nuts and seedless dried grapes (sultanas, raisins, currants) are used. In the southern end of Sicily, *caciocavallo* (a provola-type cheese) is especially common as one of the ingredients.

Suitable fish
Traditionally swordfish is used for this recipe but this is not a sustainable option. There are other versions of fish *'mpanate* made with tuna (use albacore tuna), and with sardines, both sustainable. Swordfish and tuna are both dense in texture so substitute any cutlets or thick fillets of non-oily medium- to firm-textured fish. I particularly like mackerel. And rather than using one type of fish, I like to include two or three varieties.

INGREDIENTS

SWEET SHORT PASTRY
100g (3½oz) plain flour
½ teaspoon salt
85g (3oz) sugar
grated zest from 1 lemon or
  orange
200g (7oz) butter (or a
  mixture of butter and lard)
4 egg yolks
1 egg yolk mixed with a little
  olive oil to brush the pastry
extra liquid (white wine or
  water)

'MPANATA USING SHORT PASTRY

Simply described, this is a *ghiotta di pesce* (a fish stew) encased in a sweet short pastry. The pastry is left to rest before using and the fish filling needs to be cold before it is set in the pastry.

The pastry should be compact and may not need any extra liquid, but if you feel that you will not be able to roll it out easily, add more butter and egg yolk. Some recipes use a combination of whole eggs and egg yolks, others add a little white wine or lemon juice for the extra moisture. A little water can also be used.

Small fried slices or batons of young zucchini are included in some versions of *'mpanata* and I like to include them if they are in season.

METHOD

The pastry

Mix the flour, salt, sugar and lemon zest together. Add the butter and egg yolks. I use my fingers or a blunt knife blade to rub these into the flour. A food processor also works, but do not overwork the pastry – a few short pulses are sufficient. Add more liquid as necessary. Rest the pastry in the fridge for at least 1 hour.

The filling

Heat some of the extra virgin olive oil on medium-high heat and seal the fish by shallow frying it for a couple of minutes on both sides. Remove from the pan and keep aside.

Add ¼–½ cup of extra virgin olive oil to the frying pan and sauté the onion until soft. Add the celery and stir frequently to caramelise, about 5 minutes. Add tomatoes, season with salt and freshly ground pepper, stir, and cook for about 10 minutes until some of the liquid from the tomatoes has reduced. Reduce the heat to medium and add the olives, capers and the saffron (soaked in a little water). Stir well and cook until quite dense.

Put the fish back in the pan with the sauce (preferably in one layer), and spoon some of the sauce over it. Cover and cook the fish for a little longer, 5–7 minutes – the fish will cook further in the pastry and should remain in solid chunks throughout the cooking. Cool the filling.

Cut the zucchini into preferred shapes. Add salt and sauté in hot oil in a frying pan until golden on both sides. Set aside.

Heat the oven to 200°C (400°F) and grease a circular 24–30cm (9½–12in) springform baking pan.

Divide the pastry into two; roll out one slightly larger than the other and use it to line the bottom and sides of the dish with the edge about 1cm (½in) higher than the tin. Line the pastry with foil and fill it with pastry weights or dried beans or chick peas. Bake for 15 minutes. Remove foil and weights, brush pastry with egg white to provide a better seal and bake for another 10 minutes.

Fill the pie dish with half the filling, then the zucchini if using, and top with the rest of the fish. Cover with the rest of the pastry, make a few vents in it with a knife and brush with beaten egg.

Bake for about 45 minutes until the crust is golden.

THE FILLING

1 cup extra virgin olive oil
about 1kg (2lb 4oz) firm-fleshed, non-oily fish steaks or boneless cutlets, in thick slices
2 large onions, chopped and/or 3 cloves garlic, chopped
3–4 celery stalks (pale green stalks and leaves from heart)
400g (14oz) red tomatoes, peeled, drained and chopped
1 cup green olives, pitted and chopped
¾ cup salted capers, soaked and washed
a pinch of saffron
½ cup parsley or basil, chopped
4 small zucchini, sliced into rings or batons (optional)
1 egg, plus 1 egg white
salt and freshly ground pepper

INGREDIENTS

BREAD DOUGH
800g (1lb 13oz) plain
(durum wheat) flour
10g (½oz) fresh or dried
yeast
½ teaspoon sugar
about ½ cup extra virgin
olive oil
salt to taste

THE FILLING
¾ cup extra virgin olive oil
about 1kg firm-fleshed, non-
oily fish steaks or boneless
cutlets, in thick slices
250g (9oz) red tomatoes,
peeled and chopped
3–4 tender stalks of celery,
plus the pale green leaves
(from the heart)
2 tablespoons pine nuts
2 tablespoons currants or
sultanas, soaked in a little
water
½ cup black olives, pitted and
chopped
150g (5oz) mozzarella or
fresh provola type cheese,
cubed (optional)
¾ cup finely chopped parsley
¾ cup finely chopped basil
salt and freshly ground
pepper

'MPANATA USING BREAD DOUGH

The filling is typical of Messina. The 'mpanata is not as rich and elaborate as the pastry verson. and the method is different. The fish is sealed in hot oil and the rest of the ingredients are put into the bread dough uncooked.

Ragusano, a provola-type cheese, is sometimes added. A firm mozzarella or a mild pecorino is also suitable.

METHOD

The bread dough
Place the flour in a bowl. Dissolve the yeast and sugar in ½ cup of warm water and add to the flour. Mix into a dough, adding a little water until you get a firm consistency. Sprinkle with some flour and leave under a tea towel to rise for about 1 hour.

After the dough has risen, add olive oil, a little at a time, and knead again until the oil is totally absorbed. This amount of dough will make one large 'mpanata or two smaller ones.

The filling
Heat a little of the extra virgin olive oil in a frying pan over medium-high heat and fry the fish for a couple of minutes on both sides. Add seasoning. Remove the fish from the pan and set aside to cool.

Heat the oven 220°C (420°F).

Roll out the dough to 1cm (½in) thick. Place the fish in a single layer on one side of the dough. Spread the other ingredients over the top of the fish, season and dress with oil.

Cover the filling by bringing the dough over the filling to make a half-moon (calzone) shape; alternatively, use two discs of dough and sandwich the filling between. Seal the edges by folding the dough around the edges and then pinch together. Make a couple of slits on top and place on a well-oiled baking tray. Brush with a little more olive oil.

Bake for about 25–40 minutes, depending on the size, until the crust is golden.

Cùscusu

Couscous

I can remember having lunch in an Adelaide pub in the early 1990s when couscous was all the rage. My friend asked the young waiter what couscous was. She didn't know, she told us, but she would ask in the kitchen. She came back, looking extremely serious, and said, 'The chef would like me to tell you that couscous is a small furry animal that lives at the tip of Cape York and New Guinea.'

In the meantime, I had explained couscous to my friend and thought that the young woman had been set up to amuse us. But, technically, the kitchen was right – a *cuscus* is a small furry creature, a lot like a possum and about the size of large cat.

The origins of couscous in Sicily

There is so much conflicting information about the origins of couscous – more than just the spelling. In most writings on Middle Eastern cuisine, it is referred to as 'couscous', and in those about North African cuisine it is 'couscous'. The Italians call it *cuscus* and I have seen it written in Sicilian as *cuscusu*, *cuscuszu*, *kuskus* and *cùscussú*.

Couscous are tiny spherical pellets made by rolling and shaping moistened semolina, which are then coated with finer ground flour. It is worked with the hand in a circular motion until it clumps. Semolina is coarsely ground grain – in Sicily and the Middle East it is made from semolina and hard durum wheat flour, but it can also be made from barley or maize. The pellets are usually sieved and graded and can come in a range of sizes from 1–3mm. In Sicily, the smaller size is preferred.

Couscous is also the name of an entire dish, including the aromatic broth and savoury stew of meat, fish and/or vegetables.

No one seems to agree about the origins or date of the introduction of couscous into Sicily. We know that couscous was eaten in Europe after the French occupation of Algiers in the middle of the 14th century. However, it seemed to have reached Trapani (Sicily), Sardinia and Livorno (Tuscany)

earlier than this. Many believe the Arabs brought couscous to the island. Other sources argue that the Carthaginians introduced it in the 5th century BCE and that the preparation of couscous continued to evolve during the Arab incursions, which began in the 9th century CE. Sicily remained an Arab province until the arrival of the Normans three centuries later. Another view is that couscous was brought ashore by some of the many Jewish migrants who settled in Sicily and its offshore islands over the centuries.

But it is more likely that couscous traversed the waters, in both directions, between Sicily and its North African trading partners and neighbours (what are now Tunisia, Libya, Algeria and Egypt). History supports this hypothesis. In the 11th century, the Arab-Islamic conquest helped disseminate couscous around the North African region and the development of wheat farming further accelerated this expansion.

During the Norman epoch, which began in 1129, Roger II of Sicily conquered and took control of what is now Tunisia. He was reputed to have encouraged people from different traditions and religions to contribute their wisdom and experiences to the enrichment of his court. In this period of medieval enlightenment, Jews, Muslims and Christians lived in harmony in Sicily.

I don't want to eat it. I just want to lie down beside it.
– Old Turkish saying about couscous

Sardinians call their couscous *cascá*. They also have *fregula* (or *fregola*), pellets similar to couscous, and the larger *fregulone*. *Fregula* is made with wheat semolina in the same way as couscous and is then dried in the oven and slightly toasted. Some Sardinians mix a little finely ground saffron into the semolina before making the *fregula*. The pellets are boiled, drained and served like pasta.

Could the origins be Roman? In the cookbook by Apicius there are a number of dishes that are similar to couscous, including one that uses breadcrumbs instead of grain. Wheat was grown in the Roman world in North Africa, Egypt, Sicily and Tuscany (where *manfregoli* are very similar to couscous – the Emilia Romagnia version are called *manfrigoli*).

Couscous as prepared in Sicily

Couscous in Sicily is considered to be a specialty of Trapani and other places along the north and northwest coast, from Castellammare del Golfo (north of Trapani) through Marsala, Mazara and Selinunte and to Sciacca.

Irrespective of its origins, the Arabs would have used lamb and possibly chicken to make the broth to accompany the couscous. But with the abundance of fish in Sicily this changed, and it evolved into the typical dish from Trapani province where it is served with broth made with fish.

Apart from the common practice of forming couscous into pellets, the Trapani version differs greatly from that made in Algeria, Tunisia and Morocco. Couscous in North African countries is traditionally steamed over a fairly liquid stew of meat and/or vegetables which gives aroma and flavour to the couscous.

In Sicily couscous is steamed over water and the fish and broth are cooked separately. Traditionally, the fish used is the best quality and is discarded; the broth is poured over the couscous and left to be absorbed.

Although couscous in Sicily is traditionally made with fish, it continues to evolve and is coming closer to its African roots. Between Tunisia and the Sicilian cities on the north and northwest coasts there are established links with fishermen, traders and commuters. Now that many of the migrants who work on the fishing fleets and in vineyards in Sicily are living in these cities, it is not unusual to eat different versions of couscous, sweet and savoury and made with fish or meat.

The process of making and preparing couscous
Very few Sicilians now make hand-rolled couscous, except for special occasions, and it is easy to understand why. When I have eaten it in Mazara del Vallo and in Marsala I had to pre-order it the day before. In some restaurants it is only available on Fridays, the designated day for eating fish couscous, a legacy from days of abstinence.

Forming the pellets
Preparations can take a good part of a whole day. I describe the following method for making the couscous and how it is cooked purely for interest. It truly is a labour of love.

The tiny balls of dough (the couscous pellets) are formed in a ceramic bowl (in Sicily it is called *maffaradda*) by pressing and agitating the rough ground semolina around with one hand and using the other hand to sprinkle it with a little water, salt and a little flour – the couscous pellets are formed by the action of the hand and the finger tips rubbing the mixture (this phase is called *l'incocciata*). The couscous is run through a sieve – those that fall through the holes are too small and get shaped again. Once the couscous is formed, it is rested for about an hour before steaming.

The equipment and steaming of couscous in Sicily

The word couscous is said to derive from the Arabic word *kaskasa* (meaning minced into small bits) and *kiskis*, the Arabic name for the perforated earthenware pot in which it steams. We are more familiar with the French names for the pot, *couscousière* and *couscoussier*. Most modern pots are made of metal; the more expensive versions are copper. The Sicilians use one made of pottery called a *cuscusera*, which consists of two parts: the *pignata*, the colander-like top in which the couscous is placed to steam, and a saucepan of the same dimensions which fits underneath to hold the water. A makeshift *couscousière* can be made by placing a colander or a metal steamer over a similar-sized pot. The perforated pan can be lined with a fine piece of dampened cheesecloth or muslin. The edges of the cloth pulled over the top of the couscous help to seal the pot.

Because the *pignata* has large holes on the bottom, it is customary to line it with fresh bay leaves to prevent the pellets from falling into the bottom pan. The herbs also impart flavour and aroma. The couscous is sealed and covered, and left undisturbed to steam. In order to prevent steam from escaping, the gap between the *pignata* and the lower pan is sealed with a strip of dough made of flour and water. Even this has a name. It is called a *cuddura*. The *cuddura* is made from 2 cups of flour and enough water to create a sticky putty-like paste, rolled into a long rope. The couscous in the *pignata* is also tightly covered.

The couscous is seasoned with extra virgin olive oil, salt and pepper (some variations include onion), sealed and steamed on gentle heat for 1½ hours. Once cooked, it is covered (with a lid and wrapped in plastic or foil) and then wrapped in blankets and allowed to rest for 1 more hour.

Next the couscous is placed in a large bowl (some recipes suggest using the *mafaradda)*, the fish broth (drained from the stew) is ladled over and the bowl is again wrapped in blankets and left to stand for at least another 30–40 minutes, while the pellets absorb the broth.

In Morocco and the Middle East, the couscous is prepared in several stages. The process is even more laborious – it is first wetted, then steamed uncovered, spread out and reworked, allowed to rest and steamed again.

Cùscusu

The recipe

If you wish to use instant couscous, follow the instructions on the packet: most suggest soaking it for a very short time and then tossing in butter. Alternatively you could soak it in some of the braising liquid and add a little extra virgin olive oil instead of butter. The pea-size couscous known as Lebanese couscous (*maghrabiyeh* or *moghrabyeh*) is favoured by some restaurants because it looks good on the plate and only requires boiling. It is the one used in this recipe. Israeli couscous is also cooked like pasta but requires less time. Both are sturdy enough to be cooked in two stages.

Suitable fish

In most traditional Sicilian recipes, various whole fish are used to make the stew, which is then strained. Some of the cooked fish is filleted and eaten, but most is discarded, having served its purpose of flavouring the broth. I like to serve the fish as well. Doing this will influence what fish you choose. For a stronger flavour, I add fish stock (made earlier) rather than water. In some lavish recipes, prawns (shrimp), calamari, cockles and mussels are also added. Different types of fish may require different cooking times – time the cooking so the thicker fish is put on first, then stagger according to cooking times.

Method

Make the fish stock beforehand. Alternatively, fish heads can be used for flavour and then removed before adding the extra fish.

The fish

In a large saucepan sauté the onion and parsley in the olive oil until the onion turns golden. Add the tomatoes, garlic, the bay leaves and 5 cups of fish stock. Season and bring to the boil. Add the fish (staggering the timing for different types, if necessary) and reduce the heat. Cover and poach the fish until done (Italians cook it for a long time). Take 2 cups of the liquid, strained, for cooking the couscous.

Ingredients

5 cups fish stock (see recipe,
    page 159) or water
1 large onion, chopped
½ cup finely cut parsley
½ cup extra virgin olive oil
4 large ripe tomatoes, peeled
    and chopped
2 cloves garlic, chopped
2 bay leaves
1.5kg (3lb 5oz) fish, cut
    into large chunks (if using
    whole fish, keep heads
    separate)
salt and chilli flakes to taste

THE COUSCOUS
400g (14oz) Lebanese
    couscous
1 onion, finely chopped
½ cup parsley, finely chopped
10–15 bay leaves
2–3 cloves garlic, chopped
¾ cup extra virgin olive oil
salt to taste

THE COUSCOUS

Stage 1

Parboil the *maghrabiyeh* in salted water in order to soften it so it absorbs the spices and broth; bring the salted water to a boil, add a tablespoon of oil and cook like pasta for about 10 minutes – it will be partly cooked. Drain and set the couscous aside.

Separate the grains using a large fork or with your hands. You may need to add a little more extra virgin olive oil to facilitate the process.

Stage 2

Heat the rest of the olive oil in a large pan and add the onion, parsley, garlic and seasoning. Stir gently until thoroughly mixed.

Add the drained couscous. Stir with a large wooden spoon.

Gently add the 2 cups of fish broth to the couscous. Cover and cook until it is done, checking it every 10 minutes or so (a little more broth can be added if necessary). Taste and adjust seasonings. The couscous should gradually absorb all the liquid.

SERVING SUGGESTIONS

When ready to serve, take the fish from the liquid and remove bones. Strain the broth.

Place the couscous on a large platter. Arrange the fish on top and pour over some of the hot broth. Serve with a jug of broth and a small bowl of chilli flakes mixed with a little broth (to soften). Let guests serve themselves.

VARIATIONS

- Add to the couscous pellets: 50 –100g (1¾–3½oz) chopped blanched almonds before the resting phase (a variation from Erice, north of Trapani) or a sprinkle of ground cinnamon or cloves just before serving.
- Add any of the following to the fish stew: 1–2 pinches of saffron, 1 cinnamon stick, basil leaves and/or 1 cup white wine (use less stock).

As an exceptional treat, Enzo had made couscous with eight different kinds of fish, but only for his favourite customers. These, of course, included the inspector, who, the moment he saw the dish in front of him and inhaled its aroma, was overcome with emotion. Enzo noticed but, luckily, misunderstood.

'Your eyes are shining, Inspector! Got a touch of fever, by chance?'

'Yes,' he lied without hesitation. He scarfed down two helpings. Afterwards, he shamelessly declared that a few mullets might be a nice idea.

– Andrea Camilleri, *The Patience of the Spider*

Scuntuonnu

Vegetable dishes

A VEGETABLE SIDE DISH IS CALLED A *CONTORNO*. IT HELPS TO SHAPE AND DEFINE THE MEAL AND IS INTENDED TO COMPLEMENT THE MAIN COURSE. MAIN COURSES ARE GENERALLY SERVED ON THEIR OWN WITH VEGETABLES AS A SIDE DISH SO THAT ALL THE FLAVOURS ARE DISTINCTIVE AND DO NOT SWAMP ONE ANOTHER.

Italians, like all good cooks, try to achieve an overall balance in the meal – not just in the flavours, textures and colours, but also in the ratio of vegetables to starch and protein. It is quite usual to serve more than one *contorno*, especially if the other courses do not contain vegetables or fruits. If you have eaten pasta for the first course, you probably won't be served potatoes (they are both starchy). Italians are also very mindful of not duplicating the same ingredients, even to the point of varying herbs in the different courses.

Assai terra, poca terra: poca terra, assai terra. (Sicilian proverb)
A lot of land, a little land: a little land, a lot of land.

A *contorno* can also double as an antipasto – for example, a bowl of roasted peppers or a stuffed tomato could be either. In Sicilian homes, an antipasto is rarely served; if it is, it will be just a bite. This is because it is customary to eat pasta before the main course and Sicilians see no point in spoiling dinner. But on festive occasions, the antipasto is a more elaborate affair, particularly in Sicilian restaurants where there is a self-service table called a *tavola fredda*.

What you produce from your land depends on how you treat it. Sicily has short mild winters and abundant sunshine for most of the year, the warm weather often stretching well into autumn. Most food crops – particularly vegetables such as peppers, eggplants, tomatoes and zucchini – grow to full-flavoured ripeness well before and after what would be their normal season in the rest of Italy.

There are numerous greenhouse farms (called *serre*) in Sicily and masses of vegetables are exported to Europe and the rest of Italy. .

Because of the favourable climate and the quality of its soil, Sicily is focusing increasingly on organic produce. It is Italy's second most prominent producer of organic foods after Sardinia. Of all the regions of Italy, Sicily has more than a third of Italy's total number of organic farms and many others are currently changing over from traditional methods. Some are converting to biodynamic methods of agriculture.

Fichi d'India (prickly pears)
Pericolosi ma deliziosi.
Dangerous but delicious.

Zia Niluzza has always been concerned about her health and tries to use as much produce as possible from farmers who believe that healthy soils and contented animals make healthy people. She says that many of the fruit and vegetable growers she knows still use the phases of the moon to determine auspicious planting, cultivating and harvesting times. These growers continue to grow vegetables as they have always done and many refuse to use modern ways. They may not know that they are growing their food biodynamically – or even be familiar with the term.

Her idea of quality fresh fruit and vegetables is different from what others may see as excellence. She often rejects large, uniform shapes and is more concerned about the freshness, the fragrance, and whether they have been nourished with non-chemical fertilisers and harvested in the correct season. She will tell you that the flavours of such produce is better and that it will keep fresh for longer – and, most importantly, that her health is better because of it.

What Zia Niluzza is not able to get directly from producers, she buys from her trusted seller of fruit and vegetables, the *ortolano*, who comes around in his van. Every morning, except Sunday, there is the squawk of the *ortolano* below my relatives' apartment in Ragusa. He announces himself in the very nasal Sicilian spoken by Ragusani, yelling out his list of produce.

In the early days, my two aunties and my cousin Franca, who live in neighbouring apartments, would go out onto their balconies and subject the *ortolano* to detailed questions about the quality of his produce. If satisfied, they lowered baskets tied to the end of ropes. They would haul up the filled baskets, examine the contents and only then, if they were satisfied, did they lower their baskets again with the money tucked inside. Anything that did not meet their exacting standards was sent down again and, if all went well with the sale, the change would be sent up. Then the aunties would make special requests for the next day, entreating him to visit them first so that they could have their choice of the freshest and the best. The noise would start up again almost immediately, as the *ortolano* made his sales pitch to others further down the street.

There is only one aunt now (Zia Niluzza) and Franca no longer lowers baskets from their balcony. Now they go down in their dressing gowns and slippers. The *ortolano* has a bigger van and comes earlier so they get the best produce from his trusted, best growers. The deal done, they wave him goodbye.

Alla braci

Alla brace or arrostiti

ALLA BRACE (ITALIAN) MEANS COOKING 'OVER COALS'. IN A HOME KITCHEN SOME FORM OF GRILLING IS DONE ON THE STOVE ON A GRILL PAN, AND IN FACT MOST ITALIANS GRILL THEIR FOOD THIS WAY IF AN OPEN FIRE IS NOT AVAILABLE. EVEN IN ENGLISH THERE ARE DIFFICULTIES WITH THE WORD ROASTING – IT CAN MEAN COOKING OVER AN OPEN FIRE, BUT IS ALSO USED FOR BAKING.

Pipi arrustuti

Peperoni arrostiti

ROASTED OR GRILLED PEPPERS (CAPSICUM)

I have always thought that 'charred peppers' is a much better name and description for this dish. The peppers are cooked whole to preserve the taste and juices and they acquire a smoky flavour when grilled over a flame or direct heat. They can also be cooked directly in a bed of white, hot embers. A barbecue is ideal – the peppers cook in their own juice and the flesh is protected by the skin. Do not rinse the peeled peppers.

METHOD

Place the peppers on a barbecue grill and cook over intense heat until the skin is well blistered and puffy. Turn them from time to time to ensure even blistering and charring. As you remove the charred peppers from the heat, place them in a bowl covered with a plate or lid – they will keep on cooking and will be easier to peel (leave for at least 10 minutes).

Grill the tomatoes in the same way. The skin will split and char very quickly – they only need 1–2 minutes cooking.

Peel off the skins of the peppers and tomatoes, scraping away as much charred skin as possible. Split the peppers and scrape out the seeds. Tear the peppers and tomatoes into rough strips and place in a bowl. Add the garlic and basil to the bowl. Dress with oil and season; leave to marinate for at least 30 minutes before serving. They taste even better the next day.

VARIATIONS

- Some Catanesi use mint rather than the basil.
- My relatives in Ragusa add a squeeze of lemon juice before serving – this is quite common in other parts of Sicily, especially in the south.

INGREDIENTS

6 peppers, any colour – use a
    mixture of colours (red are
    the sweetest)
2 whole, firm red tomatoes
3 cloves garlic, sliced
about ¾ cup basil leaves,
    torn
½ cup extra virgin olive oil
salt and black pepper

Cacuoccili arrustuti

Carciofi arrostiti alla brace

ROASTED OR GRILLED ARTICHOKES

Globe artichokes have been around for a long time. The Romans called them *cynara*, the Arabs *al kharsciuf* (which sounds more like the Italian *carciofo*). They contain a chemical called cynarin that is said to stimulate the production of bile. This is why artichokes are often used as the basis of *digestivi* (drinks that aid the digestion), a vital issue for the Italians (and the French). There are *digestivi* that prepare the stomach before eating (*aperitivi*) and those drunk after eating (*amari*, literally 'bitters').

Many will be familiar with Cynar, the Italian artichoke-based alcoholic *aperitivo* manufactured by Campari in Milan. There are many *amari* produced all over Italy, but Averna, the *amaro siciliano*, is a specialty of Caltanissetta (in the centre of Sicily) and is a real indulgence.

PREPARING ARTICHOKES FOR COOKING

Artichokes in Sicily are sold with long stalks often up to 1 metre (39in) long. Never discard the stalks – they are particularly wonderful added to artichoke *risotti* and braises, and, cooked, to a frittata. Remove the stalk at the base of the artichoke, clean and trim with a small sharp knife, pulling away the tough, stringy outer skin – this will expose the light-coloured centre, which is very flavourful and tender.

Working from the base, pull the tough outside leaves off the artichoke one by one, until you reach the paler, less fibrous centre. Then trim about 1cm (½in) across the top. To prevent discolouration, keep the prepared artichokes in acidulated water as you work. When ready to cook, drain by inverting the artichokes upside down for about 5 minutes. Alternatively, rub the cut surfaces with a lemon.

If you wish to stuff the artichokes, bang each on a hard surface and then gently ease the leaves apart to expose the heart (placing the artichokes in warm acidulated water makes it easier to pull apart the leaves). I start by easing the

MENU FOR GIOVANNI VERGA

Verga (1840–1922) stayed close to Catania where he was born and immersed himself in peasant life, writing social histories of fishermen, shepherds and small town people. He is best known for his novel I Malavoglia *(The Medlar Tree) and the short story* La Cavallaria Rusticana, *which he later adapted to an opera.*

Roasted or grilled artichokes
(*Cacuoccili arrustuti*)
Pasta with sardines and peas
(*Pasta ca nocca*)
Fish *alla matalotta* (*Pisci a la matalotta*)
Salad of boiled green beans
(*Fasulinu vugghiutu*)

outer leaves and working my way to the centre. There may or may not have a fuzzy choke, depending on the maturity of the plant. If there is, remove it with a teaspoon, carefully turning it without snapping the sides of the choke.

Preparing the base of the artichoke

At the markets in Italy you see men and women sitting with mounds of artichokes, skilfully wielding very sharp kitchen knives to pare off the leaves and expose the bases of mature artichokes, which are called *fondi di carciofi*. The *fondi* can be stuffed, braised, sautéed, added to frittata – their intense flavour and meaty texture are a definite taste sensation.

At the end of the season, when the artichokes are large and past their prime, they are trimmed even further. If we do not live in Italy, we have to do this ourselves. Pare off the leaves of a mature artichoke and just leave the base (no leaves) – it will look like a very shallow cup. The texture of the base will be covered with a pattern of small dots much like the eyes of flies (like a fine etching, delicate and quite beautiful).

To grill plain artichokes

If you intend to grill artichokes on a barbecue, they must be young and tender. Cook with or without stuffing. Traditionally they are kept whole. It is not necessary to remove the tough outer leaves – these will char and can be removed before eating the softer inner leaves and the heart.

Remove the stalks so the artichokes stand upright. Trim about 1cm (½in) from the top, ease the centres open, sprinkle generously with salt and pepper and drizzle about a tablespoon of oil into each artichoke between the leaves.

Place them upright on a solid bed of coals which have burned down to ash – set the artichokes directly in the ashes and give them a turn every once in a while so they cook evenly, adding more oil as they cook. The artichokes are ready when they are completely charred outside. To eat, discard the charred outer leaves to reveal the tender centre.

If using a gas or electric barbecue, grill on low to medium heat. They need to cook for at least 15 minutes on the bottom, and then equal time on each side (baste with a little oil). To test, prick them with the tip of a knife – it should slide in without much resistance and the leaves should come away with a gentle pull.

A less traditional method is to partly cook the artichokes for 15 minutes in some salted water with a dash of vinegar (the acidulated water prevents

SUMMER MENU

Rolled eggplants with a stuffing (*Mulinciani ammugghiati*)
Seafood salad (*'Nzalata di mare*)

discolouration, but don't use lemon juice, which can taste bitter). The artichoke should be softened, but not fully cooked. Drain well by placing upside down, and then either cook whole or cut the artichoke in half lengthways and proceed as above until brown and charred on the outside.

Usually the artichokes are served with a simple *salmoriglio* dressing (see page 256), but I like the mint dressings as well (see page 268).

STUFFED GRILLED ARTICHOKES

In Catania a common method of making grilled artichokes even more interesting is to stuff about two teaspoons of a mixture of finely chopped garlic, parsley and seasoning between the leaves.

When artichokes are stuffed for braising, a small amount of breadcrumbs are mixed with herbs. Some Sicilians do the same thing with grilled artichokes. Some chopped anchovies may be added or mint rather than parsley.

Always sprinkle generously with salt and pepper and drizzle about a tablespoon of olive oil into each artichoke between the leaves and on top of the stuffing before grilling.

Mulinciani, cucuzzeddi e funci 'nta braci

Melanzane, zucchine e funghi arrostiti

GRILLED EGGPLANTS, ZUCCHINI AND MUSHROOMS

Peppers are grilled whole (see recipe, page 300), but eggplants and zucchini are sliced. They are often served with *salmoriglio* dressing (see page 256).

The method of baking slices of eggplants or zucchini is not used in Italy – grilled means having grill marks from cooking over an open flame or in the home kitchen on a *ferro*, grill pan. I have a commercial 'open BBQ grill' (also called a contact grill or a high-powered sandwich press), which works extremely well for slices of eggplants and zucchini. Like all *contorni*, eat them at room temperature. When cooking, turn them only once.

EGGPLANTS (AUBERGINE)

Slice the eggplant lengthways. Put the slices in salted water, weigh down with an upside-down plate, and let sit for 30 minutes. It is not always necessary to soak them to remove the bitter taste, but it prevents the eggplant from discolouring when cooked. Dry on paper towels. Brush with olive oil and place, oil-side-down, on a hot grill. Cook until grill marks appear and the eggplant is slightly golden on that side. Then turn over and cook the other side.

ZUCCHINI (COURGETTES)

Sprinkle the slices with a little salt on one side. Rest for 10 minutes, pat dry to remove the beads of moisture and grill as for eggplants.

MUSHROOMS

Remove the mushrooms stems and clean the heads with a damp cloth. Brush them with olive oil, sprinkle with salt and pepper, and place the oiled side on the grill. Cook on both sides, turning delicately and brushing with oil again.

Fritti

Fried

ONE OF THE BEST FRIED DISHES IS SLICED EGGPLANTS (AUBERGINES) AND ZUCCHINI (COURGETTES) PREPARED AS FOR GRILLING, AND FRIED IN HOT EXTRA VIRGIN OLIVE OIL. EGGPLANT AND ZUCCHINI *IMPANATE* (ITALIAN FROM *PANE*, BREAD) ARE ALSO CALLED *MELANZANE A COTOLETTA*. THEY ARE PREPARED AS ABOVE, BUT BEFORE COOKING EACH SLICE IS DIPPED IN LIGHTLY BEATEN EGG, WHICH HAS BEEN SEASONED WITH A LITTLE SALT, AND THEN COATED WITH FINE DRIED BREADCRUMBS MIXED WITH A LITTLE GRATED PECORINO OR *PARMIGIANO*. THEY ARE SHALLOW-FRIED IN HOT EXTRA VIRGIN OLIVE OIL. TURN ONLY ONCE AND DRAIN WELL.

MENU FOR TORNATORE

Raised in Bagheria outside Palermo, Guiseppe Tonatore directed the Oscar-winning Nuovo Cinema Paradiso. He makes films that confront difficult truths about Sicilian life. This menu has some strong flavours to match the strong spirit he displays in his films.

Sweet and sour onions
(*Cipudduzzi all'auruduci*)
Pasta with *bottarga* (*Pasta ca buttarga*)
Tuna with peppers (*Tunnu che pipi*)
Potato croquettes (*Cuzzili*)

Cazzilli
Crocchette di patate

POTATO CROQUETTES

Potato croquettes were the only way my mother cooked potatoes for guests. When I was a girl, my Anglo-Australian friends loved eating them. The mother of a Dutch friend also made them, but she used to include ham in hers. These are particularly nice eaten hot.

In Sicily, *cazzulli* are one of the common *cucina popolare*. They are fried in vats of hot olive oil and sold in the streets, usually in the evenings, wrapped in a little greaseproof paper. When cooking these at home, I use a non-stick frying pan and shallow fry them.

Sicilians have a fascination with body parts. *Cazzo* is slang for penis and the word most often used as a swear word. *Cazzili* are little penises, so when you are shaping the croquettes ready to fry, keep the shape in mind. I certainly did not have this information when, as a teenager, I was helping my mother to make them. I make oval ones.

To prevent them from becoming soggy, boil the potatoes whole and then peel them once cool.

METHOD

Cook the potatoes until soft. Peel when cool enough to handle and use a ricer or a mouli to mash them. Add the eggs, garlic, parsley and seasoning. Shape into patties and just before frying roll them in breadcrumbs or flour.

Heat some olive oil in a frying pan and fry until golden, turning once. Drain on absorbent paper.

INGREDIENTS

700g (1lb 9oz) potatoes
2 eggs, lightly beaten
2 cloves garlic, minced
½ cup parsley, finely cut
fine breadcrumbs or a little
    flour to coat the croquettes
extra virgin olive oil for
    frying
salt and freshly ground
    pepper

Vegetable dishes

Purpetti ri mulinciani

Polpette di melanzane

EGGPLANT (AUBERGINE) CROQUETTES

Eggplant croquettes, like *cazzili* are particularly good eaten hot and make a good antipasto. Like most fried food, they are served with lemon wedges.

INGREDIENTS

1kg (2lb 4oz) eggplants
2 eggs, lightly beaten
1 cup grated pecorino
2–3 cloves garlic, finely
   chopped
about ¾ cup finely cut basil
   leaves
1 or more cups fresh
   breadcrumbs
plain flour for coating
1–2 cups extra virgin olive oil
   for frying
salt and freshly ground
   pepper

METHOD

Slice the eggplants and cook them in boiling salted water until soft. Drain, cool and peel, then coarsely mash them in a large bowl.

Add the eggs, cheese, garlic, basil and seasoning and, to start with, ¾ cup of breadcrumbs. Add more breadcrumbs if necessary until you have a pliable but still soft consistency – the mixture needs to hold together. Form into oval patties about the size of an egg.

Coat the croquettes with a little flour. Heat the oil in a frying pan and fry the croquettes on each side until golden. Drain on paper towels and serve immediately.

VARIATIONS

꧁ Dip into 1 beaten egg, then into fine breadcrumbs before frying.
꧁ Add a few pine nuts to the mixture.
꧁ Serve with fresh mint leaves.

Brocculi a pastella

Fritelle di cavolfiore

CAULIFLOWER FRITTERS

Brucculi is Sicilian for cauliflowers but I use this same recipe for broccoli. Zucchini flowers can also be cooked the same way.

This is the traditional way of making fritters: dipping pre-cooked cauliflower florets into an egg batter moistened with a little water (Sicilians don't use milk in batters). Another method is to crumb the florets: dip each lightly in flour, then quickly dip into beaten egg and lastly into breadcrumbs seasoned with a little salt or grated cheese; shake off the excess before frying in very hot oil. They are best eaten hot.

METHOD

Break the cauliflower into florets and cook until just tender but still with a crunch. They are usually cooked in boiling salted water, but I prefer steaming. Drain and cool.

To make the batter, mix the flour and a pinch of salt and one of pepper in a bowl, make a well in the centre, add the eggs, and as much water as you need to make a soft batter. Leave it to stand for about 40 minutes.

In a frying pan, heat the olive oil to hot. Dip the cauliflower in the batter and drain off any excess. Alternatively, add the florets to the batter then pick out with a slotted spoon and drain. Drop them into the hot olive oil and fry until golden. Remove with a slotted spoon and drain on paper towels.

VARIATIONS

- Use this same recipe for broccoli.
- Zio Pippo always placed a small piece of anchovy inside each floret before dipping it in batter. He did this with zucchini flowers too.

INGREDIENTS

1 cauliflower, any colour
250g (9oz) plain flour
3 eggs, lightly beaten
1 cup extra virgin olive oil for frying
salt and black pepper

Ficato ri setti cannola

Fegato di sette cannoli

PUMPKIN WITH VINEGAR, MINT, SUGAR AND CINNAMON

Sali e misturi mitticcinni 'na visazza, falla comu voi, sempri è cucuzza. (Sicilian proverb)

Sale e misturi metti, cucinala come vuoi, ma resta sempre una zucca. (Italian)

Add salt and any mix of flavours, cook it how you like, but it will always be a pumpkin.

This is sometimes called *zucca in agro dolce* but I prefer the more colloquial Sicilian name, *ficato ri setti canola* – literally, 'liver of the seven spouts (or reeds)'. The dish is said to have originated among the poor, in what is known as one of the *quartieri svantaggiati* ('disadvantaged suburbs') of Palermo.

Sicilians are colourful characters and like stories. It is said that the pumpkin dish was first cooked and named by the herb vendors of the Piazza Garraffello, a small square in Palermo. These were the days before refrigeration and balconies and windowsills were often used to cool and store food, especially overnight. As the story goes, the herb sellers could often smell the aroma of veal liver coming from the balconies of the rich. At home, they cooked yellow pumpkin the same way as the well-to-do cooked liver (*fegato*) and, wanting to create a *bella figura*, they hoped the fragrance of their cooking would mislead the neighbours into thinking that they too were well-to-do and could afford to eat liver. The typical way of cooking liver is to slice it thinly, pan-fry it and then caramelise the juices in the pan with sugar and vinegar to make *agro dolce* (sweet and sour sauce).

As for the seven spouts (*sette cannoli*), they are the short cane-shaped spouts of an elegant 16th-century fountain in the piazza.

Ficato ri setti canola is a colourful and aromatic dish. There is the strong colour of the pumpkin, tinged brown at the edges, and contrasted with bright green mint, its sweetness enhanced by the flavours and fragrance of garlic, cinnamon and vinegar. It is better cooked ahead of time – the flavours intensify when left at least overnight, but it can be stored in the fridge for several days.

Some recipes suggest using *cucuzza russa* (red pumpkin). In Sicily I have seen an unusually shaped, two-coloured pumpkin that looks like an overfilled cupcake. I have recently discovered an heirloom variety called Turk's turban, which may be the same sort. I generally use the butternut or Jap pumpkin, which are bright orange with a dense texture (a watery pumpkin will not do).

The pumpkin is sliced 1cm (½in) thick and traditionally fried in very hot oil (if thicker, they take too long to cook).

Although baking the pumpkin slices is not traditional, I prefer this method. It certainly saves time in the preparation (see variation below). Serve it at room temperature as an antipasto or as a *contorno*.

INGREDIENTS

1kg (2lb 4oz) pumpkin
10 cloves garlic
extra virgin olive oil (1½ cup
  if frying, ¾ cup if baking)
1 tablespoon sugar
1 cup white wine vinegar
½ teaspoon ground cinnamon
small mint leaves
salt and freshly ground pepper

WINTER MENU

Pumpkin with vinegar, mint,
sugar and cinnamon *(Ficato ri
setti cannola)*
Rich fish soup from Syracuse
cooked in the oven *(Zuppa di
pisci a sirausana 'o fornu)*
Green leaf salad – with bitter
leaves *('Nzalata virdi)*

METHOD

Peel and remove the seeds of the pumpkin and cut into 1cm (½in) slices. Peel and slice 4 cloves of garlic.

Heat the olive oil in a large heavy-based frying pan. Add the garlic cloves. Remove when it has coloured and fry the pumpkin slices, until they become soft and begin to colour around the edges; turn them only once in case they break. Add salt to taste. Remove the pumpkin and discard some of the oil, but keep any juices.

Use the same frying pan for the *agro dolce* sauce: add the sugar, stir it around the pan to caramelise it, and then add the vinegar and cinnamon. Stirring constantly, allow the sauce to thicken slightly as the vinegar reduces. Add the remaining garlic cloves and few sprigs of mint to the warm sauce.

Add the pumpkin to the sauce, and sprinkle with pepper. Allow the sauce to penetrate the pumpkin on very low heat for a few minutes. Alternatively, pour the sauce over the pumpkin and turn the slices a couple of times. Cool and store in the fridge once cool. Eat at room temperature.

When ready to serve, arrange the slices in a serving dish, remove the old mint (it would have discoloured). Scatter slices of fresh garlic and fresh mint leaves on top and in between the slices.

VARIATION

🌿 To bake the pumpkin, cut into thicker slices, about 2–3cm (¾–1in). Sprinkle with salt and place on an oiled baking tray. Bake the pumpkin and garlic in a 200°C (400°F) oven (discard the garlic when the pumpkin has cooked). Make the *agro dolce* sauce (see the above) in the baking tray instead of a frying pan.

🌿 I like the look and the taste of fresh bay leaves and bake some with the pumpkin and/or add them to the sauce.

'O furnu
Al forno

THESE ARE THE CATEGORY OF VEGETABLE DISHES THAT ARE BAKED IN THE FURNU (OR FUORNU) OR OVEN. THEY INCLUDE SUBSTANTIAL DISHES SUCH AS PARMIGIANA DI MELANZANE AND THE MUCH SIMPLER STUFFED TOMATOES. I ALWAYS FEEL I HAVE GREATER CONTROL OF REGULATING TEMPERATURES AND ESTIMATING COOKING TIMES WHEN I USE MY HOTPLATE, BUT MAYBE THIS IS BECAUSE I GREW UP IN AN ENVIRONMENT WHERE THE OVEN WAS RARELY USED.

Turticedda ri finocchiu

Tortino di finocchi

FENNEL TORTINO

A *torta* is a torte or a cake in Italian; it can also be a savoury – for example, a *torta di verdura* (a vegetable flan or pie). A *tortino* is usually smaller than a *torta* and it can be less substantial. (In Italian, when you add *-ino* to the end of a word, it indicates it is a diminutive. Remember the tiny Topolino cars? *Topo* is Italian for mouse, so the Topolino is a small mouse, an appropriate name for a very tiny car.)

In this recipe, the layers of cooked fennel and breadcrumbs form the *tortino*, which can be cut into slices. There are similar dishes called a *sformato* or a *pasticcio*, which are basically the same thing. The fennel is braised and can be cooked beforehand and left until you are ready to assemble the dish. This is a very versatile recipe and can be served hot and cold, and as an antipasto.

METHOD

Preheat the oven to 180°C (350°F).

Thinly slice the fennel lengthways and finely chop the soft green leaves. Sauté the fennel in the extra virgin olive oil until it is slightly softened and coloured. Add salt and pepper and a little water (or use stock or white wine), cover with a lid and cook for another 10 minutes (it will finish cooking in the oven).

Oil the bottom and sides of an ovenproof dish (I use one which is about 10cm/4in deep), or line it with baking paper. Lard was used once, as is common in many of the older traditional recipes. Sprinkle 2 tablespoons of the breadcrumbs over the greased surface of the baking dish.

Mix the remaining breadcrumbs with the parsley, garlic and pecorino. Place a layer of the fennel in the baking dish, then the breadcrumb mixture, another layer of fennel and repeat until you have used up all the ingredients,

INGREDIENTS

2–3 large fennel bulbs, about 500g (17½oz) each

about ¾ cup extra virgin olive oil, plus extra

about 2 cups coarse breadcrumbs, made from day-old bread

1 cup finely cut parsley

3–4 cloves garlic, finely chopped

1½ cups grated pecorino

salt and freshly ground pepper

finishing with breadcrumbs. Compress the layers with your hands and drizzle some extra virgin olive oil over the top.

Cover with a layer of baking paper or foil and then with a heavy lid or a plate with a weight on top. The liquid needs to reduce, so the fennel should not be completely covered – there should be a thin gap between the weight and the side of the pan.

Place the dish in the preheated oven for 40–50 minutes. If the fennel is not cooked (it should be soft) or if it appears too dry, add a little more liquid, cover and return to the oven.

Remove the cover, drizzle with some extra virgin olive oil and bake for a further 10 minutes until it is golden on top and all the liquid has evaporated – the *tortino* should resemble a moist cake. Leave in the baking dish until ready to serve. Cut it into slices – lift the slices out carefully.

Pumarori chini

Pomodori ripieni

BAKED STUFFED TOMATOES

Stuffing tomatoes was one of my childhood tasks. Although adding black olives, grated cheese and anchovies are common, my family liked the fresh taste of the tomatoes and herbs and only added these ingredients when the stuffed tomatoes were to accompany a dish of strong flavours. The tomatoes can be served warm or cold as a *contorno* or as an antipasto.

INGREDIENTS

6 firm ripe tomatoes
3 cloves garlic, finely chopped
½ cup finely cut parsley
1 cup extra virgin olive oil
1 cup breadcrumbs, made
   from day-old bread
1 tablespoon fresh oregano,
   finely chopped, or
   ½ teaspoon dried oregano
½ cup capers, rinsed and
   soaked if salted
salt and freshly ground
   pepper

METHOD

Preheat the oven to 180°C (350°F). Halve the tomatoes crossways, scoop out the seeds and leave them upside down to drain.

Sauté the garlic and the parsley in a little of the oil. Cool, then add the sautéed garlic and parsley to the breadcrumbs, oregano, capers, some of the oil and seasoning. Fill the tomatoes with the mixture but don't press it down – it will expand as it cooks.

Arrange the stuffed tomatoes in an oiled baking pan and dribble a little olive oil over each. Bake for about 30 minutes, until the breadcrumbs are golden.

VARIATIONS

- Add ½ cup of grated pecorino, ½ cup of chopped black olives or some finely chopped anchovies to the stuffing mixture.
- Fresh basil always goes well with tomatoes: serve with some leaves around the cooked tomatoes.

Mulinciani ammugghiati

Involtini di melanzane

ROLLED EGGPLANTS (AUBERGINES) WITH A STUFFING

There are many recipes for stuffed eggplant (*involtini*). The most famous are *melanzane a beccafico* (a small, migratory fig-eating bird: *becca* is peck and *fico* a fig). The rich stuffed the birds (with parsley, bread, currants, pinenuts and pecorino). The poor substituted sardines for the birds (see *Sarde a beccafico* page 150) and the poorer still used slices of eggplants.

A different recipe comes from Enna in the centre of Italy. Two slices of lightly fried eggplants enclose a simpler stuffing of chopped herbs and fresh pecorino. The slices are dipped in egg, coated with breadcrumbs and fried.

I prefer the method used in the west of Sicily: each slice of fried egglant is rolled around the stuffing (sometimes covered with a tomato salsa) and baked.

METHOD

Prepare the eggplant slices (see page 305) and lightly fry. For the stuffing, mix together the herbs, garlic, capers (or pine nuts) and the oil. Place a spoonful of the stuffing on each slice of eggplant. Lay a slice of pecorino on top. Roll up each eggplant around the stuffing. Arrange each roll in a baking dish with a bay leaf separating each or, cover each roll with the tomato sauce. Cover with foil and when ready, bake in a 180°C (350°F) oven for 20–30 minutes.

VARIATIONS

- Add chopped anchovies to the stuffing.
- Use a stronger tasting cheese, such as aged pecorino or provolone.

INGREDIENTS

6–12 eggplant slices, lightly fried

herbs – chopped parsley and either basil or mint

2 cloves garlic, finely chopped

2 tablespoons capers or pine nuts

½ cup extra virgin olive oil

6–12 thin slices pecorino

10 fresh bay leaves

about 1 cup thick tomato sauce (made with chopped peeled tomatoes, oil, basil, garlic and seasoning)

Mulinciani o cucuzzeddi a la parmiciana

Parmigiana di melanzane or di zucchine

EGGPLANT (AUBERGINE) OR ZUCCHINI (COURGETTE) PARMIGIANA

A *parmigiana* made with eggplants or with zucchini is a very common *contorno* all over Sicily. (See variation below if using zucchini.) I also like to serve it at the start of a meal or as a light lunch.

The dish does not contain *parmigiano* nor does it originate in Parma, the home of *parmigiano* and *prosciutto di Parma*. It is an old Sicilian dish, most likely an adaptation of the fried eggplant dishes introduced by the Persians. One common dish still prepared today in Iran is *kashk-e baadenjaan*, which consists of layers of fried eggplants (*baadenjaan* in Iranian), covered with thick whey (*kashk*, an Iranian-type of yoghurt) and then sprinkled with mint.

The layers of eggplants resemble the horizontal slats of the louvres attached to the outside of houses for blocking sunlight while allowing ventilation. These are called *parmiciane* (in old Sicilian and *persiane* in Italian), in English commonly called Persian blinds or *persiennes* (from the French) – consequently, the name *mulinciani a parmiciana*, later distorted in translation from the Sicilian into Italian to *parmigiana*. The Italian word for eggplant is *melanzana* (*Solanum melongena*), but it was once called *malum insanum*, the mad apple or apple of madness. It belongs to the nightshade family (which is poisonous and can be fatal) and was thought to bring madness to those who ate it.

To make *parmigiana*, the eggplants are fried then layered; each layer is covered with a little tomato sauce, some grated pecorino and basil and then baked. In some parts of Sicily, instead of *pecorino*, fresh *tuma* or *primo sale* is used. Both are pecorino in different stages of production. *Primo sale* is the second stage of maturation when the first sprinkling of salt is added to the outside of the cheese. Pecorino *fresco* is more widely available and is a good substitute.

Traditionally, the eggplants are fried in plenty of oil, but a little oil in a non-stick frying pan can also achieve good results.

Salting slices of eggplants to remove bitter juices was once thought necessary for all eggplants, but fresh in-season eggplant is very unlikely to be bitter when cooked. But soaking slices of eggplants in salted water while you work will minimise the absorption of oil. My relatives in Sicily use the violet-coloured eggplants they call *violette*, which are seedless and sweet. An heirloom variety called *listada di gadia* is purple striped and almost seedless.

An Italian *signora* at the Queen Victoria Market in Melbourne told me how to tell if the eggplants are going to be good ones. As well as looking at the colour (shiny and deep purple), check the eggplant's belly button (the mark at the base where the blossom was). It should be either a narrow line or a line stretched into an oval shape, but never round (evidence of seeds). I must look odd when I shop for eggplants, turning them upside down to check their belly buttons!

Method

Slice the eggplants (and soak in salted water, optional). Pat dry gently, and fry the slices in olive oil, in several batches, until golden. Drain on paper towels.

For the sauce, heat a little of the olive oil over medium heat and sauté the garlic. When it is golden, remove and discard it. Add the tomatoes, some basil leaves and season with salt and pepper. Cook until thick.

Oil an ovenproof dish and cover its base with a thin layer of tomato sauce, add a layer of the eggplants, sprinkle with the cheese and a few basil leaves. Repeat until all the ingredients are used up and you have two to three layers, leaving a little cheese for the top. Bake for about 20 minutes in a 200°C (400°F) oven. Serve at room temperature garnished with basil leaves.

Variations

- Add slices of hard-boiled eggs between the layers.
- Just layer the fried eggplant with sauce and basil (no cheese or baking).

Ingredients

2 large eggplants, peeled and
    thinly sliced lengthways
about 1 cup extra virgin olive
    oil
1 clove garlic, peeled
1kg (2lb 4oz) ripe tomatoes,
    peeled, seeded and diced
    (or canned)
about 1 cup small basil leaves
¾ cup grated pecorino cheese
salt and freshly ground
    pepper

Sautati e in umitu

Saltati e in umido

THE CULINARY TERM FOR SAUTÉING AND BRAISING
VEGETABLES IS SOMETIMES N'TIANATI OR *IN TEGAME*
(ITALIAN). IN ENGLISH IT MEANS 'IN A PAN'. THE
VEGETABLES ARE FIRST SAUTÉED AND THEN BRAISED IN
A LITTLE LIQUID. SOMETIMES THEY ARE PARTLY COOKED
BEFORE BEING SAUTÉED.

Favuzzi o pisedda in umitu

Fave o piselli in umido

BRAISED BROAD BEANS OR PEAS

Young, tender and sweet broad beans (also called fava beans) or peas are a highlight in springtime. Sicilians love to eat them raw, sometimes as a teaser to the tastebuds. This is the most common way to cook broad beans or peas as a *contorno*. They are lightly sautéed, then braised in a little liquid. Using stock instead of water and adding pancetta are modern variations.

In spring, young broad beans and peas are sold in the pod. Prominent bulging shapes inside pods are a strong indication that the beans or peas are past their best and that flavour has been sacrificed for size.

My mother always double peels broadbeans. I must be lazy, because I only buy them when they are small and peel the odd big one.

METHOD

Double peel the broad beans if they are big. Sauté the onion in the olive oil, stirring frequently, until it is golden. Add the beans or peas, parsley and salt and pepper. Toss so they are well coated in the oil.

Moisten with stock (or white wine or water) and add bay leaves, cover and braise until cooked.

INGREDIENTS

2.5–3kg (5lb 8oz–6lb 10oz) fresh broad beans or peas, shelled
1 onion, finely sliced
½ cup extra virgin olive oil
¾ cup finely cut parsley or mint
½ cup stock (or white wine or water)
2 fresh bay leaves
salt and freshly ground pepper

A SAUTÉ OF SPRING VEGETABLES

There is no direct translation for the Sicilian *frittedda* – it implies something fried and the English word 'fritter' doesn't really capture it. *Frittedda* is exclusively Sicilian and is a luscious combination of spring vegetables lightly sautéed on very low heat and with a minimum amount of stirring so the textures and characteristic flavours of each ingredient – the sweetness of the peas, the slight bitterness of artichokes and the delicate, nutty taste of broad beans – are preserved. Each vegetable should be young and fresh.

The dish is usually made at the beginning of spring, around the feast day of San Giuseppe (19 March) when peas and broad beans come into season. It is thought that it originates around the northwestern part of Sicily from Palermo to Trapani, but I have found recipes from the agricultural areas in the centre of Sicily, in Caltanissetta, Enna and across to Agrigento.

Because *frittedda* is a celebration of spring I also include asparagus – this is definitely not traditional, but when I have defied the conventions and cooked this for my mother, a traditionalist who turns up her nose at experimentation in cooking (like all Sicilians), she seemed favourably impressed.

Having being brought up in Trieste, I often add a little strong stock for extra flavour, another break with tradition – Sicilians seldom add stock to vegetables and rely on their natural flavours. They believe the sun always shines in Sicily and so their produce tastes better (and they are right).

Like caponata, to fully appreciate the *frittedda*, it is best eaten cold and as a separate course – as an antipasto or *tramezzo* (an in-between course before the main).

INGREDIENTS

about 6 young tender
   artichokes
about ¾ cup extra virgin
   olive oil
6–8 spring onions (scallions),
   with green parts, chopped
1.5kg (3lb 5oz) peas
   (500g/17½oz shelled
   weight)
2kg (4lb 6oz) young broad
   beans (700g/1lb 9oz
   shelled weight); if they are
   large, double peel
1 tablespoon white wine
   vinegar or the juice of
   ½ lemon
about 1 teaspoon sugar
   (optional)
salt and freshly ground
   pepper

METHOD

Prepare the artichokes for cooking (see page 68). Slice lengthways into thin slices, cutting each quarter into three parts and ensuring that the leaves remain attached to their stems. Also use the stalk of the artichoke (stripped of its outer fibrous layer).

St Agata (died 251), patron saint of Catania, chose to dedicate herself to Christ. She rebuffed the Roman governor of Sicily, so he had her breasts cut off and put to death. St Lucia (283–304) of Syracus distributed her dowry to the poor and her spurned suitor denounced her as a Christian. Her eyes were plucked out, before being martyred. St Rosalia (1130–66), patron saint of Palermo, lived as hermit in a cave. In 1624, she miraculously saved Palermo from the plague. There are also snails for Rosalia, eye-shaped sweets for Lucia and breast-shaped cakes filled with almond paste in honour of Agata – nothing roasted or fried.

&

A sauté of spring vegetables
(*Frittedda*)
Rice with angels (*Risu cull'anciuli*) or
Small fish balls in fish broth
(*Polpettine in brodo di pesce*) or
Fish in a bain-marie (*Pisci a bagnumaria*)
Fennel tortino (*Turticedda ri finocchiu*)

Select a wide pan with a heavy bottom, heat the olive oil and sauté the onions until softened. Add the artichokes and cook them gently for about 5–7 minutes (tossing the pan, rather than stirring, and trying not to disturb the ingredients too much).

Before proceeding to the next stage, taste the artichokes, and if they need more cooking sprinkle them with about ½ cup of water, cover the saucepan with a lid and stew gently for about 10 minutes. The artichokes are cooked when there is only be a slight resistance when pricked with a fork.

Add the peas and broad beans and season with salt and pepper. Toss and shake the ingredients around gently to ensure that the vegetables do not stick. Cook for about 5–10 minutes. Add a dash of water (or stock) if needed.

Add a dash of white wine vinegar or the juice of ½ lemon at the end of cooking. You could also add a little sugar.

VARIATIONS

& Include 1 bunch or up to 500g (1lb 2oz) asparagus (green and/or white). Snap the bottoms from the asparagus and cut the spears into 2cm (¾in) lengths. Add the asparagus at the same time as the shelled vegetables.

& Some Sicilians use vinegar, others lemon juice and some include neither.

& The Palermitani add *agro dolce* sauce made with caramelised sugar and vinegar at the end of cooking instead of the separate vinegar and sugar.

& In Enna, in the centre of the island, wild fennel is added.

& I sometimes add a little grated nutmeg to accentuate the sweetness and sprinkle the *fritteda* with chopped mint to accentuate the freshness when I am ready to serve it.

Pipironata

Peperonata

BRAISED PEPPERS (CAPSICUMS)

Peperoni (peppers) are vibrantly coloured – green to red and yellow, dark purple and even cream. The green peppers are the immature forms that change colour as they ripen – this is why, towards the end of summer and the start of autumn, there are greater numbers of yellow and red peppers, which taste sweeter.

Peperonata is made with sweet red and yellow peppers. Include a few green ones if you wish for some variation in the colour. They are braised slowly and the results are wonderful. The longer thin pepper varieties, usually lime green, yellow or red in colour, are considered to be best for frying and are suitable for this recipe. Traditionally there are two ways of making *peperonata*. In the first, all the ingredients are placed in a wide pan and cooked over a very low heat for 45–60 minutes; a little water is added and it needs to be stirred periodically so it does not stick. The second method, the one I use, is to cook the onions before adding the peppers. *Peperonata* is served at room temperature and it keeps well in the fridge for four to five days.

METHOD

Sauté the onions in a saucepan with half the oil. When the onions are soft, add more oil, increase the heat and add the peppers. Add seasoning, toss on high heat until they are well coated and beginning to fry. Add the tomatoes, cover and cook for about 20 minutes until the peppers are soft. Remove the lid, increase the heat and cook until any excess liquid has evaporated.

VARIATIONS

- Lidia, my cousin from Augusta, always adds a teaspoon of sugar and a dash of vinegar to her *peperonata*.

INGREDIENTS

3 onions, sliced
½ cup extra virgin olive oil
*1.5kg (3lb 5oz) peppers, cut
  into thin strips*
*1–2 ripe tomatoes, peeled,
  seeded and diced*
5–6 basil leaves
*salt and freshly ground
  pepper*

In other parts of Sicily it is common to add 2–3 potatoes: either partly cooked chip-size added half way through cooking, or uncooked potatoes fried at the same time as the onions.

All Italians, including children, seem to attach great importance to food. Fried peppers (as in photo above) are popular fillings for a *panino* (a bread roll or thick slice). Years ago, I taught in a school where there was a large number of Italian students. One day a girl walked into the classroom, stopped suddenly, sniffed and wiggled her nose in several directions, and exclaimed (with envy), 'Mmmmm, mmmmm! I can smell *peperoni*. Who's got this in their bag for lunch?'

Cipudduzzi all'auruduci

Cipolline all'agrodolce

SWEET AND SOUR ONIONS

Travellers to Italy may have been fascinated to see round, flat-shaped onions in the markets. A heirloom variety called 'borettana yellow' is a similar shape. This dish can be made with any small onions, but the flat ones are beautiful.

METHOD

Partly cook the onions in boiling salted water for about 5 minutes; they should still be firm. Drain. Place in a wide saucepan (to allow greater evaporation) with the olive oil, vinegar, sugar, bay leaves and a splash of water. Cook, uncovered, on medium-high heat, shaking the pan often so the onions are evenly coated with the *agro dolce* sauce. Once the onions are cooked, reduce the liquid until it caramelises.

INGREDIENTS

1kg (2lb 4oz) small pickling
  onions, peeled
½ cup extra virgin olive oil
½ cup red vinegar, dry
  marsala or red wine
a splash of water
2 tablespoons sugar
4–5 bay leaves (preferably
  fresh)

Funci trifulati

Funghi trifolati

SAUTÉED MUSHROOMS

I particularly like collecting and cooking wild mushrooms. The taste, texture and the musty, rich smell of wild mushrooms are worlds aways from that of cultivated mushrooms. Wild mushrooms thrive when there has been significant rain followed by sunny days, and they start appearing in autumn. They will grow in the same place year after year. Of the two mushrooms I find in Australia, slippery jacks are not as tasty as the saffron-coloured pine mushrooms (or saffron milkcaps) but are still pungent.

Slippery jacks are similiar to *porcini* (*cepes*) and belong to the *Boletus* genus. The cap is a dark brown-orange to mustard colour and slippery in texture; it does not have gills but instead has a sponge-like mass under the cap. I prefer to eat them when they are very young and dense, either raw or cooked, and to dry larger ones and use them like their Italian cousins, dried *porcini* ('little pigs' because of their distinctive swollen stems).

To dry mushrooms, slice them finely and place in a single layer on a tray lined with several sheets of paper. Leave them to dry near a heater (but not too close) or in a well-ventilated room. Change the paper and turn them over every other day. Their flavour and texture become more intense. They can be stored in a jar, but make sure that they are well dried.

I like to cook different mushrooms together, whether cultivated and/or wild, to maximise the flavours, textures, smells and appearance.

INGREDIENTS

½ cup extra virgin olive oil
4 cloves garlic, chopped
1 cup finely cut parsley
1.5kg (3lb 5oz) mushrooms,
    cleaned and cut into
    1–2cm (½–¾in) slices
salt and freshly ground
    pepper

METHOD

Heat the oil and when hot, add garlic and stir over high heat for 30 seconds before adding the mushrooms. Add the parsley and seasoning. Stir well, and cook until the mushroms are soft. Remove from the pan and reduce the liquid. Return the mushrooms to the pan and serve with the juices.

Cucuzzedda o fasulinu co pumaroru

Zucchini o fagiolini con pomodoro

ZUCCHINI (COURGETTE) OR GREEN BEANS SAUTÉED WITH TOMATOES

Zucchini and beans are often cooked with tomatoes. The zucchini and tomatoes are combined and cooked together; the beans are pre-cooked and placed in a cooked tomato sauce. Both these *contorni* can be eaten either hot or cold.

ZUCCHINI SAUTÉED WITH TOMATOES

Always choose small zucchini (no more than 10–12cm/4–5in long). Sicilians are also fond of a round variety, which I have not seen in other parts of Italy. When one *zucchina* grows large it is called a *zucca* (*cucuzza* in Sicilian); the different squash are identified by colour – a pumpkin is called a *zucca gialla* (a yellow *zucca*). Also popular in Sicily is *zucca serpente*, a long, snake-like squash mainly used in a wet pasta dish. It is made with the *zucca* and the *tenerumi* (tendrils of the vine); both the *zucca* and the greens are considered to be *rinfrescanti* (refreshing, cleansing) for the body.

METHOD

Heat the oil in a saucepan and when it is hot add the zucchini and garlic. Stir over high heat to combine. When the zucchini begin to soften, add the tomatoes and seasoning. Stir well, cover, and cook for 5–10 minutes until done (Italian vegetables are always soft, I like the slight crunch).

Add the basil. Rest the zucchini for at least 10 minutes before serving.

INGREDIENTS

½ cup extra virgin olive oil
800g–1kg (29–36oz)
   zucchini, cut into 1cm
   (½in) slices
3 cloves garlic, sliced
2 tomatoes, peeled and
   chopped
about ¾ cup small basil
   leaves
salt and freshly ground
   pepper

INGREDIENTS

*1kg (2lb 4oz) green beans
   left whole*
3 cloves garlic, finely chopped
½ cup extra virgin olive oil
*3–4 tomatoes, peeled and
   chopped*
*5–10 basil leaves or ½ cup
   finely cut parsley*
*salt and freshly ground
   pepper*

BEANS SAUTÉED WITH TOMATOES

METHOD

Clean and cook the beans: steam or boil until partly cooked. Traditionally Italians cook these until soft. Drain.

Make a quick tomato sauce by frying the garlic gently in the olive oil. Add the tomatoes, basil or parsley and a little salt and pepper and simmer for about 10 minutes until it is thick. Stir the beans into the sauce and toss around the pan until they are cooked.

Cacocciuli all'agro

Carciofi in agro

ARTICHOKES BRAISED IN A CITRUS SAUCE

I first acquired a version of this recipe from a Sicilian woman who I met shopping many years ago. Thinking I was Australian, she was curious to know how I was going to cook the globe artichokes. I surprised her by answering in Italian. She approved of my recipe and shared hers with me.

Most of the time I stuff my artichokes as my grandmother from Catania did, with a mixture of parsley, garlic, grated pecorino, extra virgin olive oil and fresh breadcrumbs. Then I braise them in a mixture of white wine and water or stock. The Sicilian woman I met at the market used lemon, orange juice and vinegar in the braising liquid and capers and parsley as a stuffing. As with most Italian recipes, there were no real measurements or estimation of cooking time, and no name for her recipe. Years later I found a similar, very old recipe in Mary Taylor Simeti's *Pomp and Sustenance* using citrus juice. What follows is an adaptation of my interpretation of the Sicilian woman's dish – a bit of me, and a little of Simeti. I use a combination of orange and lemon juice with a little white wine or white wine vinegar and water for the braising liquid.

There are are many Sicilian recipes for artichokes, I have selected this one because the citrus flavours do cleanse the palate and go very well with fish. I always serve artichokes on their own, either as the antipasto or between the first and main course. These are best cold.

METHOD

Prepare the artichokes (page 68) and stuff them with capers and parsley. In a large, heavy-based saucepan in which the artichokes fit tightly in a single layer, sauté the onions in the oil. Place the artichokes upright on top of the onions, together with the citrus juices, vinegar and salt. Make up the rest of the

INGREDIENTS

6 artichokes

6 heaped tablespoons capers

6 heaped tablespoons parsley, finely cut

2 onions, finely chopped

1 cup extra virgin olive oil

2–3 cups citrus juice (orange and/or lemon)

½ cup wine or white wine vinegar

2–3 tablespoons sugar depending on the sweetness of the citrus

salt and freshly ground pepper

liquid with water (or stock). The liquid should almost reach the tops of the artichokes. Braise on low heat, covered, until the artichokes are very tender, about 30 minutes. Remove the artichokes carefully with a slotted spoon and put them in a serving dish.

Reduce the sauce by about a quarter; pour into a jug and set aside. Add the sugar to the pan and allow to caramelise. Return the sauce to the pan and reduce further for another 5–10 minutes. Taste the sauce – cold food needs extra flavour, so add more sugar and salt if necessary – and/or reduce it until you have about ½ cup of sauce per artichoke.

Pour over the artichokes and serve.

VARIATIONS

- In the Simeti version anchovies are dissolved in the sauce at the very last stages.
- I sometimes scatter over any of the following: chopped black olives, toasted pine nuts, finely chopped parsley or mint leaves.

MY GRANDMOTHER MARIA'S STUFFED ARTICHOKES

Use 1 artichoke per person. Each artichoke only needs 2–3 teaspoons of stuffing. Combine the ingredients for the stuffing in a bowl: 1 tablespoon of fresh breadcrumbs, 1 teaspoon each of chopped parsley, chopped garlic, seasoning, extra virgin olive oil and a little grated cheese (you can use parmesan, but pecorino is traditionally Sicilian).

Drain the artichokes, spread the leaves (especially in the centre) and sprinkle salt and pepper in-between the leaves. Using your fingers, push the stuffing mainly in the centre and any leftovers between the leaves.

Arrange the artichokes upright in a pan, with the trimmed stalks between them and drizzle well with more extra virgin olive oil. Add enough cold water to reach half way up the artichokes. Cook slowly, covered, for about 1 hour. I always add a splash of white wine and sometimes a little stock (or a good quality vegetable stock cube) to the poaching liquid.

WINTER MENU

Artichokes braised in a citrus sauce (*Cacocciuli all' agro*)
Pasta with braised red mullet (*Pasta chi trighi o'rau*)
Salad of boiled green beans (*Fasulinu vugghiutu*)

Patati nn'o tianu

Patate in tegame

BRAISED POTATOES

METHOD

In a saucepan, toss the potatoes in some hot olive oil until they are well coated, add the remaining ingredients and some water (the potatoes should be nearly covered). Cover and braise on low heat, checking periodically to see that they are not too dry; add more liquid if necessary.

VARIATIONS

- My mother added a little tomato paste and oregano.
- I also add stock instead of water.

INGREDIENTS

6–12 waxy potatoes, peeled
   and diced
extra virgin olive oil
2 cloves garlic
chopped parsley to taste
salt and freshly ground
   pepper to taste

Cavulu cappucciu a stufateddu

Verza or cappuccio in umido

BRAISED CABBAGE OR SAVOY CABBAGE

In Sicily in winter, white cabbage (*cavulu cappucciu*) is often used raw as a salad green. Cooked cabbage is not very common but I always loved the way my mother used Savoy cabbage (*verza*) in this recipe.

When we first arrived in Australia, there was plenty of cabbage and, as silly as this may seem, I used to love this dish as a filling for a sandwich or *panino*. But I was so embarassed when my mother packed it for my school lunch because it smelt so strong. On those days, I would pretend I had forgotten my lunch and would eat it on the way home. My schoolbag always needed to be aired overnight.

INGREDIENTS

½–¾ cup extra virgin olive oil
½ cabbage or Savoy cabbage, finely sliced
3 cloves garlic, chopped
½ glass white wine or water
2 fresh bay leaves
salt and freshly ground pepper or chilli flakes

METHOD

Heat the oil in a saucepan and add the cabbage and garlic. Stir the cabbage until it begins to soften, then add the wine, bay leaves and the salt and pepper.

Cover the pan and cook on very gentle heat for at least 20 minutes (my mother cooked it twice as long). Stir from time to time so it doesn't stick; add more wine or water if necessary.

VARIATION

- In some parts of Sicily, 1 tablespoon of tomato paste is added at the same time as the wine (mainly for colour).

Vruocculi affucati

Cavolofiore affogato

CAULIFLOWER BRAISED IN RED WINE, CHEESE, OLIVES AND ANCHOVIES

Caffè affogato is coffee drowned or smothered (*affogato*) with a little ice cream. Here the cauliflower florets are *affogati* (drowned) in red wine. This dish can also be made with broccoli, but using the white cauliflower accentuates the red of the wine, which is much more spectacular! This is one of my grandmother Maria's favourite recipes and a very popular dish of the Catanesi (in Palermo, they use white wine).

My grandmother always compressed the layers of cauliflowers with a weighted ovenproof terracotta plate (slightly smaller than the saucepan to allow a little steam to escape). When cooked, the vegetables and cheese will be partly stuck together so that the *contorni* can be sliced into sections. Many recipes for broccoli *affogati* do not bother with the weights, but I like my grandmother's version better. The black olives and the anchovies are regional variations and optional.

This is a good accompaniment to a strong-tasting dish or as a *tramezzo*.

INGREDIENTS

1 cup extra virgin olive oil

1 onion, finely sliced

1kg (2lb 4oz) cauliflower
  or broccoli, separated into
  florets

½ cup finely cut parsley

50–100g (1¾–3½oz)
  pecorino pepato (with
  whole black peppercorns),
  finely sliced

½ cup or more black olives,
  pitted, to taste

3–4 anchovies

½–1 cup red wine

salt and freshly ground
  pepper to taste

METHOD

Heat some of the olive oil in a deep saucepan and cook the onion until soft. Add the cauliflower, parsley, a dash of water and seasoning (remember the other ingredients are salty). Cover and cook on very slow heat for about 7 minutes.

Layer the cheese, olives and anchovies between the vegetables. Press down the layers with your hands. Add the rest of the oil and the wine. Cover the contents with a piece of foil (slightly loose) or baking paper and put a weight on the top. Cook very slowly for 20–30 minutes; when all the liquid has evaporated, you should hear the cauliflower sizzle in the oil. Test if it is ready – stab the cauliflower stems where they are thickest.

Verdura verde saltata

SAUTÉED GREEN LEAFY VEGETABLES

Green leafy vegetables, both cultivated and wild, are very much part of the Sicilian diet. There are two basic ways of cooking them as a *contorno*. The first is boiled with a drizzle of extra virgin olive oil and perhaps a little lemon juice just before serving. The second technique is to wilt the vegetables and cook them until they are almost done (Italians cook these in boiling water until soft) and then toss the *verdura* (*saltata*, jumped or tossed about) in extra virgin olive oil, garlic and chilli (optional). A variation is to add a dash of tomato sauce as well.

I often mix two or three types of leaves when I cook them. The vegetables can include:

- chicory, escarole (endive), members of the daisy family
- spinach, silverbeet, beets (the green leaves from beetroot), from the beetroot family (spinach, *blede,* is not very common except around Syracuse and Ragusa – the wild variety is preferred)
- broccoli, broccolini
- *cime di rape*, my favourite winter greens (sometimes called *broccoli di rapa* – turnip tops – a type of mustard green with small yellow flowers); these are members of the brassica or mustard family group; this diverse group includes plants with leaves, flowers, stems and roots that are cooked and eaten (a number of Asian greens are members of the brassicas and the Chinese broccoli and mustard greens are very similar in taste to *broccoli di rapa*, but I am not likely to cook these when Italians are coming for dinner)
- kohlrabi leaves
- green leaves of radishes and turnips
- borage, which is easy to grow – it self-seeds very easily and is excellent wilted as a green or as a stuffing for ravioli (instead of spinach); it has an attractive blue-purple flower often floated in cocktails and rough and hairy foliage.

It maketh men and women glad and merry and drive away all sadnesse, dulnesse and melancholy.

– Pliny

Ingredients

*about 1–2 bunches of green
  vegetables (see above for
  varieties)*

¾ cup extra virgin olive oil

*2 dried or fresh chillies, left
  whole*

*6 cloves garlic, squashed with
  the back of a knife*

salt to taste

Method

Clean the greens: remove any bruised or brown leaves and cut off the tough stem ends. Separate into leaves, wash carefully and tear some of the bigger leaves into smaller pieces (so they cook faster).

Cook the leaves by either wilting them in the pan using a little water or by adding them to about 3 cups of salted boiling water (the traditional method). Cover and cook over medium heat until softened, about 7–10 minutes, stirring regularly so they do not stick to the bottom of the pan. Again, Italians cook these for a longer period. Drain well.

Heat the olive oil in a large saucepan, add the whole chillies (if fresh, split them) and the garlic and toss around to flavour the oil. Squeeze any remaining moisture from the greens and add them to the pan. Taste for salt, adjust, and toss them around the pan in the flavoured oil. Reduce the heat to low and cook, stirring occasionally, for about 5–10 minutes. Remove and discard the garlic and chillies before serving.

Erbe spontanie
WILD GREENS

Sicilians are very fond of wild greens – regarded as weeds by those who do not know any better. They are thought to have remarkable medicinal qualities. They are called *erbe spontanie* in Italian (spontaneous herbs). Sicilians still gather them in the countryside, take them to city markets and sell them by the roadsides in Sicily. You often see people in fields or on the

Raw marinated small calamari
(*Calamaricchi crudi e cunzati*)
Tuna *alla ghiotta* with peppers
and eggplants (*Agghiotta di
tunnu cu pipi e mulinciani*)
Sautéed green leafy vegetables –
chicory (*Verdura verde saltata*),
Wild greens (*Erbe spontanie*)

roadside collecting seasonal wild greens such as *gira* (or *giriteddi*), *sparaceddi* or *amareddi*. I love collecting them. On one trip at the end of autumn, I found *lassine, sanapu, agghiti* and *urrania* (borage). Wild fennel was just coming into season and was sold in small bunches.

Agghiti is wild spinach. It is harvested with its base (cut just above the roots) because the pink tinge found in the bottom of the stem close to the root is very tasty.

Apart from the common cultivated asparagus gone wild, there are also many types of thin spindly shoots also called wild asparagus. The young shoots are harvested and cooked. The shoots are very strong tasting, pungent and rather bitter, but bitterness is much appreciated by Italians and is considered to be very beneficial for the kidneys.

Wild rape or *broccoletti selvatici*, another member of the mustard family, resemble canola plants with bright yellow flowers. I am a bit of a hunter-gatherer because I never pass up the opportunity to collect wild foods and I usually collect these along riverbanks and roadsides. My uncle Pippo told me that *lazzane* is one of the Sicilian terms for wild rape; I have also heard them referred to as *cavoliceddi*. He warned me not to eat too many *lazzane*. According to him, they are very rich in mineral content, which he cautions has a laxative effect – this is because our digestive systems are not used to so much goodness. I do wonder about some of the stories I have been told.

Vlita is a long, leafy green weed that I can buy when it is in season (usually at the end of summer). Its botanical name is *Amaranthus palmeri* and it belongs to the Amaranth family. Although common in southern Italy, especially in Calabria, it is mainly used to feed goats but is eaten in Greece.

When I see wild fennel plants (with no evidence of herbicide spraying), I collect the young shoots (which are fluffy and light green). I collect watercress in riverbeds and use the leaves and those of purslane in salads. Nettles are very nutritious – be careful how you collect them – but their prickles disappear when cooked. I like to eat them wilted and dressed with extra virgin olive oil, seasoning and lemon juice.

Hunger and famine have always played a part in Sicilian food. Donilo Dolci, in *Sicilian Lives*, quotes a poor labourer who makes a living from selling wild greens: 'There's five or six kinds of greens … growing wild – nobody plants them – chicory, cabbage, asparagus, fennel, borage and sorb-thistle … you go out walking and what you find, you pick. That's the way life goes: fill your sack or else.'

Nzalata

Insalata

SALADS ARE MADE WITH BOTH RAW VEGETABLES OR
WITH COOKED ONES. IN SICILIAN IT IS WRITTEN AS
'NZALATA OR N'ZALATA.

Insalata verde is a green salad made from one or more type of green leaves.
The green salads in Sicily are sometimes made from a single vegetable such as
romaine lettuce, cabbage or chicory. They are dressed with extra virgin olive
oil, wine vinegar and/or a little lemon juice.

Insalata mista (mixed salad) may be the same as the *insalata verde* if it
is a combination of green leaves. It may also contain one or several other
vegetables – for example, thinly sliced fennel or the young leaves and the pale
stalks from the centre of the celery. Radishes are also common.

Tomato salads are very popular, especially during summer. There is no
vinegar in the dressing – the acidity comes from the tomatoes. Unripe, slightly
green-tinged tomatoes are preferred.

Citrus salads made from oranges, and sometimes with fennel, chicory or
other vegetables, are very popular. Salads are also made with mature large
lemons – this was one of my father's specialities. Citrons (*cedri*) are large
lemon lookalikes and have a lot of pith – these are my favourites. In Sicily
they are called *cetri*.

Boiled vegetables are also classed as salads served either hot or cold.

Dried legumes are also popular in salads, either on their own or mixed
with other cooked vegetables such as potatoes and green beans.

THE DRESSING
The most popular dressing for *insalate* all over Italy is a simple *condimento*
made with extra virgin olive oil, salt, pepper and a little lemon juice or vinegar
(two parts oil to one of vinegar).

*Insalata ben salata, poco aceto e
ben oliata.* (Old Italian rhyme)
*Salad well salted, little vinegar
and well oiled.*

'Nzalàta virdi

Insalàta verde

GREEN LEAF SALAD

In Trieste we ate salads made with very young leaves of different types of *radicchi*, especially the *radicchio biondo triestino*, together with *mataviltz* (lamb's lettuce) and the cultivated *rucola* (*arugola*, *rughetta*, rocket and *roquettte*). These were sold by the handful in the market wrapped in cones of brown paper. *Radicchio* is traditionally grown and eaten in the north of Italy and Sicilians have only recently started to use it. The cultivated *rucola* (rocket) is also not common in Sicily; wild rocket is preferred.

The Sicilians eat salads of young wild *cicoria* (chicory) or *cicorino*, Batavian endive and *frisée*. Batavian endive, or escarole, has frilly leaves, is crunchy and stays crisp. *Frisée* has even frillier leaves that are spiky, firm and mildly bitter – it is a form of chicory, also known as curly endive.

Sicilians often reserve the tender centre parts or young shoots of green vegetables – celery, chicory, endives and radishes – for their *insalate*. This is something my father taught me. After his Saturday morning visits to the greengrocer, he would clean the vegetables and separate the hearts from the outer leaves. It was his weekly ritual. But our favourite salads were from his garden and took him hours to collect – leaf by leaf – from seedlings.

My Ragusa relatives use the inside leaves of green cabbage, torn into bite-sized pieces and dressed. They also sometimes make a green leaf salad with sweet corn kernels. I also ate this salad in restaurants in Modica and Noto and first thought that the practice may have been introduced by Sicilians who had lived in America. But apparently not: *grano turco* (sweet corn) was introduced at the same time as eggplants and tomatoes from the New World and seems to be common in salads in southern Sicily.

Purslane, a common garden weed in some parts of the world (*purciddana* in Sicilian, *portulaca* in Italian, genus *Portulaca*) is eaten by some Sicilians in salads, either with vinaigrette or, in some parts of the island, with tomatoes, oil, onions and salt.

INGREDIENTS AND METHOD

Select a variety of greens. Combine different textures, the sweet with the subtle and the bitter flavours. Some examples are the tender light green leaves found in the centre of chicory, or endives and escarole, different types of lettuces, the young, pale green leaves found in the heart of celery, the young leaves of radish. Dress the salad with vinaigrette (see page 346), toss it well and serve.

VARIATIONS

Olio, aceto, pepe e sale, sarebbe buono, uno stivale. (Old Italian rhyme)
With oil, vinegar, pepper and salt, a boot would taste good.

I like to include the following:

🌿 Watercress (*crescione d'acqua*). This is not common in all of Sicily, although my father told me that before the 1960s the *lavandaie* (washerwomen) who did their washing in the river ate watercress while they worked.

🌿 Fennel (*finocchio* in Italian). A salad made with thin slices of fennel and the simple *condimento* of oil, a dash of vinegar and seasoning is also very popular and particularly suitable as an accompaniment to oily or strong-flavoured foods. Clean fennel and remove the tougher outer leaves and the hard core. Always cut the fennel vertically – into quarters and then each quarter into thin slices. Any tender green leaves can be used in the salad.

🌿 Radish (*ravanello* or *rapanello*). This is another vegetable that is often overlooked: they are available all year round but are sweeter in spring. Radishes should be crisp, juicy and peppery with sparkling white flesh. My father grew them because they reminded him of raiding the radish patch when he was a boy. My grandparents lived in the centre of Ragusa but also owned a *mulino*, an old grain mill powered by water, where they had a small vegetable patch. In spring, small firm radishes with fresh, unblemished tops are often served at the beginning of a meal, with a small bowl of salt, or extra virgin olive oil and salt for dipping. Other tender vegetables such as broad beans, fennel or peas are also commonly placed on the table in the same way – as a celebration of the vegetable and the season.

Nzalata ri lumia o r'aranci

Insalata di limoni o d'arance

LEMON OR ORANGE SALAD

Citrus grow abundantly and in many varieties in all parts of Sicily. They have been strongly identified with Sicily throughout the centuries.

Lemon salad

My father always used large mature lemons – the more pith the better. I remember first making lemon salads for my friends in the 1970s and how much they liked them, and how surprised they were at the sweetness of the lemons, brought out through the use of salt (just like balsamic vinegar brings out the sweetness of strawberries).

Peel the skin off the lemons with a potato peeler, leaving as much pith as possible. Cut the lemons in half and squeeze out some of the juice (otherwise the salad will be too acidic), then cut into quarters and into thin slices.

Dress with extra virgin olive oil, freshly ground pepper and salt.

Variations

- Add finely chopped parsley or mint.
- Add the finely chopped green leaves of fresh garlic (I grow this by sowing garlic cloves among my pot plants – they will soon shoot).

Orange salad

Use fresh, juicy oranges. Blood oranges are also good (or 'bloody oranges', as I once saw on a label at one of the fruit stalls at the Queen Victoria Market in Melbourne). They are called *sanguini* and are much appreciated by Sicilians.

Estimate ½ orange per person (depending on size) and peel the oranges, removing all the pith. Cut them crossways into fine slices; if the oranges are large, cut each slice in half.

Place the orange slices in a salad bowl and about 10 minutes before you are ready to serve, add the same dressing as for lemon salad.

Variations

- Some people, like Zia Niluzza, add a little lemon juice (she says that it brings out the sweetness!).
- Others add slices of fennel, or the tender heart of celery or chicory.
- My parents have always added finely cut parsley, my uncle dried oregano.
- Red onions can be added; others prefer strong tastes such as anchovies, or sun-dried black olives.

Spring menu

Lemon or orange salad
(*'Nzalata ri lumia or 'Nzalata r'aranci*)
Tuna alla stemperata with onions, vinegar, a few capers, green olives and mint (Tunnu 'a stimpirata)
Braised potatoes *(Patati nn'o tianu)*
Asparagus salad (*'Nzalata ri sparici*)

'Nzalata ri pumaroru

Insalata di pomodoro

TOMATO SALAD

Tomato salads are always made with firm, slightly unripe tomatoes. Interestingly, they were first called *pomo d'oro* (meaning golden apples) – apparently the first tomatoes introduced were yellow. It could also be that *oro* (gold) reflects its golden status in cuisine or the letters '*dor*' come from the verb *adorare* (to adore). Heirloom tomatoes in a mutitude of colours and variety of shapes are now widely available. Interestingly, not many are red.

From Comiso and Vittoria, towns south of Ragusa, it is common to cut large tomatoes called *cuore di bue* (ox heart) crossways into halves, remove the seeds and stuff each crevice with chopped garlic, salt and extra virgin olive oil. These tomatoes are eaten in the same way in the south of France.

In other parts of Sicily, this is the most common tomato salad.

METHOD

Cut the tomatoes into bite-sized pieces. Add the seasoning, herbs and oil and serve.

'NZALATA RI PUMARORU E CIPUDDA

This was my father's favourite version of tomato salad. *Cipudda* is Sicilian for onion (*cipolla* in Italian).

To the above salad, add 2 large 'squeezed' onions. The bitter juices are squeezed out of the onions, giving them a sweet flavour. He used large salad onions for this, the white or the red variety. Red onion is called *cipolla calabrese* in Italian, probably because it is used extensively in Calabria. This variety is sweet and odourless. To squeeze the onions, finely slice them and place in a colander, sprinkle with salt and leave for about 10 minutes. Squeeze

INGREDIENTS

6–8 large tomatoes
fresh basil or dried oregano
½ cup extra virgin olive oil
salt and freshly ground
   pepper

Vegetable dishes

the onion to remove the strong juices. If fresh onions are not in season, leave the salt on the sliced onions for longer (about 30 minutes). Expect to shed tears during this process.

VARIATIONS

- Use finely chopped spring onions instead of the squeezed onions (there is a variety of red-coloured spring onions as well).
- It is popular inland, in Enna and Caltanissetta, to add 2 cloves of finely chopped garlic.
- Add small quantities of the light green heart and leaves of celery.
- Add some finely sliced cucumber.

Casulinu vugghiutu

Fagiolini lessi

SALAD OF BOILED GREEN BEANS

Fresh beans (*fagiolini*) are a common *contorno*. In Sicilian, green beans are called *casulinu* or *fasulinu*. For a more attractive dish, and depending on their availability, I often use a combination of green beans and the pale yellow ones, sometimes called wax or yellow or butter beans.

METHOD

If you are using two different varieties of beans, cook them separately as they may take different times.

Steam the beans. Or drop them into salted boiling water, as Italians do, and cook them, uncovered (like pasta), until tender.

Drain and cool – some plunge them into cold water to stop the cooking process – I prefer to let them cool and cook a little more, slowly).

Dress with a simple *condimento* (see page 346).

VARIATIONS

- Very common additions are cooked dried beans (borlotti or canellini) and/or boiled potatoes. Fresh borlotti are also suitable.
- Add a little finely chopped garlic and parsley or mint in the dressing.

INGREDIENTS

about 6 handful of tender green and/or yellow beans of the same size (about a handful per person)

Nzalata ri sparici

Insalata di asparagi

ASPARAGUS SALAD

The Italian season for asparagus lasts for only about six weeks in the spring. Often it is served on its own as an antipasto or *contorno*. In Sicily, I have only eaten asparagus cooked simply – never baked or grilled or topped with grated cheese. You can buy thin or thick asparagus and in different shades, from dark green through mauve to light cream. The colour doesn't affect the flavour, but it can make a difference to the price. I see masses of the thin variety in Sicily and my relatives are of the opinion that these are the best.

I prefer to steam asparagus until tender but still firm. This is where I part company from my Sicilian relatives, who prefer them soft and limp. I always cook vegetables for longer when my mother comes to stay. Irrespective of how soft the vegetables are, I can't bear to watch her take a bite and wince and declare: *Ma sono crudi. Io non li mangio.* ('But these are raw. I am not going to eat them.') Tradition is everything for Sicilians, who have a reputation for having a *testa dura* (a hard head, impenetrable).

INGREDIENTS

about 200g (7oz) asparagus
(4–6 spears per person)

METHOD

Steam/boil the asparagus until tender but still firm. If you are cooking different colours and thicknesses for visual effect, cook them separately (to allow for different cooking times). Drain and cool.

I do not dress the asparagus until ready to serve them as the acid in the dressing may affect their colour. A simple olive oil and lemon juice dressing doesn't mask the fresh taste of the asparagus. Or replace some of the lemon juice with orange juice, especially *sanguini* (blood oranges). I also like to add thin slices of 1–2 oranges to the salad – blood oranges look spectacular. Cut the slices into halves or quarters and add with dressing just before serving.

Una caponata per ogni stagione

A caponata for every season

THE SUPERIORITY OF SICILIAN CAPONATA IS ACKNOWLEDGED THROUGH THE ENTIRE LENGTH OF ITALY. THOSE WHO ARE FAMILIAR WITH CAPONATA MOSTLY ASSOCIATE IT WITH ONE PARTICULAR SICILIAN VERSION MADE WITH EGGPLANTS. THERE ARE MANY VARIATIONS AND OTHER SICILIAN CAPONATE THAT ARE MADE WITH DIFFERENT VEGETABLES. THE PRINCIPAL FLAVOURINGS REMAIN THE SAME: CELERY, CAPERS, GREEN OLIVES AND THE SWEET AND SOUR CARAMELISED AGRO DOLCE SAUCE MADE WITH VINEGAR AND SUGAR.

Caponate are also traditional in other parts of Italy but these are very different to the Sicilian versions. The better known ones are Neapolitan *caponata*, sometimes called *aqua sale* (literally 'salt water') and the Ligurian *capponalda* or *caponadda*. These *caponate* resemble other Italian bread salads and are very similar to the summer Tuscan *panzanella* made with unsalted country bread (a day or two old), revived with water and combined with a mixture of fragrant tomatoes, basil and red onions.

Instead of bread, the Neapolitan and Ligurian versions use *pane biscottato* and a similar mixture of summer ingredients. *Caponadda* usually contains anchovies or tuna as well. Another Ligurian dish is *cappon magro*, a very elaborate *caponata*-like dish made with layered boiled vegetables, with a layer of *pane biscottato* on the bottom layer to soak up the juices. *Pane biscottato* is similar to a rusk or hard biscuit (baked as bread and when no longer fresh, sliced, left to dry out and re-baked in a slow oven). The difference between the *pane biscottato* from the two regions is the shape: the Neapolitan version, *friselle*, are round with a hole in the centre and look like bagels or doughnuts.

Pane biscottato is common throughout Italy and has been around for a long time. My mother gave it to me as a baby to keep me quiet and when I was teething. For breakfast my relatives use the rusk as if it were toast, spread with jam, or they break it into their milk and coffee. Although it is commercially made, it is also prepared at home and is a convenient way to use stale bread. Bread is never thrown away in Italy. The Italians, being nominally Catholic,

SPRING MENU

Artichoke caponata (*Capunata di carioffuli*)
Pasta and prawns with goats' milk ricotta or curd (*Pasta e gammareddu ca ricotta*)
Trout with olives and wild fennel (*Trota in padella con olive e finocchio selvatico*)
Zucchini sautéed with tomatoes (*Cucuzzedda cu pumaroru*)

associate bread with the body of Christ (through communion). The twice-baked bread was also once a convenient and lasting food for sailors and fishermen, who reconstituted it with seawater and ate it with some fish. This could be one of the reasons why some versions of *caponate* include fish.

In the Sicilian *caponata*, good-quality bread is considered to be the best accompaniment and is *un'altra forchetta* (like another, or a second, fork) – the bread serves as an edible utensil. In some parts of Sicily, it is customary to scatter toasted breadcrumbs over the top of the dish.

The explanations of the derivation of the name *caponata* and the origins of this dish are as numerous as the variations of ingredients.

THE ORIGINS OF *CAPONATA*

The earliest description of *caponata* appeared in 1709 in *Etimologicum Siculum* by Jos. Vinci: *acetarium et variis rebus minutium conficis* (describing a recipe using vinegar and various things). Another early recipe for a *caponata*-like dish is the *Cappone di galera alla siciliana* in Francesco Leonardi's *L'Apicio moderno* published in 1790. Here is his recipe:

> Dip a few fresh new beans [freselle maiorchine, *an esteemed bean from Majorca*] *in Malaga wine, then arrange them on a serving platter, and put over them a garnish of anchovy fillets and thin slices of tuna salami, rinsed of its salt, capers, pieces of citron zest, stoned olives, fried shrimp and squid, oysters poached slightly in their own liquid and several fillets of fried* linguattola [a kind of flatfish] *until the platter is well garnished and full. At the moment of serving pour over it a sauce made as follows: in a mortar pound two ounces of peeled green pistachios soaked in olive oil, vinegar, and tarragon or vinegar, salt and ground pepper.*

Compare this with Elizabeth David's recipe for *Caponata alla marinara* in her book *Italian Food*, which she calls a 'primitive fisherman's and sailor's dish'. She describes soaking ship's biscuits in water, then moistening with olive oil. 'Garlic, stoned black olives, anchovies, and oregano or basil are added. … It is no bad dish, rough though it is, to accompany coarse red wine,' she says.

Clifford A Wright, in *A Mediterranean Feast*, cites a reference to *capón de galera* by Juan de la Mata in *Arte de Reposteria*, published in 1791: 'The most

MENU FOR
GIUSEPPE TOMASI DI
LAMPEDUSA

*Lampedusa (1896–1957)
wrote one novel. Il Gattopardo
(The Leopard) is set in Sicily
during the Risorgimento. The
novel was sumptuously filmed
by Luchino Visconti and starred
Burt Lancaster and Claudia
Cardinale. Lampadusa loved
elaborate dishes. I think he would
have been happy with this menu.
There would be more than one
choice for each course.*

Stuffed mussels with *besciamelle*
(*Cozzuli chini*)
Mixed seafood salad ('*Nzalata
di mare*)

Eggplant caponata in pastry
(*Pasticcio di caponata di
melanzane*) between courses

Roasted or grilled artichokes
(*Cacuoccili arrustuti*)
Baked sardines with cheese,
breadcrumbs and eggs (*Crostata
di sarde*)
Fennel tortino (*Turticedda ri
finocchiu*)

Tuna braciole with Emmenthal,
anchovies and citrus (*Braciole
di tonno*)

Salt-crusted fish *(Pesce incrostato di sale)* and mayonnaise

Asparagus salad *('Nzalata ri sparici)*

Caponata made with green, leafy vegetables *(Capunata di virdura)* or Green leaf salad *('Nzalata virdi)*

common gazpacho was known as *capón de galera*,' Wright explains. It consisted of 'a pound of bread crust soaked in water and put in a sauce of anchovy bones, garlic, and vinegar, sugar, salt and olive oil', which was softened. Then 'some of the ingredients and vegetables of the Royal Salad' [a salad composed of various fruits and vegetables] were added.

Giuseppe Coria, a respected voice on Sicilian cooking, suggests that *caponata* derives from the Latin word *caupo* (Roman tavern) where *cauponae* (tavern food for travellers) was served.

In *Midnight in Sicily*, Peter Robb captures the essence of a Sicilian *caponata*: 'It was the colour that struck me first. The colour of darkness ... glimmerings from a baroque canvas, that comes from eggplant, black olives, tomato and olive oil densely cooked together, long and gently.'

Sicilian caponata made with eggplants (aubergines)

Whatever the derivation, *caponata* has evolved over the ages to become the dish that typifies Sicilian cuisine. As you'd expect, there are many regional variations and flourishes of what must have been a very humble dish, as well as the personal, innovative touches from the chefs of the aristocracy.

Eggplant is the purple heart of Sicilian *caponata* – and it is the principal ingredient. The eggplant is said to be the queen of vegetables, second only to the tomato. Some traditional recipes use tomato paste rather than chopped tomatoes. Some add garlic, others chocolate (or cocoa). Many contain nuts – almonds or pine nuts or pistachio – used fresh in some recipes and toasted in others. Herbs are often added: sometimes basil, or oregano or mint. Raisins or currants may be included and some feature slices of pears. In one version found in Palermo the *caponata* is sprinkled with ground cinnamon or cloves.

Several *caponate* include fish, singly or in combination: prawns (shrimp), octopus, canned tuna, salted anchovies and *bottarga*. Many sources state that *caponne* fish (Italian; scientific name *Triglia lucerna*) was one of the basic ingredients of an ancient *caponata* made by fishermen's wives using damaged fish. In baronial kitchens, fish was also a principal ingredient, especially shellfish.

'Caponata is like religion ... you can not change it,' the Sicilian chef Giovanni Naurato commented. You don't have to be religious or Sicilian to understand what he is saying: whenever anyone cooks *caponata* they are bound by family and local traditions – you cannot introduce different ingredients or change the cooking process.

This is the way it is, and will always be.

Caponata catanese

RECIPE FROM THE LEONE FAMILY OF CATANIA, MADE WITH EGGPLANTS (AUBERGINES) AND PEPPERS (CAPSICUM)

Caponata is a family thing! My favourite version of *caponata* originates from my mother's family in Catania. It is interesting that my father's family, from Ragusa, two hours' drive from Catania, do not cook *caponata* at all. My recipe for *caponata* has been strongly influenced by Zio Pippo Leone, an adventurous cook and one of my mother's brothers.

In some of the most common recipes for *caponata*, especially those of Palermo and northern Sicily, there is just one principal ingredient (eggplants), but the *caponate* made by the Leone family include peppers. On one trip to Sicily I tried as many *caponate* as possible and ate it in restaurants in Syracuse, Catania, Sciacca, Mazara del Vallo, Agrigento, Ragusa Ibla and Caltagirone and was very pleased to find that the best tasting versions all contained peppers.

Like my zio Pippo and my grandmother, I fry the vegetables separately because they cook at different rates. It is also better to sauté them in batches: if the pan's too full the heat will drop and they will steam, not brown.

All vegetable *caponate* need to be given time to develop their flavours. I make mine at least a day before it is to be eaten because it gets better with age. The dish does take a considerable amount of olive oil, but the oil functions as a preservative and adds to the flavour. I like to make large quantities and keep some in the fridge for other times. Many older Sicilians say that it was not unusual to make *caponata* in mid-autumn and store it in a stone crock in a cold cellar (it had to be totally covered with oil); the last of the *caponata* would be eaten on Christmas day in deep winter.

The type of olives affects the flavours. Green olives (squashed and pickled for only a few weeks in salted water) will add a slightly bitter taste. The celery is usually pre-cooked in salted boiling water before being added to the other ingredients. I don't do this because I like the taste of the crunchy celery.

I make *caponata* through the summer and am very fond of an early autumn version when the peppers are red and yellow and sweet and the eggplants are still prolific. I usually serve it as a cold antipasto, as a separate course.

INGREDIENTS

1–2 large dark-skinned eggplants, unpeeled and cut into 3cm (1¼in) cubes

about 1½ cups extra virgin olive oil

3 peppers, preferably 1 green, 1 red, 1 yellow, cut into 2cm (¾in) slices or rectangular shapes

2–3 tender celery stalks and pale green leaves from the heart, finely sliced

1 large onion, finely sliced

2 medium red tomatoes, peeled and chopped, or 2 tablespoons tomato paste mixed with a little water

½ cup capers, salted or in brine, soaked and rinsed

¾ cup green olives, pitted and chopped

2 tablespoons sugar

½ cup white wine vinegar

salt and freshly ground pepper

METHOD

Use a deep, large frying pan. If you use a non-stick frying pan, you will not need as much oil, but it will be more difficult to caramelise the juices. Although the vegetables are fried separately, they are all added to the same pan at the end.

Soak the eggplants in water with about 1 tablespoon of salt. Leave for about 30 minutes; this will keep the flesh white and the eggplant will absorb less oil. Drain and squeeze them to remove as much water as possible – I use a tea towel.

Heat a large frying pan over medium heat with ¾ cup of the extra virgin olive oil. Add the eggplant and sauté until soft and golden, about

10–12 minutes. Drain on paper towels (reserving the oil, optional), then place in a large bowl and set aside.

Add oil to the frying pan (or reuse the oil from the eggplants) plus a little salt and sauté the peppers until wilted and beginning to turn brown, about 10–12 minutes. Remove the peppers from the pan, draining the oil back into the pan. Place the peppers in the bowl with the eggplants.

Add a little more oil to the pan. Sauté the celery gently for 5–7 minutes so that it retains some of its crispness. Sprinkle the celery with a little salt while it is cooking. Remove from the pan and add it to the eggplants and peppers.

Again, add a little more oil to the pan and sauté the onion. Add a little salt and cook until translucent. Add the tomatoes or tomato paste to the onions, and allow their juices to reduce. Add the capers and olives. Cook gently for 1–2 minutes. Add the tomato and onion mixture to the bowl with the eggplant, peppers and celery.

To make the *agro dolce* sauce, add the sugar to the frying pan, which is already coated with the caramelised juices from the vegetables. Heat it very gently until it begins to melt and bubble. Add the vinegar and let it reduce.

Add the eggplant and other cooked vegetables to the pan with the *agro dolce* sauce. Add ground pepper and check the seasoning. Gently toss all the ingredients together over low heat for 2–3 minutes to blend the flavours.

Spoon the *caponata* into a bowl and cool before placing it in one or more containers. Store in the fridge until ready to use. I like to serve the *caponata* piled onto one large plate.

VARIATIONS

As the mood takes me, I add:
- finely torn basil or mint leaves (stirred through the *caponata* as well as on top)
- generous amounts of toasted pine nuts or blanched chopped almonds sprinkled on top – customary in different parts of Sicily
- 2–3 finely chopped anchovies added at the same time as the olives and capers (favoured by some modern chefs)
- coarse breadcrumbs toasted in a hot frying pan in extra virgin olive oil (a cheaper alternative to nuts, and/or it was a way of using stale bread).

SUMMER MENU

Caponatina with roasted peppers and fried eggplants
Fish soup with a soffritto of garlic and parsley (*Zuppa di pisci*) or
Pasta with sardines, from Palermo, made with fennel, pine nuts and currants (*Pasta chi sardi*)
Green leaf salad (*'Nzalata virdi*)

A caponata for every season

Caponatina with roasted peppers (capsicum) and fried eggplants (aubergines)

Most Sicilians use the words *caponata* and *caponatina* interchangeably, even in the same family. There does not seem to be an obvious reason why some Sicilians call this dish *caponata* and some *caponatina*. Some sources imply that in a *caponatina* the vegetables are cut into smaller pieces (as in this recipe) and that it does not include any other additional ingredients, which would change the simplicity of the dish (for example, costly fish). A few suggest that *caponatina* may have been cooked in the oven rather than the frying pan, which is certainly less arduous.

Whatever, this recipe is interesting. The eggplants are fried, the peppers are roasted, the rest of the vegetables are sautéed and the sauce is made. When the separate components are combined, the flavours remain distinct. Although the recipe may seem complicated it is not. In fact, the different elements can be cooked at different times and combined at least an hour before serving.

Ingredients

1kg (2lb 4oz) tomatoes, peeled and chopped (or canned)

fresh basil leaves

1½ cups extra virgin olive oil

3 eggplants, unpeeled, cut into small cubes and soaked (see page 305)

6 peppers, a variety of colours

1 onion, finely chopped

2 tender celery stalks and pale green leaves from the heart, finely chopped

3 tablespoons capers, salted or in brine

½ cup green olives, pitted and chopped

½ cup wine vinegar

3 teaspoons sugar

2 cloves garlic, flattened with the back of a knife

salt and freshly ground pepper

Method

To make the sauce, combine the tomatoes, basil, ½ cup of oil and some salt and pepper in a saucepan. Cook on a low to medium heat, uncovered, for about 20 minutes, until the sauce is thickened.

Fry the eggplants in ¾ cup of oil, then drain (reserving oil, optional). Store until ready to use. Chargrill the whole peppers (see page 300). Peel and store until ready to use.

For the *caponata* base, sauté the onions and celery in fresh olive oil or the oil drained from the eggplants. Add the capers and olives and a little water. When water has evaporated, add vinegar and sugar. Store until ready to use.

At least 30 minutes before serving, combine all the elements and add more basil.

Caponata di melanzane

EGGPLANT (AUBERGINE) CAPONATA

The ingredients and method for making *caponata di melanzane* are the same as those for *caponata catanese* (page 362). Use the same ingredients, but omit the peppers and use 2–3 large eggplants. In the traditions of Palermo, just before serving top with coarse breadcrumbs, which have been toasted in a pan in a little extra virgin olive oil, or almonds (blanched, toasted and chopped). Grated *bottarga* (see (page 102) is also a popular addition. Here are some variations.

CAPONATA DI MELANZANE CON CIOCCOLATA (CAPONATA WITH CHOCOLATE)

Lu mònacu sciala e lu cummentu paga. (Sicilian proverb)
The monk feasts and the convent pays.

In Sicilian cuisine there are a number of recipes in which chocolate enriches the dish. Chocolate in eggplant *caponata* is a common variation in certain parts of Sicily. In the 1500s, the Spanish conquistadors introduced exotic foods from the New World to Europe. Among these was *xocolatl*, which means 'bitter water' (chocolate), obtained from ground cacao seeds. Although many Sicilian dishes are said to be Spanish legacies, I think it is more accurate to say they were conceived in Sicily and incorporate both Sicilian and Spanish traditions.

INGREDIENTS AND METHOD

Follow the *capanata* recipe above (adapted from *caponata catanese,* page 362) and add cocoa or good-quality bitter chocolate. Most recipes suggest using cocoa powder; I add it (a thick paste of 2 tablespoons of cocoa and 2 tablespoons of sugar dissolved in a little water) after I have made the *agro dolce* sauce.

My favourite method is to add 50g (1¾oz) of dark, extra fine chocolate (70% cocoa) pieces to the *agro dolce* sauce and stir it gently as it melts, and then I add the vegetables. This results in a smooth, luscious *caponata*. In a modern restaurant in Sicily I have eaten an eggplant *caponata* with the chocolate grated on top, much like parmesan on pasta.

Pasticcio di caponata di melanzane (caponata encased in pastry)

Pasticcio includes pastry or is assembled in layers and baked (such as *pasticcio di pasta*, in which different layers of pasta are layered with sauce and other ingredients and then baked). In the 19th century, in the homes of the wealthy, there was a fashion for embellishing traditional Sicilian dishes and one of the common elaborations was to encase cooked ingredients in shortcrust pastry. They were often extravagant, opulent and monumental dishes. This is a majestic *caponata di melanzane* and was originally prepared for the nobility of Palermo. It makes a wonderful luncheon dish and it is a great way to make leftovers impressive.

Pasta frolla

This shortcrust pastry was traditionally made with lard or a mixture of lard and butter (popular with the French). Using lard and a little sugar is still common in Sicily. This is enough for a medium *pasticcio* for six. If you have a larger circle of aristocrats around your table make two so the pastry cooks evenly. Although not traditional, small individual ones are also fun.

METHOD

Mix flour, sugar, cinnamon and salt into a bowl or onto a marble slab. Rub the lard and/or butter into the dry ingredients until the mixture resembles coarse breadcrumbs. Form a depression in the centre and add the egg and the wine bit-by-bit and work into the flour to make the pastry. Do not overwork the dough.

Divide the pastry into two – one portion to line the base of the baking tin (make it slightly bigger) and one to cover. Seal the pastry in plastic wrap and leave it to rest in the fridge for 30–60 minutes. Roll the pastry into two circles. Line the bottom of a well-greased 28cm (11in) baking tin wide with the pastry. Bake blind in a moderate oven for 10 minutes. Let the pastry cool.

Fill the pastry with warm *caponata* and cover with the other round of pastry. Brush the pastry with a little oil. Make a couple of slits in the pastry to allow steam to escape. Cook in a 180°C (350°F) oven for 30–40 minutes until golden. Serve warm or cold.

INGREDIENTS

THE PASTRY
500g (17½oz) plain flour
200g (7oz) lard or butter or
  a mixture of the two
1 egg, plus 1 yolk
1 tablespoon sugar
1 cup white wine
1 teaspoon ground cinnamon
  (optional)
salt

THE FILLING
caponata di melanzane
  (page 367), warmed

A caponata for every season

Capunata 'duchessa' ca sarsa di san bernardo

Caponata duchessa con la salsa di san bernardo

THE DUCHESS' CAPONATA WITH SAINT BERNARD'S SAUCE

Capunata 'duchessa' ca sarsa di San Bernardo is a famous *caponata*. It is appropriately named after Maria Carolina, the granddaughter of King Ferdinand, who spent most of her childhood in Sicily during the mid-1800s and became the Duchess of Berry, when she married Charles Ferdinand, Duke of Berry.

Maria Carolina was reputed to be a bit of a glutton (just a bit). Her favourite *caponata* was an eggplant version to which her chefs added artichokes, wild asparagus tips and fish (swordfish, crayfish, shrimps and bottarga). The *caponata* was coated with Saint Bernard's sauce and decorated with slices of hardboiled eggs (marinated for ten days in red wine vinegar and cumin seeds), stuffed olives (with capers, anchovies, red peppers, gherkins) and prawn tails.

Salsa di san Bernardo was an odd combination of almonds, sugar, anchovies, breadcrumbs, vinegar and chocolate. My research suggests the sauce was also used with cooked vegetables and was particularly popular spread over artichokes or potatoes or as an accompaniment to meat.

I cannot help making associations between Maria Carolina's *caponata* and the Ligurian *cappon magro*. And I see similarities between *cappon magro* and *insalata russa* (Russian salad), which my mother used to serve as an antipasto on any festive occasion.

Cappon magro is an elaborate dish made with boiled vegetables and fish and traditionally served as an antipasto on New Year's Eve. The components of the dish are cooked separately and assembled into a monumental multi-layered pyramid. The base is a layer of dried oven bread moistened with oil and vinegar mixed with garlic and salt. The vegetables are boiled separately

A caponata for every season

and may include all or some of these: potatoes, carrots, green beans, white cauliflower (not the purple or green cauliflowers found in Sicily), artichokes, mushrooms, celery, salsify and beetroot. One of the fish used is the capon fish (*pesce cappone*), hence the name *cappon magro*. The other fish are: prawns (shrimp), scampi, oysters, molluscs, salted anchovies and a lobster, placed on the very top of the pyramid.

A green dressing (much like *salsa verde*) coats the entire dish. It is made of hardboiled eggs, capers and olives, pine nuts, garlic, lemon juice, olive oil, vinegar seasoning and some white breadcrumbs.

A very detailed recipe, dating from 1880, is found in *Cucina di Strettissimo Magro* by Father Gaspare Dellepiane, from the San Francesco da Paola order of monks. The title of the book (perhaps the first collection of 'lean cuisine') literally translated is 'Cuisine of very strict magro'. *Magro* ('lean') is the opposite of *grasso* ('fat') and was the term used for the meat-free foods eaten at times of fasting. The dishes served in some rich monasteries may have been without meat, but they matched the bourgeoisie in extravagance.

SARSA DI SAN BIRNARDU (SALSA DI SAN BERNARDO)

Saint Bernard's sauce is said to have originated in the monastery named after the saint in Catania where the monks were reputed to revel in wealth and opulence, gluttony and greed. Most of the recipes for this sauce do not include method or quantities of ingredients.

The recipe in Correnti's book, *Il Libro d'Oro della Cucina e dei Vini di Sicilia*, appears to be the most detailed and is likely to be the most authentic recipe. The sauce is first made into a pesto – the ingredients are pounded, the liquids are added and the mixture is amalgamated into a smooth paste (pounded almonds, breadcrumbs, anchovies, dark chocolate, a little vinegar and oil). The ingredients are then thickened over a bain-marie. In some of the older recipes, the vinegar is infused with tarragon (*dragoncello*, also called *estragone*), a herb generally associated with the French which is sometimes used in the northwest of Italy but is not common in Sicilian cuisine. The use of chocolate in savoury foods has Spanish origins.

To eat, to love, to sing, and to digest; in truth, these are the four acts in this opéra bouffe that we call life, and which vanishes like the bubbles in a bottle of champagne.
– Gioacchino Rossini (1792–1868)

Lu mònacu sciala e lu cummentu paga. (Sicilian proverb)
The monk feasts and the convent pays.

Caponatina 'o fornu
Caponatina al forno
CAPONATINA COOKED IN THE OVEN

This is an easy *caponatina* cooked in the oven. It includes *caciocavallo ragusano* cheese. If you can't find this cheese, substitute *provola*.

METHOD

Place all the ingredients, except the wine, in an ovenproof dish and dress with sufficient oil.

Bake in a 200°C (400°F) oven for 20 minutes, add the wine and return to the oven for another 20–30 minutes.

Once again, this *caponatina* is eaten cold.

INGREDIENTS

2 large dark-skinned eggplants, cut into cubes and soaked (see page xxx)
3 large red tomatoes, peeled and chopped
3–4 red and yellow peppers, sliced into strips
100g (3½oz) caciocavallo ragusano (or provola), cut into small cubes
1 large onion, finely sliced
2 cloves garlic, chopped
½ cup white wine
fresh basil leaves
1 cup extra virgin olive oil
salt and freshly ground pepper

A caponata for every season

Caponata di patate

POTATO *CAPONATA*

This *caponata* can be eaten hot or at room temperature. It also keeps well refrigerated for several days.

The potatoes are fried until lightly golden. The ingredients commonly used to make *caponata* – onions, celery, olives, capers, tomatoes and the vinegar and sugar for the *agro dolce* sauce – are cooked together separately. The potatoes are then added to the other cooked vegetables.

INGREDIENTS

1.5kg (3lb 5oz) potatoes, peeled and cubed
1 cup (or more) extra virgin olive oil
2 large onions, chopped
1 celery heart (the centre pale green stalks and some of the fine leaves)
1 cup finely cut parsley
1 cup tomato passata
½ cup capers, salted or in brine
¾ cup green olives, pitted and chopped
3 tablespoons sugar
200ml (7fl oz) white vinegar
salt and freshly ground pepper

METHOD

Dry the potatoes well and fry in hot extra virgin olive oil and sprinkle with salt – do not crowd the potatoes; use a wide frying pan or cook in batches. Turn occasionally until they are cooked and golden. Drain and set aside.

Use this same oil to braise the vegetables (purists would use new oil). Heat the oil and add the onions and celery. Cook over moderate heat, stirring frequently, until the onion is golden and the celery has softened. Season and add the parsley. Add the tomato passsata, capers and olives and toss the ingredients together for about 5 minutes.

Add sugar and vinegar and increase the heat to high to reduce some of the vinegar. Add the potatoes and cook for about 4–5 minutes to blend the flavours.

Serve at room temperature.

VARIATIONS

- Add chopped, toasted almonds or pistachios just before serving (either sprinkled on top or mixed through the *caponata*) and scatter the dish with fresh mint leaves.

Caponata di natale

CHRISTMAS CAPONATA MADE WITH CELERY, ALMONDS AND SULTANAS

INGREDIENTS

½ cup extra virgin olive oil

1 celery heart, including pale green leaves, very finely chopped

1 large onion, chopped

¾ cup green olives, pitted and chopped

¾ cup sun-ripened sultanas

½ cup capers, salted or in brine

3 tablespoons sugar

60ml (2fl oz) white vinegar

1 cup blanched almonds, toasted and chopped

2 tablespoons coarse breadcrumbs, toasted in a frying pan in hot oil

salt and freshly ground pepper

Eggplants and peppers are summer vegetables and not in season in winter for Christmas, so this very unusual *caponata* is made with celery hearts, traditionally boiled first before being sautéed (I do not do this). Once again, this *caponata* would be eaten on its own, but I have served it with small fish, lightly dipped in flour, fried in very hot oil and served cold (see page 236).

METHOD

Heat the olive oil in a deep frying pan and sauté the celery with the onion until it has softened, then add salt and cook for about 10 minutes. Add the olives, sultanas and capers and cook for another 2 minutes. Place in a bowl.

To make the *agro dolce* sauce, add the sugar to the frying pan and heat it very gently until it begins to melt and bubble. Add the vinegar and allow it to reduce completely. Add the vegetables to the sauce with some of the almonds, reserving some for decoration.

Leave the *caponata* in the fridge, at least overnight. Mix in the remaining almonds and top with toasted breadcrumbs when ready to serve.

Caponata di virdura

Caponata di verdure

CAPONATA MADE WITH GREEN LEAFY VEGETABLES

This *caponata* is from the Madonie (in Palermo province, also called Monti Madonie), a mountain range in northwest-central Sicily. It is made with green leafy, winter vegetables and is traditionally served cold as part of the Christmas evening meal. It would be considered cleansing after the rich foods eaten on the *Vigilia* (Christmas eve) and during Christmas day. The chicory and endive would be particularly appreciated, because bitter vegetables are considered particularly beneficial for the liver. They also include cardoons (the flowerless relative of the artichoke).

I have used this *caponata* as a filling for a *torta di verdura* (vegetable pie). Use the recipe for short pastry on page 368.

METHOD

Prepare the spinach, chicory, endives and cauliflower: wash, tear or cut them into bite-size pieces.

Wilt the vegetables individually (Italians would cook the vegetables in boiling salted water): place with a little water in a covered saucepan over high heat and shake the pan – it should only take a minute or two. If you wish to save time, boil or steam them together: cut the less tender vegetables into smaller pieces, or add the ingredients to the pan in descending order of cooking time. Drain and squeeze out as much liquid as possible.

Sauté the onions and celery in the olive oil, season with salt and pepper (or chilli flakes), then add the capers, sugar and the vinegar. Add the cold cooked vegetables, check seasoning and leave to cool.

Toss the pine nuts and anchovy fillets through the *caponata* and arrange on a serving dish. Just before serving, scatter with the toasted breadcrumbs and top with lemon slices.

INGREDIENTS

500g (17½oz) spinach, washed then squeezed dry

500g (17½oz) chicory

1 small endive, about 250g (9oz)

1 small cauliflower, about 500g (17½oz)

1 large onion, chopped

3 celery stalks and pale green leaves from heart

¾ cup extra virgin olive oil

¾ cup capers, salted or in brine (if salted, rinsed, soaked and drained)

1 tablespoon sugar

½ cup white wine vinegar

¾ cup pine nuts

5–6 salted anchovies, bones removed, rinsed and finely chopped

¾ cup toasted breadcrumbs (fried in a little extra virgin olive oil)

1 lemon, finely sliced

salt and freshly ground pepper or chilli flakes to taste

A caponata for every season

VARIATIONS

- I sometimes add seedless raisins or sultanas (½ cup) soaked in a little water and then drained.
- Use the juice of 1–2 lemons instead of vinegar.
- Replace the sugar with honey.
- I have seen a much more elaborate recipe for this *caponata* (called *cunigghiu*) from the Madonie Islands. As well as green vegetables, it contains *baccalà*, potatoes and dried tomatoes.

Capunata di cacuocciuli

Caponata di carciofi

ARTICHOKE CAPONATA

I always sauté each of the vegetables separately as is the traditional method of making *caponata* (as in a well-made ratatouille). I have provided an alternative method as a variation.

METHOD

Thinly slice the trimmed, quartered artichokes for sautéing. Trim the stalks, pulling away the tough, stringy outer skin and leave attached to the artichoke. Drain the artichokes and squeeze dry.

Place some of the extra virgin olive oil a large shallow saucepan and sauté on low heat until they are tender (do this in batches if they do not fit comfortably). This may take up to 10 minutes or more (add a little water or white wine if drying out). Remove and set aside.

Add a little more extra virgin olive oil to the pan and sauté the other vegetables in the same pan separately. First, sauté the onions until they begin to colour; remove from the pan and add to the artichokes. Add a little more oil and sauté the celery. Add the olives, capers and tomatoes to the celery and season with salt. Simmer gently for about 7–10 minutes. Add a little water if needed (it should have the consistency of a thick sauce). Add to the sautéed artichokes and onions.

To make the sauce, add the sugar to the pan and caramelise by stirring it until it melts and begins to turn a honey colour. Add the vinegar, swirl it around and reduce it (2–3 minutes). Return all the sautéed vegetables to the pan and gently toss with the sauce. Simmer on very gentle heat for about 3–5 minutes to allow the flavours to amalgamate.

Place the *caponata* in a sealed container or jar and store in the fridge. Leave it for at least a day but preferably longer before serving.

INGREDIENTS

9–10 young artichokes, with stalks, trimmed and quartered (see page xxx)

1 cup extra virgin olive oil

2 large onions, finely chopped

4–5 tender celery stalks and some pale green leaves from the heart, finely chopped

1 cup green olives, pitted and chopped

1 cup capers (if salted, rinsed and soaked)

500g (17½oz) ripe tomatoes, peeled and chopped (or canned)

½ cup sugar

½ cup wine vinegar, white or red

salt to taste

A caponata for every season

To make the *caponata* without frying the ingredients separately, proceed as follows: Prepare and sauté the artichokes as in the preceding recipe. Add a little more extra virgin olive oil and when it is hot add the onion and celery and sauté until they begin to colour. Add the olives, capers, sugar, salt, vinegar and tomatoes. Cover and simmer gently until tender, 5–10 minutes or more, depending on the freshness and age of the artichokes.

VARIATION

❧ Use fennel instead of artichokes. Some pre-cook the fennel beforehand.

The menu

The menus scattered throughout the book will give you an idea of how Sicilians compose a meal.

They may eat two or three seafood dishes at one sitting, but, like all Italians, they try to achieve an overall balance in the meal – not just in the ratio of protein, vegetable and carbohydrates but also in flavours, textures and colours. Courses that are lighter or drier are contrasted with heavier dishers or wetter ones, alternating the crisp with the soft, setting off the bland with the highly flavoured.

If the pasta sauce includes fish or meat and there's an antipasto, it will be something light, probably vegetables, which may be raw (a bowl of radishes, a fennel bulb cut into quarters, some young broad beans, served with some good-quality salt and extra virgin olive oil). The vegetables for the antipasto and the contorno will be different — and may also differ in texture and colour. Italians avoid duplicating ingredients, to the point of varying herbs in the different courses.

Seasons count. A local species of fish caught in peak season will be much fresher and cheaper than one from some distance away, frozen or packed in ice. There may also be some variation in the taste of fish caught in different seasons — in summer the fish is eating different food than in cooler seasons and its flavour and ratio of fat may also be different.

A meal can be as simple or as complicated as you like. A course could be dropped or there can be many courses with servings kept small, especially if a meal is to be enjoyed over a long leisurely time.

This is a book about fish and it is included as an ingredient in the pasta sauces. However, the tuna can be omitted from Pasta with artichokes and tuna or Spaghetti with tuna and lentils; similarly the bottarga can be left out of the Pasta with tomatoes, eggplants and bottarga – and so on.

And although there are no desserts included, it is taken as a given that cassata and cannoli are on the menu.

Index

Acciughe condite 217
Agghiotta
    di pisci a missinisa 131
    di piscistoccu 134
    di tunnu cu pipi e mulinciani 133
Ammaru 'nta brace 244
Ammogghia e mataroccu 271
Ancidda in brouet 169
Anciovi cunzati 217
Anguilla in brouet 169
Artichoke
    braised in a citrus sauce 336
    caponata 378
Asparagus salad 355
Aubergine, *see* Eggplant

Baccalà al forno 193
Baccalaru 'o furnu 193
Bad weather pasta
    from Messina 111
    from Palermo 109
Baked
    baccalà 193
    fish with meat broth 188
    fish with potatoes, vinegar and
        anchovies 187
    sardines with cheese,
        breadcrumbs and eggs 199
    stuffed tomatoes 319
Boiled tuna as the Capo Rias
    ate it 221
Braciole di tonno 144
Bracioline 143
Braciulittini 143
Braised
    broad beans 326
    cabbage 339
    peas 326
    peppers 330
    potatoes 338
    Savoy cabbage 339
Brocculi a pastetta 310

Cacocciuli
   all' agro 336
   arrustuti 301
Calamaretti
   crudi e conditi 214
   ripieni con marsala e mandorle 149
Calamaricchi
   chini cà marsala e mennuli 149
   crudi e cunzati 214
Caponata
   catanese 362
   di carciofi 378
   di melanzane 367
   di natale 375
   di patate 373
   di verdure 376
   duchessa con la salsa di San Bernardo 370
   from the Leone family of Catania 362
   made with green leafy vegetables 376
Caponatina 365
   al forno 372
   cooked in the oven 372
   'o furnu 372
   with roasted peppers and fried eggplants 365
Capunata
   'duchessa' ca sarsa di San Bernardo 370
   di cacocciuli 378
   di virdura 376
Carciofi
   arrostiti alla brace 301
   in agro 336
Capsicum, *see* Peppers
Cauliflower
   braised in red wine 341
   fritters 310
Cavolfiore affogati 341
Cavulu cappucciu a stufateddu 339
Cazzilli 308
Christmas *caponata* 375
Cipollata 265
Cipolline all'agrodolce 332
Cippudata 265

Cipudduzzi all'auruduci 332
Courgette, *see* Zucchini
Couscous 284
Cozze ripiene con besciamella 148
Cozzuli chini 148
Crispeddi di nunnata 238
Crocchette di patate 308
Crostata di sarde 199
Cucuzzedda cu pumaroru 334
Cucuzzeddi a la parmiciana 321
Cùscusu 284

Dressing
   cooked tomatoes and chilli 259
   oil, lemon and oregano 256
Duchess *caponata* with Saint Bernard's sauce 370

Eel *in brouet* 169
Eggplant
   caponata 367
   caponata in pastry 368
   croquettes 309
   parmigiana 321
Erbe spontanie 344
Estratto di pomodoro 59

Fagiolini
   con pomodoro 334
   lessi 354
Fasulinu
   cu pumaroru 334
   vugghiutu 354
Fave o piselli in umido 326
Favuzzi o pisedda in umitu 326
Fegato di sette cannoli 311
Fennel tortino 316
Ficato ri setti cannola 311
Fish
   alla ghiotta from Messina 131
   alla matalotta 200
   in a bag 190
   in a bain-marie 205
   made of eggs 152
   poached in broth with capers 162
   soup with a *soffritto* 157
   stock 159

   with broad beans 172
Fried fish, mixed 236
Fritelle
   di cavolfiore 310
   di neonata o bianchetti 238
Frittedda 327
Fritto misto di pesce 236
Funci trifulati 333
Funghi trifolati 333

Gamberi alla brace 244
Green beans sautéed with tomatoes 334
Green leaf salad 348
Grilled
   artichokes 301
   eggplants 305
   fish 242
   mushrooms 305
   prawns 244
   tuna with oregano 245
   zucchini 305

Insalata
   di asparagi 355
   di mare 220
   di polpo 223
   di pomodori 352
   ri limoni o d'arance 350
   verde 348
Involtini 143
   di melanzane 320

Lemon salad 350

Maccarruna che caccocciuli 67
Maccheroni coi carciofi 67
Maionese 272
Mayonnaise 272
Melanzane, zucchine e funghi arrostiti 305
'Mpanata
   using bread dough 283
   using short pastry 279
Mulinciani
   a la parmiciana 321
   ammugghiati 320
   cucuzzeddi e funci 'nta braci 305

'Nzalata
    r'aranci 350
    ri lumia 350
    ri mari 220
    ri pumaroru 352
    ri pumaroru e cipudda 352
    ri sparici 355
    virdi 348

Octopus
    braised with tomatoes 173
    salad 223
Orange salad 350

Parmigiana
    di melanzane 321
    di zucchine 321
Pasta
    a la norma ca bottarga 119
    a la palina 113
    al nero di seppie 78
    alla norma con la bottarga 119
    alla paolina 113
    and prawns with goats' milk
        ricotta 96
    ca buttarga 114
    chi brocculi arriminata 106
    chi sardi 55
    chi trighi o'rau 60
    co pumaroru cruru e pisci friuti 63
    col pomodoro e pesce fritti 63
    col sugo di tonno 74
    con la bottarga 114
    con le sarde 55
    con spada e menta 73
    cu niuru di sicci 78
    cu tunnu no sucu 74
    del cattivo tempo 109
    e gamberi colla ricotta di capra 96
    e gammareddu ca ricotta 96
    e trigle al ragù 60
    how to make 45
    rimestata coi cavolfiori 106
    ro' malutempu 109
    with a tuna stew 74
    with artichokes and tuna 67
    with black ink sauce 78

    with *bottarga* 114
    with braised red mullet 60
    with cauliflower, sultanas, pine nuts
    and anchovies 106
    with tomatoes and fried fish 63
    with sardines from Palermo 55
    with sardines from Syracuse 58
    with swordfish and mint 73
    with tomatoes, anchovies,
        cinnamon and cloves 113
    with tomatoes, eggplants and
        bottarga 119
Pasticcio di caponata de melanzane 368
Patate in tegame 338
Patati nn'o tianu 338
Peperonata 330
Peperoni arrostiti 300
Pesce
    a bagnomaria 205
    al cartoccio 190
    al forno con brodo di carne 188
    all'agliata 208
    alla brace 242
    alla ghiotta alla messinese 131
    alla matalotta 200
    con le fave 172
    e capperi 162
    incrostato di sale 194
    infornato con patate 187
    spada con agrumi e pistacchi 174
    steccato e con marsala 180
Pesto
    garlic, parsley and mint 268
    potatoes, almonds and garlic 267
    tomatoes, basil, pine nuts or
        almonds 271
Pipi arrustuti 300
Pipironata 330
Pisci
    a bagnumaria 205
    a la matalotta 200
    all'agghiata 208
    che favi 172
    che' patati 'nfurnatu 187
    chi chiappareddi 162
    d'ovu 152
    'nta braci 242

    o'furnu co bruoru ri carni 188
Polpette
    di melanzane 309
    di tonno con la salsa 248
Polpettine in brodo di pesce 165
Polpi in sugo 173
Pomodori ripieni 319
Potato
    caponata 373
    croquettes 308
Pumarori chini 319
Pumpkin with vinegar, mint, sugar and
    cinnamon 311
Purpetti
    di tunnu cà sarsa 248
    ri mulinciani 309
Purpi' no sucu 173
Purpu vugghiutu 223

Ravioli
    di ricotta col nero di seppie 80
    di ricotta cu niuru di sicci 80
Raw marinated
    sardines 217
    small calamari 214
    tuna 213
Rice
    with angels 88
    with black ink sauce 78
Rich fish soup from Syracuse 161
Ricotta ravioli with black ink sauce 80
Riso con gli angeli 88
Risu cull'anciuli 88
Roasted artichokes 301
Rolled eggplants with a stuffing 320

Salad of boiled green beans 354
Salamurrigghiu 256
    russu 259
Salmoriglio 256
    rosso 259
Salsa
    di capperi 260
    fatta a freddo 258
    per i pesci 262
    saracina di olive bianche 263
    verde siciliana 261

Salsicette di tonno 250
Salt-crusted fish 194
Saracen green olive sauce 263
Sarde a beccafico 150
Sardi a beccaficu 150
Sardines a beccafico 150
Sarsa
    a friddu 258
    di chiappareddi 260
    ppi'i pisci 262
    saracina d'alvi janchi 263
    virdi siciliana 261
Sasizzeddi du tunnu 250
Sauce
    capers and anchovies 260
    cooked, almonds, green olives,
        capers and tomatoes 262
    thick, green olives, capers, carrots
        and vinegar 266
    thick, onions, sugar and vinegar 265
    uncooked, tomatoes, herbs and
        garlic 258
Sauté of spring vegetables 327
Sautéed
    green leafy vegetables 342
    mushrooms 333
Scurdalia 267
Seafood salad, mixed 220
Shrimp, see Prawn
Sicilian green sauce 261
Small braciole stuffed with herbs 143
Small fish balls in fish broth 165
Soused fish 208
Spaghetti
    a vonguli 92
    al cartoccio 75
    alle vongole 92
    c'arausta 98
    ca sarsa murisca 116
    chi ricci 93
    col granco fritto 100
    colla salsa moresca 116
    con l'aragosta 98
    con le uova di ricci di mare 93

cu granciu frittu 100
e tonno con le lenticchie 70
e tunnu chi linticchi 70
in a bag 75
with cockles 92
with crayfish 98
with fried crab 100
with Moresca sauce 116
with sea urchins 93
with tuna and lentils 70
Spaghettini
    e cozze 90
    e cozzuli 90
    with mussels 90
Stimpirata 266
Stoccafisso alla ghiotta 134
Stockfish alla ghiotta with green olives,
    capers and potatoes 134
Stuffed
    calamari with cheese, almonds and
        nutmeg in marsala 149
    grilled artichokes 303
    mussels with besciamelle 148
Sweet and sour onions 332
Swordfish with citrus and pistachios 174

Tomato
    paste 59
    salad 352
Tonno
    ala ghiotta con peperoni e melanzane
        133
    alla griglia con origano 245
    alla stemperata 138
    con peperoni 171
    cunzato 213
    in ragu, con cannella 181
    lesso del Capo Rais 221
    sott'oli, cucinatto nel forno 227
    sott'olio, lesso con aceto 229
Tortino di finocchi 316
Trota del manghisi 232
    in padella con olive e finocchio selvatico
    233

Trotta d' u manghisi 232
Trout from the Manghisi River 232
    with olives and wild fennel 233
Tuna
    alla ghiotta 133
    alla stemperata 138
    balls in salsa 248
    braciole with Emmenthal cheese,
        anchovies and citrus 144
    braised in marsala 180
    poached in oil and vinegar 229
    poached in the oven 227
    ragout with cinnamon 181
    sausages 250
    with peppers 171
Tunna
    ammattunatu 180
    'a stimpirata 138
    a' raù ca canneddà 181
    che pipi 171
    rigatanu 245
    sutt' ogghiu o furnu 227
    sutt' ogghiu vugghiutu cu acitu 229
    vugghiutu d'u capu rais 221
Turticedda ri finocchiu 316

Verdura verde saltata 342
Vermicelli alla siracusana 112
Vermicelli as cooked in Syracuse 112
Verza o cappuccio in umido 339
Virmiceddi sirausani 112
Vruocculi affucati 341

Whitebait fritters 238
Wild greens 344

Zogghiu 268
Zucchini
    con pomodoro 334
    parmigiana 321
    sautéed with tomatoes 334
Zuppa di pesce 157
    alla siracusana 161
Zuppa di pisci 157

Acknowledgements

This book has been a long time in the making and I would like to thank all my friends and family who sustained me during the project, especially my partner Bob Evans, and Caro Llewellyn who gave me the confidence to begin it. I also want to thank my relatives in Sicily and particularly my father's only living sister in Ragusa, Zia Niluzza, who has always been a great inspiration and a valuable source of all things Sicilian. Finally, my indefatigable editor Mary Trewby.

Most of the location photography, including the front cover photograph, were taken by Bob Evans. Additional photography of Sicily by Barrie O'Gorman and Angela Tolley.

This PB edition published in 2014 by New Holland Publishers (Australia) Pty Ltd
Sydney • Auckland • London

First published in 2011.

www.newhollandpublishers.com

The Chandlery Unit 114 50 Westminster Bridge Road London SE1 7QY United Kingdom
1/66 Gibbes Street Chatswood NSW 2067 Australia
218 Lake Road Northcote Auckland New Zealand

A record of this book is held at the British Library and the National Library of Australia.

ISBN 9781742576602

Senior Editor: Mary Trewby
Design concept: Emma Gough
Designer: Celeste Vlok
Cover design: Celeste Vlok
Front cover photo: Bob Evans
Stylist: Fiona Rigg
Publisher: Lliane Clarke
Production Manager: Olga Dementiev
Printed by Toppan Leefung Printing Ltd

10 9 8 7 6 5 4 3 2 1

Keep up with New Holland Publishers on Facebook
www.facebook.com/NewHollandPublishers